FROM HOT AIR TO
HELLFIRE

FROM HOT AIR TO
HELLFIRE

The History of Army Attack Aviation

JAMES W. BRADIN

★
PRESIDIO

This book is dedicated to the brave soldiers who have fought and died flying in America's armed helicopters.

Copyright © 1994 by James W. Bradin

Published by Presidio Press
505 B San Marin Drive, Suite 300
Novato, CA 94945-1340

Library of Congress Cataloging in Publication Data

Bradin, James W.
    From hot air to hellfire : the history of army attack aviation / James W. Bradin.
        p.   cm.
    Includes bibliographical references and index.
    ISBN 0-89141-511-4
    1. United States. Army—Aviation—History. 2. Attack helicopters—United States—History. 3. United States. Army—Aviation—Ground support—History. 4. United States—History, Military. I.Title.
    UG633.B697 1994   94-10050
    358.4'00973—dc20   CIP

Typography by ProImage
Printed in the United States of America

Contents

Acknowledgments

To pull together the information necessary to write this story required that I call on the talents of many people. It was especially important to have exemplary support during the early phase, that special some- one who knows where everything is, or who knows someone who might know. For me that person was Mrs. Regina G. Burns, the library technician and archivist at the U.S. Army Aviation Museum, Fort Rucker, Ala- bama. Regina helped me plot a proper course and kept me on it. Likewise I would like to thank Ms. Beverly Hall of the Fort Rucker Technical Library for her kind assistance. Together these ladies made my tasks less difficult.

To record recent events important to this story, I turned to those involved. A special salute to Col. Jay D. Vanderpool, USA (Ret.), for telling of the early days at Rucker, but more importantly for being the kind of officer who made good things happen. Apache would have never become an indispensable battlefield force had Vanderpool not fought to arm the helicopter. Rightly, Colonel Vanderpool has been inducted into the Army Aviation Hall of Fame.

I owe Lt. Cols. Thomas Stewart, Richard Cody, and William Bryan, all commanders of Apache helicopter battalions during Operation Desert Storm, my sincere thanks. Not only did they share their experiences, they ensured that I was able to interview men who had been at the point of the sword. Numerous young officers, warrant officers, and enlisted men—those who flew the long and dangerous missions and kept the aircraft ready—lent me their assistance. Soldiers like Tom Drew, Tim Vincent, Bob Glover, Kevin Woods, Newman Shufflebarger, Adam Heinicke, Doug Gabram, Scott Hanling, George Hodge, Mike Davis, Bob Gage, Eric Henderson, and David Bently took the time to tell their stories and the parts played by others during Desert Storm. These brave, high-tech warriors also deserve the thanks of the nation.

Others (too many to mention) not directly involved in this writing assisted Apache in making its contribution to the Allies' success. One might say that the line of credit stretches from Mesa, Arizona, via Forts Rucker and Hood to the deserts of Iraq.

Subject matter experts, participants, and eyewitnesses are important to document any historic event. (I was fortunate in having assistance from key players during Apache's development days.) Generals Samuel G. "Sammy" Cockerham and Edward M. "Ed" Browne, former Apache program managers, were generous with their time and documents dealing with Apache development. The nation and all who go to war in Apache owe these two great soldiers their thanks.

Lieutenant Colonel John R. "Jack" Burden, USA (Rct.), another brave soldier, true son of West Point, and one of the most honest officers I ever met, assisted me with TOW Cobra and Cheyenne. My old boss, Lt. Col. Nick J. Primis, USA (Ret.), now at Bell Helicopter, helped me recount the exciting story of Cobra, our first attack helicopter. Nick, too, was a great soldier and leader. Carl L. Harris, director of public relations for Bell Helicopter, also provided excellent support. Dr. Harrison N. Hoppes made available the information concerning the Ansbach trials. These tests were decisive, a watershed for army aviation and the attack helicopter. In particular Hal Klopper of McDonnell Douglas was supportive in providing documents and pictures. Brigadier General Charlie Canedy, USA (Ret.), another former boss and brave soldier, helped by sharing his experiences with the 1st Armored Division and in the early days of Cobra. Likewise his daughter, Dr. Susan Canedy, of the office of the Training and Doctrine Command historian, was another of the special people who knew where to look.

Colonel James R. "Ron" Hill, USA (Ret.), qualifies as special. Ron is one of the unsung heroes who nurtured the development of attack helicopters as a staff person. He did this while doing the same for a host of other projects within Fort Knox's Armor Agency. Ron is a smart, honest, and brave soldier—and funny as hell.

My thanks go to Col. Thomas "Tom" Green, commander, 18th Aviation Brigade, Fort Bragg, North Carolina, also a brave warrior who, as a captain, taught the stateside army how to fly nap of the earth. In helping me with this book, Tom was a "door buster" who made things happen. Our army is in good hands with leaders of the quality of Tom Green. Lieutenant Colonel John Powell, USA (Ret.), an old and treasured friend, made things happen at Fort Campbell, Kentucky.

To Angela Williams goes my sincere appreciation for patiently reading all this and making sound suggestions. Major Williams, director of The Citadel Writing Center, the college's most important asset, is a great teacher and a charming lady who taught me that it is never too late to learn. Major, where were you when I was but a lowly "Knob"?

Lastly, none of this could have happened without the support of my wife and best friend. In her own way Jervey is the best soldier of them all.

All quotations not otherwise annotated are from personal interviews conducted by the author.

Chapter One

APACHE AMBUSH

The four AH-64 Apache attack helicopters hovered across the desert. Their cockpit lights gave off a faint, eerie glow. (It was important for the Apaches to remain unseen and unheard.) Deep in enemy territory, part of a daring helicopter raid on two Iraqi early warning air defense radar sites, the blacked-out Apaches sneaked forward slowly. As yet there was no sign they had been detected.

As the helicopters cautiously approached their unsuspecting prey, flying fifty feet above the desert floor at twenty knots airspeed, the powerful downwash from the main rotor blades picked up the powdery desert sand and blew it skyward, making forward airspeed necessary to stay in front of this self-generated cloud. The Apache crews worried that the large, billowing cloud forming in their wake might be seen.

Because stealth is an important component of raids, they are in and of themselves the most difficult of military operations to conduct. This particular operation was certainly no exception. It had been months in preparation and, if successful, would save the lives of a great many American and Allied airmen. This raid was to be the first Allied strike of Operation Desert Storm against military forces of Saddam Hussein.

Officially the raid was dubbed Task Force (TF) Normandy, a title that might suggest large size. In reality, the raiding party was a small

1-101st AVIATION TF NORMANDY OPERATION
17 January 1991

force of eight U.S. Army Apaches, and four air force MH-53J Pave Low helicopters. The mission sounded simple. In fact, it was not. It was part of a sophisticated plan driven by world events.

On August 2, 1990, Saddam Hussein, the Iraqi leader, had sent his armed forces into neighboring Kuwait, claiming the small independent country as a historical part of Iraq. World reaction had been swift. The United Nations (UN) passed thirteen resolutions condemning Iraq, and set January 15 as the day that Iraq was to be out of Kuwait. The UN deadline had come and gone, with Iraq's brutal occupation forces still in Kuwait. By January 15, a large Allied military force had been assembled by UN members and was poised to move against Iraq.

The Allied plan was twofold: First, a massive air campaign would be unleashed. Next, powerful ground forces would assault the Iraqi army wherever it was found.

To begin the air war, Allied strategy called for the creation of a radar-free corridor twenty miles wide and reaching deep into the interior of Iraq. Once this aerial road was established, Allied fighter-bombers would use it to launch a massive air campaign against the infrastructure of the Iraqi government. To create this darkened corridor required the destruction of two Soviet-installed early warning ground control intercept radar sites (part of a much larger system). The two target sites were separated by sixteen kilometers and were key components of the Iraqi air defense system guarding the approaches to Baghdad, the capital of Iraq.

The task force, divided into two teams of four Apaches and two Pave Low helicopters each, was to take the two sites off the air at 2:38 A.M. on the morning of January 17, 1991. Inasmuch as these radar sites provided overlapping coverage, it was essential that they be attacked and silenced simultaneously. If one or both sites broadcast attack warnings, then all would be for naught. The alarm would put Iraqi defense on alert.

But why use attack helicopters to perform a mission this complicated? Early warning radar sites are designed to detect approaching aircraft. Positioning them on high ground usually allows the radar to see farther and with less interference from ground objects—"ground clutter." The sites, of necessity, orient their antenna skyward. This positioning makes it difficult for conventional aircraft to approach or conduct an undetected, surprise attack. Additionally, early warning radars are built to "see" aircraft moving above a predetermined altitude and airspeed. It was these characteristics that the Apaches hoped to exploit. By flying nap of the earth (NOE), using the terrain as a shield from the radars' preying electronic eyes, and by approaching at reduced airspeed, the raiding Apaches hoped to slip undetected under the radar cover.

Once within range, the Apaches' target priority was to first destroy the sites' ability to communicate, then to destroy the electrical generators providing power to the sites. To ensure that enemy communications were silenced, these targets had to be destroyed in the first seconds of the attack. Remaining facilities and equipment would be attacked step-by-step until everything was destroyed.

The raid plan had built-in redundancy to ensure the destruction of all primary targets. Each attacking aircraft was assigned one primary target and another aircraft's primary target as a backup. After destroying its primary target, each aircraft was to shift its sights to the prearranged primary target of adjacent aircraft. If the crew determined that its backup target was undamaged, it would engage and destroy it. If, on the other hand, the backup target had been neutralized or destroyed, the backup crew was free to engage other targets within their assigned sector of the Iraqi radar site.

The Russian built, top-of-the-line equipment provided the Iraqis a system laid out to protect Baghdad and other vital installations. It had to be destroyed. Undamaged, the equipment would bring havoc to attacking Allied fighter-bomber aircraft. With the equipment neutralized, the Allies could operate with impunity and a better-than-even chance of reaching Baghdad uncontested.

Down through the ages, surprise has been the one principle that warring parties have sought to achieve. With surprise, the attacker not only gains the initial advantage, he gains the initiative, the upper hand. In surprise attacks, timing and sequencing are fundamental. In this raid, simultaneous attacks against two sophisticated radar sites demanded surprise and accurate timing.

Economy of force, another principle of war followed by most successful warriors, was part of TF Normandy's reason for being. Loss of men and aircraft to Iraqi air defense would be minimal if the Allied air forces could achieve surprise in their initial attacks. Friendly forces and equipment would therefore have been economized while Iraqi assets were being destroyed.

Economy of one's own forces has become especially important to warring democracies. The value of human life drives commanders representing democratic societies. In today's world, a commander from a true democracy, who loses too many soldiers, finds himself unemployed. Prudent leaders seek ways to minimize loss of human life. Task Force Normandy's purpose was to do just that—save lives.

A total of fourteen aircraft—ten army and four air force—were dedicated to TF Normandy. At first, plans called for attacking three sites, but just before the mission was to go, the third site, determined to be nonessential, was canceled and the aircraft were redistributed among the remaining two teams. The army contingent consisted of nine army AH-64 Apaches and one UH-60 Black Hawk. The aircraft and crews came from the elite 1st Battalion, 101st Aviation Regiment, 101st Airborne Division (Air Assault). Eight Apaches would make the raid, with one spare. The UH-60 was to provide support: Initially the Black Hawk would transport maintenance personnel and parts, but during the raid it would remain airborne near the Saudi Arabian–Iraqi border with the spare Apache, ready to rescue downed airmen if needed.

The AH-64 Apache, the most sophisticated attack helicopter in the world, lacks state-of-the-art, long-range navigational systems. Apache has a Doppler inertial navigation system. The Singer Kearfott ASN-128, old technology by today's standards, is a completely self-contained system designed to provide the crew velocity, heading, and current position information. For TF Normandy this system had two major drawbacks. First, as time passes, the ASN-128 tends to drift, requiring frequent updates during long flights. In a desert with few recognizable reference points, updating on a dark night becomes a difficult feat. But more important, the Doppler radar is not passive. It emits detectable electronic energy, which, if detected by the enemy, could eliminate surprise, compromise the mission, and endanger lives.

To gain the navigational precision required for a mission of this duration, four U.S. Air Force MH-53J Pave Low helicopters, belonging to the 20th Special Operations Squadron and equipped with the satellite-activated Global Positioning System (GPS) equipment, were integrated into TF Normandy. The Pave Lows were to lead the Apaches to a point fifteen kilometers from the target sites, and after the attacks, lead them out. In addition to having the GPS, Pave Lows are equipped with a fixed forward-looking infrared (FLIR) and terrain-avoidance radar.

The GPS-equipped Pave Lows would cover Apache's navigational gaps. In fact, the GPS made Pave Low essential to the success of TF Normandy. At best, and under ideal conditions, Apache's Doppler is accurate to one hundred meters. Pave Low's GPS, on the other hand, is accurate to ten meters, the level of precision required for this mission.

The mission folders prepared for the army–air force teams, labeled Red Team and White Team, called for the White Team to depart Al Jouf, the mission headquarters, first at 12:56 A.M. on January 17. White Team's target was the easternmost of the two. Red Team would lift off minutes later. Both teams were to have first missiles impact at 2:38 A.M. Al Jouf, little more than a remote desert airstrip, ironically means "starting point" in Arabic.

For missions of this importance, it is not unreasonable that participating crews would be handpicked. The pressure to ensure success might well be enough to cause some commanders to violate crew integrity, selecting and sending only the most experienced people. For this mission, Lt. Col. Richard A. "Dick" Cody, or as his soldiers nicknamed him, "Commander Cody," commander of the 1-101st, opted to keep his highly trained crews together.

From his first day in command, Dick Cody insisted that flight crews be paired and assigned to one aircraft. He assigned new aviators to an aircraft commanded by an experienced aviator. This permanent crew was then held responsible for its aircraft. The policy resulted in crews of varied experience levels within the cockpit, but basically balanced across the battalion. More importantly, by maintaining crew stability, crews learned to work with each other, their aircraft, and the enlisted crew chief who maintained the aircraft. This is how second lieutenants and warrant officer ones, the personnel with the lowest level of flight experience, found themselves taking part in this mission.

A word about these fledgling aviators. Second lieutenant and warrant officer one are the first rungs of the ladders for their respective rank structures. Second lieutenant needs little explanation. Warrant officers, on the other hand, are a special group whose role is often not understood. Warrant officers are selected and issued a warrant rather than a commission because of their unique technical qualifications. The warrant rank bridges the gap between noncommissioned officer and the commissioned officer corps. In days gone by, warrant officers were described as "neither fish nor fowl." Today they are a most important part of the high-tech army. In army aviation, warrant offiicers are not only important, they are absolutely essential. The aviator warrant is the professional backbone of the aviation branch. Just as second lieutenants are jokingly referred to as shavetails, the warrant officer one carries the moniker Wobbly One.

At thirty-two years, WO1 Timothy L. "Tim" Vincent was, by most standards, a relatively old warrant officer one. In 1980 Tim Vincent left his home in Kentucky and enlisted in the army. He served six and a half years in a Ranger battalion, one of the army's most elite forces. He was good enough at his craft to be selected to serve two years as an instructor at the Ranger School.

Being on the cutting edge of something exciting and dangerous had been Vincent's lifelong goal. The desire for high adventure is what lured him out of rural Kentucky and into the army. The call of adventure is why he became a Ranger.

However, after several years of what he considered disappointing duty, no war, Vincent left the army. A few months later he was back. He had come to realize that civilian life was equally without adventure; in fact, he found it tedious. Reenlisting in the army, Vincent discovered while he was away that his old Ranger unit had led the invasions of Grenada and Panama. Determined to make up for lost opportunities, Vincent sought adventure in a new endeavor, army aviation. Completing flight school on October 3, 1990, he was assigned to the 1-101st at Fort Campbell, Kentucky, and was further assigned as co-pilot-gunner in the tandem-seated Apache.

At five feet, seven inches, Vincent was ideal for the copilot-gunner's station. However, being muscular, he fit snugly in the front seat. His size, supplemented by the required wartime protective equipment—survival vest, flak jacket, and heavy ceramic chest protector—made the Apache front seat even tighter. What is more, the added bulk made bending over to look through the gunner's target acquisition and designation sight (TADS), his primary sighting device, difficult, not to mention uncomfortable. But deep in enemy territory, none of this seemed to matter. Tim Vincent was now in sight of his target. This was true high adventure.

On this unusually dark night, the attacking teams had closed to within seven thousand meters of their targets without discovery. As the target complex came into view, Vincent's eight years of Ranger training automatically kicked in; all thoughts of personal discomfort disappeared. As a Ranger, Vincent had come to know discomfort as his constant companion. After all, the unofficial Ranger creed states it pretty well: "If you ain't hurtin', you ain't tryin'."

But this mission was too important to allow nonmission concerns to interfere. Vincent was more than aware that for a brief few minutes, his actions would have great impact on the lives of hundreds of fellow aviators. Their safety would depend on how well he and seven other frontseaters worked their magic.

As an Apache copilot-gunner, Vincent's duties required him to search for enemy targets, identify them as enemy, and attack them with the best weapon system available from the multiple systems carried by Apache.

Apache weapons loads are tailored for each mission. The aircraft can carry sixteen Hellfire missiles, eleven hundred rounds of 30mm for the cannon, and several 70mm folding fin aerial rockets (FFAR). Trade-offs between fuel and ammunition allow flexibility for the Apache.

For this crucial raid each Apache carried eight Hellfire antitank laser-guided missiles, nineteen of the 70mm rockets, and eleven hundred rounds of 30mm cannon ammunition. A 230-gallon external fuel cell, or ferry tank, was added on the right side. The fifteen hundred pounds of additional fuel carried in this tank gave Apache a four-hundred-mile range, enough for the round-trip.

Chief Warrant Officer Three Shawn Hoban, flying in the backseat, sat above and behind Vincent. As the aircraft commander and pilot, Hoban was to fly and navigate the Apache to the target area and to position it where the copilot-gunner could best employ the weapons system.

With the target complex in sight and range, Hoban worked to fly the aircraft as smoothly as possible. It was important that he provide Vincent a stable firing platform.

In the process of the attack, once the target was identified, Vincent's duties became much like those of a bombardier riding in the nose of a World War II B-17. He had to lay the crosshairs on the target, activate the fire control equipment, and finally, when all was in order, pull the trigger. But unlike any aircraft ever seen, Apache can operate as well at night as it can during daylight.

When serious mission planning first began, during September and October, planners selected a night for the mission, which optimized Apache's night-fighting capabilities. Darkness, or low ambient light, enhances Apache's FLIR night targeting system. The FLIR performs so well that the Apache is able to fly at night or in bad weather and see well enough to identify and engage targets at great distances. Unlike the ANVIS-6 night vision goggles, which depend on ambient light— that faint quantity of light reflected to earth by the stars—the FLIR measures differences in temperature between objects, and portrays what it sees onto a small cathode ray tube (TV screen) called an optical relay tube (ORT). The process is also called thermal imagery. The image can be portrayed onto the crewman's integrated helmet and display sight system (IHADSS), a one-inch-square screen suspended from the helmet and positioned in front of the right eye. The FLIR does all this passively and without any visible onboard source of light. It was Apache's night capability that allowed the mission planners to pick such a dark night for the endeavor. It was this same onboard equipment that allowed Hoban, Vincent, and the others to fly to the radar sites undetected and open fire at extended distances.

Bending over to look through the TADS, Vincent could clearly see buildings and vehicles in the target area. People unaware of the Apache's presence walked between buildings, some smoking.

The planning and training for the mission had been so exacting that it left nothing to chance. After weeks of assiduous map reconnaissance and endless hours of sand table rehearsals, the fourteen crews took to the air and flew repeated rehearsals. These demanding repetitions went on until sequence became routine—second nature. Between flights Cody reviewed aircraft mission folders, updated them with the latest intelligence, and reissued them to the crews. Night gunnery exercises took place with increasing frequency. Hellfire missiles, heretofore scarce for training, were suddenly available. For many crew members, this was their first opportunity to fire a real honest-to-God Hellfire. At secluded desert ranges, surplus air force trucks disappeared into the night as Hellfires found their mark.

As Chief Warrant Officer Three Hoban continued to maneuver the darkened Apache forward, Vincent felt as if gallons of adrenaline raced through his body. Sitting in the gunner's seat, he knew that this was true high adventure and he was here and ready. He was pumped!

Viewing the target for the first time, Vincent sensed something awry. At one minute before the scheduled launch time, he was still unable to identify his primary target. Rangers do not panic, Vincent reminded himself: It's their hallmark. But he was worried just the same.

The four Red Team Apaches were now within sixty-five hundred meters of the still placid radar site. Glancing about, Vincent realized that their run into the site would not be as good as he would have liked. To reduce their dust signature, Hoban had added 100 feet to their planned altitude, putting them at 150 feet above the desert floor. Their airspeed remained at twenty knots. Even at 150 feet, they would initially be in a low spot looking uphill at the target array. This should correct itself somewhat as they got closer. Even so, the radar site would stay slightly uphill. Vincent wondered if his low vantage point was why he could not find his first target.

The Apache, like all weapons systems, suffers a slight degradation in accuracy when forced to shoot uphill. For most weapons, an uphill shot is difficult. However, if the gunner understands this limitation and is trained to compensate for it, he can overcome the disadvantage and hit the target. Remembering this, Vincent continued to search for his elusive first target.

From the instant that their Apache came into line of sight with the target radar facility, the onboard APR-39 radar warning receiver had been giving off audible signals of incoming radiated energy. The still placid activities around the site led Hoban and Vincent to disregard the warnings. If they had been discovered, the target area would be in high gear. The fact that the Apaches were approaching from low ground with the radars above them, their antenna pointed skyward, apparently was enough to mask the helicopters. On the other hand, it might be good luck, thought Vincent. Whatever the cause, it was show time. The curtain was about to go up.

At the last second, Vincent spotted his target. It was right where the mission folder said it would be. Both he and Hoban were aware that their first target was the most critical of all the targets—the radar site's command-and-control (C&C) van. It was the C&C van that housed the site's ability to communicate with the outside world; it was the site's nerve center.

Information collected from outlying radar sites was transmitted to the C&C van, where it was evaluated, decisions were reached, and orders were issued. Failure to destroy this key center first might have allowed the Iraqis an opportunity to alert the Iraqi high command in Baghdad, resulting in the sending of messages to scramble MiG fighters from four nearby airfields and alerting antiaircraft missile units. But once the C&C van lost its voice—its ability to sound an alarm—life would be much safer for attacking Allied aircraft.

Once the C&C van went down, Vincent was to shift to his secondary target, the power generators that provided electrical energy for the entire site. With neither power nor communications, the site would be totally out of action. With the site blinded, dark, and helpless, the Apaches would then be free to systematically destroy what remained of the site's fragile and sophisticated electronic equipment. More importantly, the Allied fighter-bombers to follow would have a clear route, overflying unwarned enemy airfields and antiaircraft missile units.

Without warning, Red Team's radios came to life for the first time since engine start-up at Al Jouf: The prearranged code word, "Joy," broke through the intercom chatter. Ten seconds to first missile launch.

As the flyers closed on the target, Vincent's aviation training overrode all other instincts. Aiming at the doomed C&C van, he pulled the laser trigger button to its first detent, activating the laser range finder/designator and squirting a short burst of laser energy. At the speed of light, laser energy went out to the van and came back, allowing the range finder to accurately determine the aircraft-to-target distance. This information was then automatically fed to the fire control computer. On command this firing data was passed to the onboard weapons systems.

During his transition into the Apache, Vincent had been taught that the most reliable method of firing the Hellfire missile was to use the image auto tracking (IAT) system. He decide to follow that advice.

The IAT works by causing the FLIR system to lock onto the targeted hot spot or heat source. When the system is in lock-on status, the copilot-gunner sees a set of brackets appear on his screen to each side of the target. For the Hellfire to home to its target, laser illumination of the target is still needed.

With the helicopter inching forward, Vincent ranged and verified that his missiles were ready. At launch time, Vincent pulled the trigger, sending the first Hellfire roaring off its launch rail to begin its flight to the unsuspecting C&C van. After a short pause Vincent pulled the trigger a second time. Two Hellfire missiles were now in the air, ripping through the quiet night. Watching the seconds-to-missile-impact countdown in the lower right corner of his ORT, Vincent, every muscle tense, was sure that he had his first target killed. There was no way he could miss. But a split second before the first Hellfire was to impact, there was a tremendous flashing explosion to the left of, but close to, the C&C van. The heat from that explosion, greater than the heat coming from his target, caused his IAT to lose its lock. His missile disappeared into a cloud of debris.

Looking quickly again, Vincent was unsure if his missile had hit the van. An old army adage, dusted off for each new war, says, "When in doubt, shoot and then shoot again." More out of reflex than conscious thought, a now-cursing Vincent switched from image tracking to manual mode, relaid the crosshairs of the TADS where he knew the C&C van center of mass to be, and watched as his second missile streaked into the van. This time, there was no doubt. The subsequent explosion inside the van sent parts flying. When the dust cleared, there was no van.

Shifting his sights to the second target, the site's electrical generation system, Vincent confirmed what he had suspected. The Apache to his immediate left had taken care of the generators. Fire engulfed the entire power generation area. All lights in the target area were out. There was no sign of electrical power remaining.

Thick, dark smoke drifted across the target area. This obscuration forced the Apache crews to hurry their attacks against the remaining targets. With one Hellfire remaining but no suitable target in view, Vincent readied the 70mm unguided multipurpose submunitions (MPSM) rockets for launch.

The 70mm rockets, stored in fixed nineteen-round pods suspended under Apache's stub wings, require that the aircraft be aimed at the target to attain accuracy. The pilot is in the best position to aim and fire the rockets. Although the 70mm is a World War II–era weapons system originally called the 2.75-inch rocket, it saw service in Korea and Vietnam. A great deal of work went into its improvement. By its very nature, free flight, only modest improvements could be made in accuracy. However, much has been accomplished in improving fusing, range, and payload. Once fired the 70mm leaves its launcher tube and goes where it is aimed or where wind drift takes it.

Receiving range data from the fire control computer, the 70mm MPSM travels to a preset distance, where a small internal charge explodes, rupturing the rocket body and dropping shaped-charge bomblets over a wide area.

Still flying at twenty knots, Hoban aimed the Apache and let fly with the multipurpose rockets. His intent was to cover areas not damaged by the Hellfires. The explosions of the multiple submunitions were clearly visible through the TADS and pilot's night vision system as the dust kicked up on the desert floor.

Unlike the Hellfire missile, both the 70mm rocket and the Apache's 30mm gun are best described as area weapons vis-à-vis point target weapons systems. A point target weapon can hit the point at which it is aimed, whereas an area weapon will strike within a given area. With effort the munitions of the 70mm rocket and 30mm cannon can be made to impact in a reasonably small area, but both systems lack the surgical precision of the Hellfire.

As Hoban's last MPSM rocket roared out of its launcher tube, Vincent began firing at likely targets with the 30mm cannon. This cannon, which hangs directly beneath the copilot-gunner seat, is electronically linked to the gunner's crash helmet. When activated, the cannon will follow the movements of the gunner's head, aiming wherever he looks. Smoke from burning equipment obscured much of the target area, but with their Apache four thousand meters from the near side of the radar complex, Vincent had little difficulty indentifying targets suitable for the 30mm. With each slow bark of the cannon, the Apache quivered. But Vincent could see his rounds impacting and knew that he was adding to the destruction of the sensitive electronic radar equipment.

Suddenly a slight wind shift cleared a small area hidden by the smoke. Sitting in the middle of the clearing, an undamaged radar antenna reached for the sky. Fearing that the smoke might again close around this target, Vincent quit the cannon, reactivated the Hellfire system, and loosed his last Hellfire missile. The startled Apache crewmen, close enough to witness the violence of the Hellfire's destructive warhead, watched as the warhead struck home, sending large pieces of the antenna twisting into the air and floating back to earth in slow motion. Smoke and flames filled the spot where seconds before the large antenna had stood.

Senses restored, Hoban, with the ease and confidence of a veteran, again took control and switched to another type of 70mm rocket, a flechette, and fired it into the burning target site.

Flechette rockets are designed as antipersonnel munitions. Each warhead carries hundreds of small steel darts. Little in their path escapes one or more of these deadly shafts. Like the MPSM, the flechette receives data from the fire control computer. Based on the aircraft-to-target range, the pilot sets the time of flight to a predesignated point of desired detonation, and when the rocket arrives at that point, an internal charge ignites. With the rocket body acting like a shotgun barrel, detonation of the second charge propels the flechettes forward, with their speed greater than the carrier rocket. These darts have enough mass and velocity to penetrate normal vehicles and buildings, not to mention uniform shirts. Although Hoban could no longer see people moving about, he knew that the darts would find any of the exposed Iraqi. The hundreds of impacting darts added to the mounting clouds of dust and smoke.

With their flechettes all gone, and the Apache still closing on the damaged radar complex, Vincent returned to firing the cannon at remaining likely targets. One reason for having the cannon on Apache was for protection of the aircraft from close targets. Remembering his preflight mission briefing, Vincent began to search for one weapon in the area he knew could do them great harm—the Russian-built ZPU-4 antiaircraft gun–carrying vehicle.

Earlier photos of the target sites revealed that each site was guarded by three ZPU-4s, positioned in a large triangle around the site perimeter. Of all the equipment at each site, the ZPU-4 antiaircraft gun was the one weapon best equipped to fight helicopters, and the thin-skinned Apache was vulnerable. However, with the impact of the first Hellfire missile, the crews of the ZPUs not only did not attempt to return fire but abandoned their vehicles and fled on foot.

To prevent these guns from being remanned, Vincent and other gunners raked them with cannonfire. Vincent and Hoban were close enough to see cannon rounds impacting on the three deadly vehicles. No attempt was made by the Iraqis to return to these vehicles. It seemed that no one wanted to become the Iraqi John Wayne.

Finally it was time to leave. Hoban had run in pretty close to the site, close enough. Any closer and they would be within small-arms range. Although it felt as if they had been firing for hours, the elapsed time since 2:38 A.M. was less than five minutes.

As Hoban began their departure turn, Vincent ceased firing to look up to view the results of their grisly work. The entire site was ablaze. Every vehicle or building appeared to be either burning or full of holes. In Vincent's estimation, it would be a long time before this site would be a danger to Allied aircraft.

While Vincent gazed at their evening's work, Hoban put the aircraft into an even steeper left turn. They were close to one hundred feet in altitude. Both Hoban and Vincent felt good. The success of their mission exceeded their wildest expectations and, so far, no one had been hurt. All they had to do was to get back to Al Jouf and safety.

But war is replete with the unexpected. Without any warning Hoban's pilot's night vision sensor (PNVS) failed. In an instant, Hoban was flying blind. Immediately he announced the failure to Vincent, while simultaneously pressing the TADS override switch, giving him control of Vincent's TADS, and redirecting it to his IHADSS. The elapsed time for this to happen takes three seconds. In a blacked-out helicopter in a steep banking turn one hundred feet off the ground, these three seconds seem an eternity.

With Hoban's announcement, Vincent ended his sight-seeing and returned to his sensor screen. In the few seconds that Hoban had been blinded, the Apache entered a shallow dive, with the altimeter passing through fifty feet. As Vincent watched, the ground seemed to be rushing up to meet them. Pushing his push-to-talk switch, Vincent screamed: "Pull up!"

Hoban obeyed; he rolled out of the turn and pulled back on the cyclic stick, moving the Apache into a nose-up attitude. In seconds the Apache reached five hundred feet, with its tail and engine exhausts pointed directly back at the radar site. The aircraft's hot spots were now exposed to danger if someone behind were to fire a heat-seeking missile. This time Vincent screamed, "Get down!" Again Hoban complied. Minutes later, without explanation, the PNVS restored itself. Looking back at the incident months later, Hoban and Vincent claimed being the army's first and perhaps only Apache to have "mooned" their Iraqi enemies.

With the aircraft again under control, the next task for Vincent and Hoban was to regain their composure and link up with the rest of the team and the air force MH-53J Pave Low helicopters. Again everything went as planned, and the return flight to Al Jouf, led by the Pave Lows, was without further incident. Red Team had succeeded in its mission. Their half of the corridor was open.

Meanwhile, sixteen kilometers away at the other site, adventures of equal dimensions were also drawing to a close.

Earlier, Lt. Tom Drew, leader of the White Team, was tense as he and his team lifted off for their journey into Iraq. Drew elected to ride in the gunner's seat to allow himself the freedom of action needed to provide leadership to his team. Drew's pilot, CWO3 Timothy "Zeek" Zarnowski, was another highly skilled aviator. Drew felt comfortable flying with Zarnowski. He also had equal trust in the remainder of White Team. He knew that they were well trained and up to the mission. Only Murphy's Law or that unforeseen, off-the-wall happenstance could keep them from accomplishing their raid against the eastern radar site. With Tom Drew's experience and leadership, there could be little doubt of a successful mission.

Tom Drew is a ruggedly handsome man. His size is what one expects to see in a college football line. He speaks softly but with authority. He exudes competence. His picture belongs on army recruiting posters.

Drew enlisted in the army in 1982 at age eighteen for the "High School to Flight School" warrant officer program. But in a way, Drew had been an aviator all his life. He had grown up an army brat, the son of an army aviator. His father flew Cobras in Vietnam, retiring as a colonel. Figuratively, Drew had cut his teeth on his dad's aviator helmet bag, all the while listening to flying stories of the war in Vietnam.

Graduating from flight school as an AH-1S Cobra pilot, Drew reported to C Company, 229th Attack Helicopter Battalion, 101st Airborne Division (Air Assault). In a few weeks, Drew found himself back in school at Fort Rucker transitioning to the Apache. Upon return to Fort Campbell, Drew was temporarily assigned to Task Force 1-112, a special group assembled to test employment of the attack helicopter battalion. The experience gained flying the Apache in TF 1-112 qualified him for reassignment to the Aviation School at Fort Rucker, Alabama, as an Apache instructor pilot.

After a few years instructing, Drew was asked to return to Fort Campbell and the 101st to help them in their transition from Cobra to Apache. Shortly after completion of the Apache issue and training, Drew found himself being selected to attend officer candidate school to become a commissioned officer.

By the time Operation Desert Shield came along, Drew had eight years of service, seven of them flying the Cobra and Apache. His experience gained flying in the deserts of California with TF 1-112 proved to be invaluable to the battalion in Saudi Arabia during their initial in-country training.

Low-level flying over desert or open water is similar—depth perception is difficult. Too often the inexperienced and untrained fly into the water or ground. This proved to be especially true in the desert at night. Using night vision devices seemed to compound the problem. Drawing on Drew's expertise, a carefully prepared training program was devised and implemented, resulting in none of the 1-101st's pilots or aircraft being hurt or damaged during both Desert Shield and Desert Storm.

Thirty-five minutes after takeoff from Al Jouf, as Drew was racing through his mental checklist to ensure that he had not overlooked some minor detail, he was startled at the sight of small-arms tracers arcing up from the dark desert floor. The fire seemed to be aimed at one of the air force Pave Lows, in front of the Apaches. Drew's aircraft was the third Apache in the loose formation. Turning his TADS toward the source of the tracers, he could see a Bedouin camp consisting of one tent with a few frightened goats nearby. The gunfire was coming from the door of the tent.

Pave Lows are manned on their sides and rear by scanner-gunners, airmen trained as observers and machine gunners. The rear scanner-gunner on the aircraft singled out by the Bedouins wasted no time returning fire. The Bedouin fire ceased immediately and, except for the terrified goats scattering about, the camp became still.

Jeeze, we're still in Saudi Arabia. This mission is gonna be a real bitch, Drew recalls thinking. But unknown to him at the time, things were worse than they appeared.

During the postmission debriefing, one of the gunners from the number two Pave Low reported seeing what appeared to be an SA-7 antiaircraft missile being fired from near the tent. This sighting was confirmed by others. Apparently the missile failed to lock on and flew harmlessly past the formation.

The White Team's inbound route to the target required them to pass near a known Iraqi outpost. Drew had carefully programmed the location and loaded it into the memory of his fire control computer. Approaching the outpost, Drew called up the stored information and caused his FLIR to point to the outpost location. Sure enough, hot spots appeared on the FLIR screen. Lasing it with the range finder, Drew stored the updated information for use on their way out. If ammunition remained on the return trip, he would enliven the Iraqis' otherwise dreary evening. But all that would have to wait. Drew needed to first reach and destroy his assigned target.

The routes for both teams into and out of Iraq were subdivided by preselected locations called checkpoints. The last location, instead of being called a checkpoint, is entitled release point (RP) and is that point where subordinate units break their march formation and move off to their assigned routes or positions. For TF Normandy, the RPs were the points where the Pave Lows provided the Apaches one last Doppler position update before the Apaches started their final leg toward the targets. The Pave Lows would then move to a second designated location to await the Apaches' return.

Arriving at the RP, the lead Pave Low slowed to a hover, dropped a chemically activated light stick to the ground, and hovered aside. One by one the Apaches passed over the glowing stick, updating their ASN-128 navigation systems. From here on, Doppler would be their primary navigational tool.

White Team's route in and out would take them around the right side of the targeted radar site, causing them to approach their target from the northeast. The idea was to confuse the Iraqis into believing that the aircraft coming from the northeast were friendly. There was some danger in this approach. Allied intelligence had indicated that an Iraqi tank battalion was deployed along the last few kilometers of a road the team planned to follow to reach their objective. Sure enough, as the team raced along on either side of the road, they observed armored vehicles dispersed nearby. The sudden sight of two BMP armored personnel carriers parked on the road caused a rapid increase in anxiety levels. A quick glance at the FLIR showed these vehicles to be warm, not hot enough to have their engines running, but warm just the same.

Drew recalls worrying that these vehicles would be directly at their backs and close enough to reinforce the radar site during White Team's attack.

At twelve kilometers from their target, each Apache went to its assigned attack position and began identifying individual targets. Lack of light discipline and relaxed security within the Iraqi radar site gave Drew a good indication that the Iraqis had not yet detected the Apaches' presence.

Identifying his first and second targets, Drew turned his attention to his watch and began counting the seconds as the numbers in the small window of his watch climbed to 2:37:50 A.M., ten seconds to fire. As team leader, it fell to Drew to broadcast this key time check to the other three aircraft.

At 2:37:50 A.M., Drew pushed his push-to-talk switch, breaking radio silence, and announced, "Party in ten."

At precisely 2:38 A.M. the night awoke as if all triggers were pulled by one finger. Four Hellfire missiles roared off launch rails, streaking toward unsuspecting Iraqis. Again as one, each aircraft launched a second Hellfire. Eight of the deadly missiles headed toward critical targets. As soon as one missile struck its intended target, the gunner shifted his laser guidance beam to a second target in time to capture his second Hellfire. Altering course, the second missiles followed the shifted laser beam to its new location. All Apaches reported destruction of their targets.

Drew's initial target was the radar site's command-and-control van. He remembers it looking like a "large eighteen-wheeler." A slight shift of his sights ensured that his second missile completed target destruction.

Drew recalls crew members scrambling off their ZPU-4 antiaircraft gun as soon as the first Hellfires were launched. "One guy I watched jumped out of his seat on the gun and hit the ground running. He didn't get too far before the flechettes got him," Drew remembers.

After ensuring the destruction of his initial target, Drew shifted his TADS to Cody's primary target to see if he needed backup. He didn't. Cody, in the aircraft to Drew's immediate right, was assigned one of the site's larger and more important radar antennas as his primary target. Cody's target had disappeared. Next Drew shifted to his second target, a prefabricated structure used as a troop barracks. As soon as the crosshairs came to rest on the target, he let two more Hellfires fly. As the missiles arced toward the barracks, an unlucky Iraqi soldier could be seen entering a side door. The barracks collapsed in a cloud of dust.

Crews began shifting to their 70mm rockets. MPSM rockets rained into the target area until all those targets declared essential—the C&C van, radar antennas, and generators—were gone. Next flechettes filled the air, and Drew saw several Iraqi soldiers drop under their impact. The bump-bump-bump of the slow and steady 30mm cannons became the dominant sound as yet more destruction pounded into the flaming former radar site. But all too soon, it was time to break for home.

On order, two of White Team's Apaches turned toward the rendezvous point and the two waiting Pave Lows. Drew and Cody elected to remain behind long enough to verify the destruction of all essential targets. A quick inspection revealed that nothing remained untouched. Nothing moved . . . nothing.

Outbound, the Apaches discovered that the personnel on the two BMPs parked along the road had been aroused by the sounds of the battle at the radar site. Alert to possible danger, and probably quite scared, the BMP crewmen opened fire with the 12.7mm machine guns mounted on the top of their vehicles, firing at the sound of the passing but invisible Apaches. Cody, being closest to the BMPs, turned away and passed by them at a safe distance. Once they were out of range of the 12.7s, catching the Pave Lows became the next challenge.

The operational plan had established 120 knots as the agreed cruise airspeed. With the Pave Lows flying at that airspeed, Cody and Drew were forced to fly at 150 knots to catch up. Under normal circumstances that would be no problem. But in Drew's case, it was becoming one. Something unusual had touched his Apache.

Racing across the desert at 150 knots, hugging the ground, completely blacked out, Drew kept his eyes glued to the FLIR. The run to catch the Pave Lows was proving to be more difficult than he had imagined. In fact, the distance separating the two trailing Apaches was enough that Drew could barely make out the tiny hot spots he assumed to be the Pave Lows and White Team's other Apaches. He was determined not to lose sight of his distant comrades. But as he watched, two somehow became four, then six, then nine, and finally his entire screen blanked out from too much heat. Looking up and outside the cockpit, Drew witnessed the first wave of Allied fighter-bombers streaking down the radar-free corridor, en route to targets in Baghdad. Close behind, a second wave, an "aluminum overcast," appeared to Drew. There were more than a hundred fighter-bombers in the two waves.

Racing to catch the Pave Lows, Drew's Apache began to experience vibration. Normally an in-flight vibration on a helicopter indicates that some component of the rotor system is out of balance. If the vibration occurs after takeoff, it is reasonable to assume that one or more of the rotor blades has experienced some trauma. In Drew's case, the vibration was barely noticeable at first. But with each passing minute it seemed to increase. Soon there was no doubt that one of the main rotor blades was way out of balance and getting worse. By the time Drew and Zarnowski crossed the Saudi-Iraqi border, the vibrations were severe enough that neither could read their instruments. By the time they touched down at Al Jouf, they were convinced that one or more of their blades was about to fail.

Postflight inspection revealed that one of the main rotor blades had sustained severe damage. Neither Drew nor Zarnowski remembered being hit, but one blade had a fist-sized hole. The cause of the damage remains unknown, but the damage had reached the point that the blade was beginning to separate.

One of Apache's most important built-in features is survivability. A few bureaucrats, people whose lives and jobs are seldom in danger, have charged that the Apache is too costly due to needless overengineering. Apache airframe and drive components were designed to sustain damage and get home safely. In Drew's and Zarnowski's case the built-in survivability worked. Their Apache had been damaged, but it brought them home. In fact, the damaged blade outlasted the army's maximum damage specifications. The lives of two valuable aviators and an expensive aircraft had been spared. They would live to fight another day.

Drew's Apache was back in operation twenty-four hours after returning to Al Jouf, most of that time spent waiting for a replacement blade to be flown in. It took him a while longer to forget the size of the hole in the damaged blade.

Fourteen aircraft had gone out and fourteen returned. The mission was executed flawlessly. The Apache attacks lasted a total of four and a half minutes.

Back on the ground at Al Jouf, Task Force Normandy enjoyed a short celebration. Although the air force fighter-bombers were already en route to targets deep in Iraq, Cody needed to notify Central Command (CENTCOM) that the TF Normandy mission had succeeded. Two code words, California AAA and Nebraska AAA, meaning that the mission had been a success, were relayed to Headquarters CENTCOM via the Pave Lows' special long-range radios. When informed, General Schwarzkopf was heard to breathe, "Thank God."

The war was on. The rejoicing crews at Al Jouf had started it. But Cody was worried. He was convinced that Saddam Hussein would not thank the coalition for the sharp stick that they just stuck in his eye, and he wanted to get into position to support the 101st Division if Hussein attacked.

Cody allowed the tired, jubilant crews only a few minutes for backslapping and handshaking. When the celebration ended, the helicopters were refueled and rearmed and then they lifted off for the long flight to King Fahd. After all, if the Iraqis counterattacked, the 101st Division would need the TF Normandy Apaches.

When, at 4:00 P.M., the task force finally touched down at King Fahd, the crews had been flying since 1:00 A.M., a total of fifteen hours. Landing and taxiing to their tie-down area was like something out of a scenario for the air force's Thunderbirds. Members of the battalion who had remained behind lined the taxiways and ramp, rendering the hand salute to each Apache as it taxied to its assigned tie-down. There tired flight crews worked their way through shutdown checklists, and the unfailing Apaches grew quiet. Crew chiefs, smiling ear to ear, rushed to open cockpit hatches. These, the unsung heroes, could barely contain their pride—pride in their aircrews and greater pride in knowing that their hard work had kept their crews and aircraft safe.

It took weeks before word about Operation Normandy reached the public's attention. A veil of secrecy had been draped over the operation and, for a while, had worked. But word leaked out and belatedly the participants became known. They were hunted down and interviewed by aggressive media representatives. Many found this attention embarrassing. Much of the credit rightly went to the brave Pave Low and Apache crews. Equal acclaim was given to the tremendous success of American technology represented in the mission's aircraft. Unfortunately the media gave all too little credit to those hardworking and dedicated men and women who maintained these wondrous aircraft under conditions never before imagined. Searing heat, blowing sand, and poor living conditions were the Apache crew chief's way of life. But the quality of maintenance never suffered. Lieutenant Drew recalls that during Desert Shield/Desert Storm, not one of his Apaches was grounded for maintenance. A truly remarkable feat accomplished by remarkable soldiers.

Together, crews from the 1st Battalion, 101st Aviation Regiment, and the 20th Special Operations Squadron accomplished the first of many extraordinary feats that would take place during Operation Desert Storm. In the words of General Schwarzkopf, the Apaches "plucked out the eyes" of Iraq's air defense. To the curious, skeptical American taxpayer, long programmed to doubt the costly high-tech equipment of the armed forces, this was the first visible example that they had bought their sons and daughters equipment that worked. There was no repeat of the disastrous Desert One, the attempted rescue of the Iranian hostages, which had failed. This time, America had its collective act together.

For army aviation, it all came wrapped in aircraft called Apache, Sioux, Black Hawk, and Chinook. But helicopters are inanimate objects. They are capable of nothing until manned by good soldiers.

Operation Desert Storm would see other battles in which Apache would play an important role. A total of fourteen Apache battalions were deployed in support of the liberation of Kuwait. Some were decisive players. Others belonged to units that played less glamorous supporting roles. It had been the lot of the 1-82d, 1-101st, and 1-24th Aviation Regiments to come early and take great risk. By the time Desert Storm ended, Apache and the men who flew it earned their place in history. In the hundred-hour ground war that destroyed the world's fourth largest army, Apaches led the way, leaving in their wake hundreds of smoking craters where much-feared T72 tanks had died.

Chapter Two

SADDLE UP, WE'RE OUTTA HERE

To the soldier, the profession of arms is a calling, one that assures the soldier a life of challenge and, on occasion, danger. The soldiers' day-to-day life alternates from near boredom to intervals of great difficulty and danger. It's a lifestyle often fraught with stress.

Units with quick reaction missions (strategically deployable) live on the cutting edge of danger. They attract the intrepid. But over time even those who fear little come to know stress. Tucked away in the deployable soldiers' subconscious is the concern about an early morning phone call with a voice saying "Shotgun" or some other code word that tells the soldier to report immediately and be prepared to be outbound to some world hot spot. Even if the day begins without the early call, the soldier might spend it wondering if, at day's end, he will return home.

When individual soldiers are organized into units, the unit, like the soldiers who compose it, carry their own unique reputations—reputations that are often driven by a sense of mission. The reputation a unit carries either attracts adventurous soldiers or repulses those seeking a more staid lifestyle.

Mission anxiety is common to units like the 2d Infantry Division, deployed along the demilitarized zone separating the two Koreas; forward-deployed air force fighter pilots of the Tactical Air Command; the Ranger battalions stationed in the United States; the three divisions making up the XVIII Airborne Corps, stationed in three locations within the United States; or, until recently, the two U.S. Army Armored Cavalry Regiments deployed along the East-West German border. All these units (and many others) literally live with bags packed.

For the most part, all light, rapidly deployable forces based within the continental limits of the United States belong to Headquarters, XVIII Airborne Corps. As expected, this three-division corps was the first army force ordered to Saudi Arabia as part of Desert Shield. To fully understand the risks involved during the early days of this operation requires an examination of the mission of XVIII Airborne Corps during the first days of the Allied buildup.

Fort Bragg, North Carolina, home base for the XVIII Airborne Corps and the 82d Airborne Division, has a forty-plus-year history of its soldiers being primed to move on short notice. In every international crisis involving the United States since World War II, the 82d Airborne has usually been first to load and depart. Often these preparations were for real, with the division becoming involved in combat in places like the Dominican Republic, Vietnam, Grenada, and Panama. Other times the loading is done for practice, or sometimes as a ruse. Would-be troublemakers know from experience that the alert assembly and deployment of the 82d marks the first step in America's making a serious military commitment.

The 82d's reputation for being fast movers and tough fighters keeps it at the top of the army's "ready" units. Light, lean, and quick to react, the airborne division allows the national command authority, the president, through the army, to project combat power anywhere in the world within hours. An airborne division arrives at its destination either by parachute or by air force transport aircraft on a friendly-held airfield.

The 82d is the last of the army's airborne or parachute-trained divisions. (Although the 101st Airborne Division [Air Assault] is still an active division, it no longer parachutes into battle.) During World War II there had been five airborne divisions with all but one serving in Europe. The 82d returned in 1946 with a distinguished combat record. But the threat of the massive tank formations created by eastern bloc Communist countries soon after World War II saw the need for the U.S. Army to maintain a higher number of heavier armor and mechanized divisions, so the number of airborne divisions declined. Unlike the 82d Airborne, these heavy divisions take longer and are more difficult to move overseas. Instead of moving by aircraft, heavy divisions require ocean shipping and good ports on both ends of the journey.

Airlanding, as arriving by aircraft is known, was how the 82d came into Saudi Arabia. They arrived first, days before other U.S. or Allied ground forces began their moves. Within hours of their arrival, units of the 82d were deployed forward along the Saudi-Iraqi border between the massive offensively equipped forces of Iraq and the smaller defensive forces of Saudi Arabia. Being first, the 82d became a thin line of military force representing the determination of the United Nations and the United States to protect Saudi Arabia and eventually to free Kuwait. During those early tentative days and weeks of the Allied buildup, the 82d Airborne faced peril. With the exception of a small Marine Corps landing force, tactical air, and the Saudi Arabian National Guard, the 82d "All-American" Division stood alone. Its first major army reinforcement came in the form of the 101st Airborne Division (Air Assault).

Like the 82d, the 101st Division, also one of the five World War II airborne divisions, had fought in Europe. The 101st Airborne distinguished itself on several occasions, especially during the Battle of the Bulge in December 1944. The 101st earned its unquestionable place in American military history by winning the Presidential Unit Citation for its heroic defense of the Belgian village of Bastogne. Following World War II, the 101st remained one of two airborne divisions in the postwar army force structure until its deployment to Vietnam. Technological advances and another type of war were to fundamentally alter how the army and the 101st would fight in the future.

Because entry into battle by parachute has always been difficult and sometimes confusing, large airborne assaults often found paratroopers and their supplies widely dispersed from their intended objectives. It was not uncommon for an airborne force to be inadvertently dropped miles from its intended drop zone by confused transport pilots. Frequently individual soldiers discovered that they had landed far from the rest of their unit and were forced to join and fight with whomever they chanced to find. By the 1960s, much to the chagrin of the airborne community, the army had developed a better vehicle for the tactical delivery of troops into battle, the helicopter. However, strategically the parachute remained the best, and sometimes the only means of entry.

When the 101st arrived in Vietnam in the mid-1960s, the war had evolved to one of movement—movement dominated by the helicopter. The UH-1D and later the UH-1H Huey and the CH-47 Chinook provided the primary means for moving men and material to battle. The helicopter brought speed and agility to the battlefield and also cured the ills found of airborne (parachute) operations. For example, with combat assaults by helicopter, the scatter or dispersion problem common to airborne operations disappeared. The helicopter landed soldiers in squads, platoons, or companies at the designated objective while maintaining unit integrity, one of the intangibles required for successful fighting units.

The helicopter offered other advantages. When the World War II paratrooper jumped into battle, he carried—strapped to his body—150 pounds of equipment and supplies. This additional load increased his chances of injury during landing. For the modern 101st heliborne trooper, that weight has been reduced. The helicopter allows for frequent and quicker resupply to units in the field, eliminating the need for the soldier to carry several days' worth of supplies.

During World War II, the 101st Artillery, as part of an airborne division, was delivered in separate aircraft. Personnel arrived in one aircraft, guns in another, and often ammunition in another. Today's 101st artillerymen, equipped with larger and more powerful weapons, are delivered by helicopter and arrive with their equipment completely assembled. What is more, each artillery piece arrives accompanied by its crew and ammunition, and can be firing within minutes of touchdown.

Soon after the arrival of the 101st in Vietnam, General Westmoreland, commander of the Military Advisory Command Vietnam (MACV), and a former divisional commander of the 101st, authorized the conversion of the 101st to an air assault division, one that goes into battle by helicopter. Since then, the division has kept its air assault designation. Historically, the 101st Airborne Division (Air Assault), home stationed at Fort Campbell, Kentucky, is a part of the XVIII Airborne Corps' strategic capability. Like the 82d, the 101st maintains a fixed percentage of units on ready status, prepared to load and move in hours.

Rounding out the three divisional XVIII Corps is the 24th Infantry Division (Mechanized), home stationed at Fort Stewart, Georgia. The 24th Division is a heavy division equipped with tanks, armored personnel carriers, and many other tracked and wheeled vehicles. It takes longer to transport overseas than an air assault division.

In a world where armored forces dominate ground warfare, prudent leaders know that a light division must never be committed to combat without the means for rapid reinforcement. Under normal conditions, the order of deployment for the XVIII Corps might see the light 82d load and move first to establish a lodgement for the arrival of the remainder of the corps. Next would come the somewhat heavier 101st, followed later by the heaviest 24th Division.

During August 1990, with Iraq threatening to invade Saudi Arabia, the XVIII Corps moved to Saudi Arabia. Alert notification had gone out to the 82d, 101st, and 24th Divisions on August 7, five days after Iraq had brutally overrun Kuwait.

Assembling in the heat and humidity of August, soldiers of the XVIII Corps' three divisions hoped that this would be but another emergency deployment readiness exercise (EDRE), a test of the unit to assemble and load with no notice. Not this time. The skies and loading ramps at Forts Bragg and Campbell grew crowded with large air force C-5 and C-141 jet transport aircraft. The 24th Mechanized moved equipment to the docks of nearby Savannah, Georgia. The tone of the talk in briefing rooms was deadly serious.

By August 8, 1990, members of the 82d Airborne Division's 1st Battalion, 325th Parachute Infantry Regiment, were on the ground in Saudi Arabia. By August 13 most of the division's fighting elements had completed their move. Once in Saudi Arabia, the nearly alone 82d Airborne Division became a light infantry division, a long way from home and standing face-to-face with the world's fourth largest armored force. If Saddam Hussein had elected to continue his quest for the control of Mideast oil and had invaded Saudi Arabia, the 82d, the marine landing force, and the Saudi Arabian National Guard would have been the sole defense against him. The grim humor of hardened paratroopers manifested itself when describing their circumstances, viewing themselves as "speed bumps." Quick reinforcement of the 82d was essential.

Meanwhile at Fort Campbell, the 101st Division, understanding the urgency of its mission, was packing and nearly ready to load aboard air force transport aircraft for the flight to Saudi Arabia.

Lieutenant Colonel Richard A. Cody, commander of the 1st Battalion, 101st Aviation Regiment (1-101st), the divisional AH-64 Apache battalion, was notified on August 15 that his battalion would be the first battalion of the 101st to go, a departure from normal divisional deployment procedure. Usually the infantry led, secured the division's lodgement area, and was followed by the remainder of the division. With the 82d already on the ground, the lodgement mission was moot. However, the armor threat faced by the 82d dictated that the 101st's tank-killing Apaches be moved quickly to reinforce the 82d.

At 6:00 P.M. on August 15, the 1-101st went into lockup status. Battalion members were restricted to the marshaling area, a tightly guarded enclosure where units make their final preparations. No one is allowed in or out. All communications with the outside are cut. In the marshaling area the officers and men of the 1-101st went about the business of preparing for their departure. The news coming over the Cable News Network (CNN) informed them of the 82d's arrival in Saudi Arabia. The urgency of the activity told the soldiers of the 1-101st that they were going next. They were also aware that until Allied armor arrived, both divisions would be playing a high-tech and high-stakes game of David and Goliath. If war began before the strength of Allied armor reached adequate levels, it would take unusual men and leaders to fight, hold, and defeat the large Iraqi army. If war came, Cody was convinced that the 1-101st was prepared and would leave its mark in the desert sands. Cody is one of those remarkable men who seem born to lead.

In 1968 Dick Cody, a man of great energy and strong ambition, left the beauty of Vermont's mountains to become a cadet at the United States Military Academy at West Point, New York. Graduating in 1972, he was commissioned in the infantry. Hampered by bad knees—enough to limit his useful service to the infantry—Cody was temporarily detailed to service with the Transportation Corps. With good medical treatment, his troublesome knees were healed enough to pass the entrance physical for flight school. He graduated as an army aviator in 1976.

Cody's early experience in aviation began in aircraft maintenance. Too adventuresome to spend life fixing aircraft someone else had flown, he set his sights on becoming the leader of an attack helicopter unit. Although time would prove him good at both, Cody's killer instincts won out over his mechanical talents. He was assigned to the 24th Infantry Division in Georgia, where he flew AH-1 Cobras, gaining experience while participating in several special tests involving attack helicopters. Alternating between flying attack helicopters and serving as maintenance officer, he established himself as an officer with unusual qualifications and superb leadership skills, enough that his superiors decided he was capable of leading war fighters. Moving to the 101st at Fort Campbell, Cody was given command of an attack company and later served as an attack battalion operations officer (S-3). After a short diversion as aide-de-camp to a general officer in Korea, Cody returned to Campbell, this time assuming command of the 1-101st Battalion in 1989. He had been in command less than a year when the Apaches and crews of the 1-101st departed for Saudi Arabia and war.

Getting ready took the 1-101st a full day and night of furious, round-the-clock finding, fixing, and packing, each task sprinkled with liberal laughter, occasional profanity, and silent, gut-twisting apprehension. The battalion readied its equipment to board the seven giant C-5 and seventeen medium C-141 air force transports allocated for its move. Finally it was all done. The aircrafts' huge clamshell loading doors were swung shut, and the big fan-jet engines began their low whine leading to takeoff.

Silence and fatigue swept over the men as the aircraft whisked them eastward through the short night to an early dawn. During that ride, the soldiers, like soldiers through the ages waiting to go into battle, sat and wondered—some of what lay ahead, others with thoughts of home and family. The dark interior of the windowless aircraft added to the gloom of the flight. No soldier likes war; damn few care for darkness.

On August 17 at 4:30 A.M., the coolest time of day, the C-5s and C-141s bearing the 1-101st began landing at King Abduhl Aziz Air Base, Dhahran, Saudi Arabia. As the engine sounds of the air force transports died away, the men of the 1-101st deplaned into the eighty-seven-degree air. For the soldiers from Kentucky, 4:30 A.M. in Saudi felt like an August afternoon. The real surprise would come a few hours later. In the meantime, the first order of business was to unload their Apaches, reassemble them, and get them ready for combat. After that, soldiers could worry about personal comfort and living facilities.

By 8:00 A.M. the temperature reached 135 degrees, making work in the direct sun difficult. The 1-101st's soldiers were not prepared for temperatures this high. Lack of shade added to their discomfort. It would take days before the soldiers acclimatized to the harsh desert environment.

Within twelve hours, Apaches from the 1-101st "Expect no Mercy" battalion were reassembled, test-flown, and ready to be loaded with fuel and ammunition. Once the Apaches were inspected and cleared by maintenance officers, the armament specialists moved in and loaded each aircraft with Hellfire missiles, 70mm rockets, and 30mm cannon ammunition. This done, the 1-101st reported themselves ready.

Later they were startled to learn that the only Hellfire antitank missiles available in Saudi Arabia were the two hundred they had brought with them from Fort Campbell. In an intense antitank fight, this small supply could be expended within an hour. The problem was that the 1-101st arrived in Saudi Arabia ahead of the logistical system's ability to sustain it. The good news was that an additional supply of missiles was scheduled to arrive by air soon.

Three days after their arrival, the 1-101st moved to King Fahd International Airport. As it turned out, they were the first army helicopters assigned to King Fahd. Arriving at their new home, they were comforted to learn that air force tank-killing A-10 Warthogs preceded them. Apaches and A-10s routinely trained together, so the 1-101st was glad to see these air force tank-killing warriors. If events caused the Allies to fight the Iraqis, these two forces—Apaches and Warthogs— were familiar with each other's capabilities and spoke a common tactical language.

For the next several days, the Apache-Warthog combination would be the Allies' primary tank-killing systems. The only restriction was that the A-10, the only aircraft ever built by the air force to provide direct close air support to the army, lacked built-in night vision equipment. Although A-10 pilots train with the ANVIS-6 night vision goggles, the A-10 is better suited to daytime use.

The Apache crewmen faced another serious problem: Desert flying is dangerous. Flying low level over the flat, featureless desert surface is much like low-level flight over water where the pilot's depth perception is adversely affected. Blowing sand compounds the problem. To be effective, Allied pilots had to learn how to fly in the desert, and they had to learn quickly. Apaches, vital to the divisions' mission, simply could not be allowed to become victims of needless accidents.

With the exception of Lt. Tom Drew, who had gained experience flying in the deserts of California, the flight crews of the 1-101st lacked any desert flying experience. Also, Fort Campbell had trees; Saudi Arabia had few. It would take time and practice to learn to navigate safely in an endless brown sea devoid of recognizable landmarks. Flying low level at night proved to be an even greater challenge. The secret to success lay in sharpening individual depth perception. Drew found himself the resident expert and selected to develop the battalion's desert training program.

As if these obstacles were not enough, Allied forces had a problem of even greater consequences. Saddam Hussein was threatening to use chemical weapons; intelligence sources believed that he also had nuclear weapons ready to strike. Hussein appeared desperate enough to employ these weapons. The nuclear, biological, chemical (NBC) threat brought additional discomfort to the soldiers' already uncomfortable lifestyle. The seriousness of this threat required that the level of NBC alert remain high. Additional NBC training began in how to fly and fight in a chemically contaminated environment. The realities of NBC warfare affected everything the soldier did. The heavy, hot, charcoal-lined chemical protective suit became part of the uniform of the day and night. Aircrews were instructed to fly wearing their NBC equipment. Soldiers kept all protective equipment close at hand at all times. All this added anxiety to an already strenuous situation. But the spirit of the soldier dominated, and preparation for war moved ahead.

A unit's success in combat depends first on its level of training and second on the operational availability of its equipment. During times of peace, the ideal is to train the soldier to a keen edge while maintaining his equipment in a ready-to-fight status—goals that sometimes work against each other. In practice, too much of one erodes the other: Use of equipment in training causes equipment readiness status to suffer; too much time spent maintaining equipment reduces training readiness. Successful commanders learn where to place the fulcrum and how to balance one against the other. Not an easy job. However, some of the army's problem in keeping equipment ready is the result of its failure to procure an adequate density of high-use parts. On the other hand, some of the problem is caused by overuse, the result of poor leadership and asset management.

Aircraft availability—readiness—is based on many variables, some of which the commander may not be able to influence. The availability of spare parts, allocated flying hours, required maintenance, and the presence of skilled maintenance personnel are all factors with which the commander must contend. One truth of success in the army shines like an airfield beacon: Unit reputations, and therefore commanders' reputations, are won or lost on the roll of the equipment availability dice. Naturally, the army is most sensitive to this problem and works hard to keep all its fleets, including Apaches, ready.

Going into Desert Shield, the 1-101st owned one of the most consistently high Apache availability rates in the army. One might speculate what impact Cody's maintenance background had on these numbers. Although this is difficult to measure, the understanding of what best keeps systems in proper working order comes from having to maintain them. In that regard, Cody had years of experience. Not open to speculation is the fact that Cody could not have done it alone. The success of the 1-101st in keeping its equipment in fighting condition took the collective efforts of every member of the battalion. Good leadership helps, but hard work and caring soldiers are what win the daily maintenance numbers battle.

One might also speculate on the impact of Cody's innovative training program for flight crews and his insistence on holding them responsible for their assigned Apaches' availability. But Cody attributes the battalion's success to "the best damn crew chiefs and maintenance crews in the world." Whatever the reason for its success in being good at both training and maintaining, the 1-101st was selected for Operation Normandy, the raid against the radars, because of its overall reputation. But every soldier knows that one other intangible is involved in this selection—luck. It is also a truism that people and units sometimes make their own luck. In addition to good maintenance habits, Cody and the 1-101st practiced night raids long before Desert Shield.

For much of the year preceding the battalion's departure to Saudi Arabia, the 1-101st had been unknowingly preparing for its role in the opening hours of the war. Cody's knowledge of possible employment of the 101st Division in several other regions of the world caused him to quietly analyze the 1-101st's role in accomplishing divisional missions. This analysis led him to conclude that raids were a possibility in several mission scenarios. In addition, several of the division's possible missions might require the 1-101st to self-deploy.

To prepare for such contingencies, Cody planned a series of long-range night training raids. The Apaches' night vision systems and auxiliary, or ferry, tanks made such extended missions possible. Although these auxiliary tanks were not designed for use in combat, Cody visualized using them just as air force fighter aircraft use them: Fuel from the auxiliary tanks would be consumed en route to the target and the tanks jettisoned before the attack.

To make these night missions realistic, Cody selected a target several hundred miles away from Fort Campbell—the municipal airport located on the outskirts of Vidalia, Georgia, a small town located midway between Macon and Savannah and known worldwide for its sweet onions. From Fort Campbell the Apaches crossed the Tennessee-Kentucky state line headed south. Flying low level through Tennessee and Alabama, they would turn east into Georgia. The flight crews were forced to use all of their navigational skills to reach Vidalia. The airfield, located on the southeast side of town, is typical of most small Southern airports—a small terminal building and two small hangars. The rotating beacon and runway lights drew the Apaches the last few miles. Once the Apaches were in position, the crews conducted their simulated attack on airport buildings and parked aircraft before withdrawing and returning to Fort Campbell.

During these long, grueling flights, copilots used the army's ANVIS-6 night vision goggles, while the pilot flew using the pilots night vision sensor (PNVS). This combination of goggles and PNVS ensured that the crew could function if the weather favored one system over the other. It also added a degree of safety insurance. If the pilot's onboard system failed while flying low level, the copilot could take over the piloting duties before events got out of hand. Once in the target area, the copilot would remove his PNVS goggles and shift to his TADS for target identification and attack. Once in Saudi Arabia, it did not take the crews long to wonder whether Cody was a training prophet or just lucky.

By September 1, thanks to Tom Drew's training program, the 1-101st aircrews were operating with great confidence in the Saudi desert. Still concerned with the threat posed by the massed Iraqi army, Cody ordered one of his companies to move to a forward support base, positioned to provide quick reaction to any threat against the overextended 82d Airborne Division. The forward support base was initially called Camp Hell, but it was officially named Camp Bastogne. The 1-101st Apaches were to fly surveillance of the Saudi Arabian–Iraqi border. Then on September 27, the 101st Division relieved the 82d of its covering force mission, and the 82d moved to the rear to become the XVIII Corps reserve and to receive a well-deserved rest.

In the spectrum of military operations, a covering force mission serves as a trip wire. When an enemy approaches, the covering force first sounds the alarm and then engages the attacking force by fire, but does not allow itself to become so entangled that it cannot disengage and move. This phase has the covering force acting as a buffer, protecting the larger force by attacking the approaching enemy, forcing him to deploy and then moving to new ground and repeating the process. The covering force defends the main force in this way as long as possible, allowing the main force time to prepare its defense. Finally, when the main force is prepared to meet the enemy force, the covering force disengages and moves to the rear of the main body to prepare for other missions. By relieving the 82d, the 101st became the buffer for the force arriving to its rear, a force not yet a match for those facing the 101st across the ill-defined desert border.

The covering force mission caused the bulk of the 101st Division to take up positions along the Saudi-Iraqi border joining the Apaches of 1-101st. As the division occupied its new positions, it was reinforced by elements of the Apache-equipped 12th Aviation Group, recently arrived from Wiesbaden, Germany, and two artillery brigades just off their ship from Fort Sill, Oklahoma. Although these reinforcements were most welcome, the balance between Allied and Iraqi forces was still tilted in the Iraqis' favor.

Situations like the Saudi Arabian covering force mission can become extremely hazardous for relatively light divisions like the 101st or the 82d if they are attacked by armor. Even though both divisions were equipped with 180 tube-launched, optically sighted, wire-guided antitank missile launchers (TOWs), mounted on high mobility multi-purpose wheeled vehicles (HMMWVs), neither could stand toe-to-toe and slug it out with heavy armor for very long. The antitank TOW is capable of defeating most known armor, but mounted on the thin-skinned HMMWV it lacks the protection required to stand in the open, especially open desert, and fight tanks. The 1-101st and the attached Apaches from the 12th Group added to the division's tank-killing capabilities, but more antitank systems would be required before they could engage and defeat Hussein's massive armored formations.

The covering force mission did not inhibit Cody from continuing to conduct challenging desert training. It did, however, require that the battalion be poised to drop what it was doing and react quickly over a wide sector if the need arose.

As weeks passed, more Allied armored and mechanized forces arrived in Saudi Arabia, lowering the level of danger to the 82d and 101st

Divisions. Even so, the 101st Division remained the covering force until January 17, the day after it helped begin the war and the air campaign.

This forward deployment forced the 1-101st to continue living and maintaining equipment in the open desert under the worst conditions. Commanders had to train their units to deal with the complexities of desert warfare in an environment seemingly designed by the Creator to purposely destroy man's machinery. Time and the harsh elements showed their effects. The incessant and abrasive dust took its toll on everything mechanical. Powdery dust kicked up by the downwash from the main rotors and ingested into the turbines adhered to the parts deep within the engines. As this dirt built up, the smooth flow of air through the combustion and compression chambers of turbine engines was disrupted, eventually causing them to lose power.

But the damage done by dust and sand was not limited to turbine engines. The swirling, abrasive clouds caused by rotor blade downwash ate away at the composite materials along the leading edges of rotor blades. This happened despite the innovative field expedients coming from pilots and ground crews alike, ideas like not landing in remote, unimproved areas if possible. At their home base, diesel oil was sprayed to "pave" the runway and taxiways, greatly reducing dust. Using the Apache's wheeled landing gear to make running takeoffs and landings, just as an airliner would, reduced the dust somewhat. Even with these innovative techniques, it was only by the herculean efforts of the mechanics and crew chiefs that the battalion maintained its high availability of Apaches.

Time became an enemy. After several weeks operating in the grating environment, commanders came to realize that the scope and intensity of training and the use of aircraft had to be scaled back if the equipment was to be ready for the coming war.

All the while, even before the hurried arrival of Allied forces in Saudi Arabia, work had been going on in General Schwarzkopf's CENTCOM headquarters to develop plans that would put to good use the experience gained by the 1-101st during the long night flights across Tennessee, Alabama, and Georgia. Unknown to Cody, the training and maintenance status of the 1-101st was being carefully tracked and had been for some time.

Starting several weeks before the 1-101st's departure from Fort Campbell, Cody received unusual telephone calls. The caller identified himself as belonging to a staff section located within the Pentagon and questioned Cody about particulars of the 1-101st's monthly Apache readiness status. Basically, Cody was asked to verify his reports that showed the battalion's Apaches to be at 85 percent availability, fifteen percentage points above the army's goal and 35 percent above the average. During one call, the caller hinted to Cody that the battalion's readiness was being closely monitored. At the time, none of this made sense to Cody, except that the Government Accounting Office (GAO) spent a great deal of its effort challenging the army's reported Apache readiness.

One month and six days after landing in Saudi Arabia, Cody and his brigade commander, Col. Tom Garrett, were told to report to Col. Jessie Johnson, commander of the Theater Special Operations Command (COMSOCCENT). Johnson, an army colonel, briefed Garrett and Cody on the top secret plan to destroy the radar sites guarding the approaches to Baghdad. This raid, they were told, would be the opening of the Allied campaign to free Kuwait. COMSOCCENT's mission was to eliminate these radars, an action critical to the success of the air campaign.

The plan for the raid was daring and, if successful, would open a radar-free corridor from the Saudi border to Baghdad, allowing Allied fighter-bombers to conduct their initial attacks deep within Iraq with little interference. According to Johnson, the 1-101st's high Apache availability rate was what brought Cody and Garrett to the meeting.

Raids are high-risk operations normally conducted by a small party against a cardinal objective. Raid tactics are based on striking a quick blow with surprise against isolated enemy. The plan must be clear and concise. Whenever practicable, movements and attacks are made at night. The use of aircraft in a raid compounds the risk. The raid of the 1-101st against the Iraqi radar sites was indeed high risk. It was to be a night raid, using totally blacked-out helicopters, penetrating deep into Iraq, attacking two widely separated radar sites at the same instant. No mean feat and enough to cause one to wonder what they smoked in Schwarzkopf's war room.

To make matters worse, the Soviet-supplied Iraqi radar system was state of the art. Operating in conjunction with other systems, it provided complete early warning coverage all along the Iraq borders between Saudi Arabia and Kuwait. Additionally, it gave the Iraqis the means for control of their intercept aircraft and surface-to-air missiles (SAMs). The total system consisted of radars positioned well forward along the border, which were subsequently linked to sector operations centers (SOC). The SOCs were in turn linked to intelligence operations centers (IOC). Information from the radar sites was passed to the SOC and IOC; if the information was determined to be hostile, alerts were sent to Iraqi SAM launch sites and MiG-24 airfields. These centers then assigned targets using the radars that had initially acquired the targets. Finally the centers would direct the interception and destruction of the hostile intruders.

Posing a theoretical question to Cody, Johnson asked, "Could Apaches eliminate these radar sites?" Without hesitation Cody answered: "Yes, they could do it!" Johnson then dropped the other shoe. "I am not talking about 50 percent; they have to go down 100 percent." Cody replied, "I don't see any problem." Johnson then drove home the point that the mission would not only have to be done at night, but on the darkest night of that period. Once more Cody expressed his confidence in being able to make it all happen.

At this point Johnson raised concerns of the Apache's reliability. Speaking directly to Cody, Johnson asked if the aircraft availability rate of the 1-101st was correct. A confident Cody answered, "Yes, sir!" Satisfied with Cody's response, Johnson ended the mystery of the strange calls received at Fort Campbell, explaining that he had been tracking the 1-101st's readiness reports. Johnson, convinced that Cody and his troops could handle the raid, ended the meeting instructing Cody to commence planning the details for the mission.

Some time later, in October, while General Schwarzkopf and air force Col. George A. Gray, commander of the 1st Special Operations Wing, were discussing the feasibility of the pending raid, General Schwarzkopf asked Gray if he could guarantee "100 percent success." When Gray assured Schwarzkopf that he could, Schwarzkopf responded, "OK, Colonel, you get to start the war." It would be up to Cody and his task force of Apaches and air force Pave Lows to prove Gray correct.

Following Cody's meeting with Johnson, Cody's life became far more complicated. He was a man with two missions and two masters, not the best of situations for a promising young lieutenant colonel. The raid mission had not relieved the 1-101st of its responsibility to respond if the division was attacked. Cody was forced to look in two directions: his activities under the operational direction of Headquarters COMSOCCENT to prepare the detailed plan for the raid, and his duties as battalion commander. Cody was assisted in his planning role by a small number of COMSOCCENT staff members, but in the final analysis, the burden rested with him.

In the meantime, Cody had to lead a battalion without raising suspicion; he had to maintain visibility around the battalion area while at the same time going undercover to work on the raid plan. By building a tightly guarded workroom located within his battalion headquarters building, Cody somehow accomplished both.

The time soon came to select crews for the raid. Once the final plan was accepted, crew training would begin. For Cody, crew selection involved difficult choices. No "special" crews or special aircraft existed in the 1-101st. Basic to the profession is the understanding that keeping crews together and keeping crews with the same aircraft is a sound practice. Just as individual crew members can have their own idiosyncrasies, so can machinery. Men need time to get used to each other, to become comfortable with each other as well as with their machines. The longer they are together, the better they work together. Cody's belief in this philosophy was strong, and he worked hard to ensure that crews and aircraft melded into a functional team. When it came time to decide which crews could meet the demands required for this mission, Cody considered three-part teams, each with a flight crewman, a crew chief, and an Apache. If one element of a team was weak, Cody would pass the team by and select another.

Secondary to Cody's decision of whom to assign to Task Force Normandy, code name for the raid, was his concern that the raid might trigger a retaliatory response by the Iraqis. To Cody, it was clear that TF Normandy had top priority, but equal in his mind was the survival of the 101st Division. If TF Normandy returned from Iraq intact, it would take him seven to ten hours to fly back east to where the bulk of the 101st Division was arrayed along the border as the corps' covering force. If Hussein retaliated against the 101st Division, the Apaches of TF Normandy would be needed by the division. Cody reasoned that both scenarios—the raid and the defense of the division—would require competent crews. With this criteria fixed in his mind, he selected crews from across the battalion's experience spectrum, ensuring a balance in both the raiding party and those remaining behind.

Cody's mission analysis determined that Normandy would require ten crews—nine AH-64 Apaches and one UH-60 Black Hawk. The remainder of the battalion would be left under the command of the battalion's able executive officer, Maj. Michael H. Davis. If, indeed, the division were attacked during the absence of TF Normandy, the 1-101st Battalion, minus the task force, would provide excellent antitank support to the 101st Division. Additionally, Apaches from Wiesbaden's 12th Aviation Group were tasked to support the 101st.

Cody recalls that the selection of at least one company commander for the raid was a tough call. All of the serving company commanders were good men and good leaders. Because Capt. Newman Shufflebarger, commander of Company A, was the most experienced Apache pilot, Cody chose him. However, since the other line company commanders, Capt. Doug Gabram, commander of Company B, and Capt. George Garcia, commander of Company C, had spent months working for Davis in California as part of a special task force, they stayed with him while the raiding party was away.

With Shufflebarger selected to lead one team—Red Team—Cody needed another leader for White Team, one capable of operating independently. Lieutenant Tom Drew filled the requirement. Obviously Cody would lead the third team himself. With the crews and leaders selected, Cody began the training program he had developed to get TF Normandy ready.

Just days before the mission was to launch, word would come from COMSOCCENT to drop the number of targeted radar sites from three to two. The crews from the now unneeded third team were distributed among the remaining two. With this done, Cody's major concern remained timing. The distance between the targeted sites required the teams to operate independently. The extraordinary requirement to ensure that both sites be eliminated simultaneously made the mission difficult. But somehow Cody felt confident that his team leaders would make it work. However, he would not rest easy until they had.

At the time of its fielding, Apache was considered the most advanced attack helicopter to be found. It still is. However, it was built and issued lacking state-of-the-art navigational equipment. Mission analysis during Apache's early development indicated that some Apache missions would require a self-contained navigational aid. At the time, the Singer Kearfott ASN-128 lightweight Doppler navigational system (LDNS) was considered adequate and was selected to be installed during manufacture. The system operates by entering data for a known location and then, as the aircraft moves about, it directs radar beams to the ground below and processes the returned signal. The twenty-eight-pound radar system then provides the crew with information on aircraft velocity, present position, and heading. But programming the system at a known start point, and being able to provide position updates, are essential for the ASN-128 Doppler to provide adequate information. In Europe, with its many landmarks to aid in determining location, Apache's onboard Doppler system is sufficient, but not so in the faceless desert. On a long mission, in the dark of night, across the vast deserts of Saudi Arabia and Iraq, accurate update input coming from the crew would be unlikely. For a mission as delicate and finely tuned as TF Normandy, a more precise system was needed. Task Force Normandy would have to have outside navigational assistance.

The aircraft most compatible with Apache for a mission like the raid was the air force MH-53J Pave Low helicopter. Several of these most special aircraft belonging to the 20th Special Operations Wing were already in-country. As mentioned earlier, two Pave Lows were selected to lead and assist the Apaches in navigating to and from their targets.

When units from separate services are brought together for an operation, time and training are needed to allow them to become used to one another; Task Force Normandy was no exception. But for TF Normandy, time was becoming a most scarce commodity. Getting the units used to working with one another and gaining an understanding of their strengths and weaknesses was critical to a successful mission. Even so, time was made available and joint training was conducted to bring the army Apache and air force Pave Low crews together as a team.

On October 1, Apache and Pave Low crews met for the first time. The pilots of each service first needed to gain an understanding of the other's aircraft and its capabilities. Additionally and most importantly, they learned each other's jargon. Failure of something as simple as human communication could not be allowed to endanger the mission. With this done, the crews from both services discussed and rehearsed techniques for recovery of downed crew members. Next they took to the air and flew joint missions at night, over courses of varying lengths and terrain. Although the crews still were not aware of what all this "special" training was for, they flew demanding dress rehearsals.

Specialized training was conducted separately. This training, done mostly at night, included extensive live-fire gunnery for the Apaches. Hellfire missiles, heretofore scarce, suddenly became plentiful. For some Apache crewmen, including the much experienced instructor pilot Drew, it was their first opportunity to use the Hellfire. To protect the security of TF Normandy, Cody would occasionally bring the entire battalion together for training. Otherwise that segment not involved with Normandy conducted routine Apache unit training.

During the detailed mission planning following his meeting with Johnson, Cody sought every means possible to avoid being put into the position of having a plan too complicated to work. After taking stock of his concerns, Cody decided that they fell into two categories: psychological and material. Perhaps unconsciously Cody was carrying the baggage of the failed Desert One operation.

In the 1980s the army, in conjunction with the navy, Marine Corps, and air force, attempted to rescue American hostages held in Tehran by Iranian "students." This rescue attempt was a colossal failure. Afterward much finger-pointing and denial occurred. Postmission analysis determined that the operational plan was so complicated that it was doomed from the beginning. There were too many services involved, too much turf protection, and too little leadership with authority to knock heads together. One of the weakest links was the quality of the helicopters assigned to the mission, several of which failed to reach Desert One, the scheduled refuel point deep in Iran. The final calamity was the tragic collision of a marine-piloted navy helicopter with an air force C-130 on the ground at Desert One.

All of the services involved with the rescue mission have carried emotional scars from that experience. No member of the Department of Defense wanted TF Normandy to be a repeat performance. The breakdown at the refueling site at Desert One was one thing that Cody was determined to avoid during TF Normandy's raid.

The time of flight from Al Jouf (the launch point) to the targets, plus the time required to conduct the attack and then return, was beyond the Apache's internal fuel carrying capability. To make the plan work, the Apaches would either have to refuel en route or find the means to carry enough fuel to complete the mission. Cody decided to fly the mission with the ferry, or external, tanks used on his raids against the Vidalia, Georgia, airport. He had forgotten about them until he was reminded by Lt. Tim De Vito. Luckily they had been brought along from Fort Campbell.

Ferry tanks, by definition, are used in ferrying aircraft from one point to another. They lack ballistic tolerance; they are not intended for use in combat. Those designed for use with the Apache are neither bulletproof nor immune to damage from weapons fired from the Apache. Because of this, Cody had to convince the army to allow their use on this mission. The advantage gained in range was more than enough to compensate for the aircraft's flying slightly out of trim. If flown properly, the Apache with ferry tank would have fuel for four hours of flight, more than enough to complete the mission. But first, regulations required Cody to seek authorization from Aviation Systems Command (AVSCOM) in St. Louis, Missouri.

Responding to Cody's initial inquiry, AVSCOM asked that he configure one of the 1-101st Apaches just as it would be flown during the mission and test-fly it. Cody was to report the results back to AVSCOM.

De Vito recommended rigging the aircraft with one of the fifteen-hundred-pound, 230-gallon tanks mounted under the right stub wing, suspended from the inboard pylon. Four Hellfire missiles were then loaded on the right outboard pylon. Under the left wing, one thirty-eight-round 70mm FFAR pod was hung on the inboard pylon and four more Hellfire missiles were hung outboard. All this brought the aircraft weight to 19,000 pounds, 4,555 pounds over mission gross weight.

Preflight calculations indicated that the weight of the 230-gallon tank on the right side should cause some lateral center of gravity differential. However, with the pilots being made aware beforehand, this should not be a problem; they would easily be able to correct for this temporary condition.

Cody did the test-flying himself. Finding the aircraft flight characteristics little changed, he reported the results to AVSCOM and was granted the air worthiness release needed to fly the loaded Apache on the raid. Interestingly, all this paperwork was handled by fax from Saudi Arabia to St. Louis. (The gods of technology be praised.)

With the AVSCOM approval, the need for refueling points along the ingress or egress routes inside Iraq disappeared. But Cody still had one last hurdle to clear before he could gain peace of mind. Would the Apache's own weapons systems cause enough damage to the external tanks to endanger the aircraft and crews? The Apache's external fuel tanks were not designed to withstand the pressures generated by the back blast of either the Hellfire or the 70mm rocket motors. Likewise the back blast of both types of rockets contains flame and burning debris. Cody needed assurance that firing rockets from the pylons adjacent to the external tanks would not rupture the tanks and result in a catastrophic explosion. Once more Cody elected to act as test pilot and ordered his aircraft up-loaded with the mission ammunition. Flying to a nearby range, he test-fired all weapons systems with no adverse effect. With that, Cody was sure that TF Normandy could succeed without refueling en route and without endangering aircraft and crews.

With the raid aircraft configuration now settled, the remainder of the task force aircraft were mission rigged. Flight crews practiced becoming accustomed to flying and firing their "heavy" Apache. When all were comfortable, training moved to the next phase—long-range flight operations with the air force Pave Lows.

From the day that Cody and Garrett had first been briefed on the mission, operational security (keeping it secret) had weighed heavily on Cody's mind. Cody was sure that his comings and goings were noticed. In addition, Southwest Asia is a region rich in the history of spying and intrigue. Cody knew well that compromise could spell tragedy, that good men might die.

All too soon the security situation reached the point where the need to inform the soldiers outweighed the need for continued attempts to portray events as something else. Cody reasoned, and events proved him correct, that the rumor mill was working overtime and had to be shut down. The time for the task force to move to Al Jouf was drawing near, and the departure of ten aircraft and crews would add grist to the rumor mill. Men of the caliber found in the 1-101st could not be fooled for long, and guessing aloud would become increasingly popular.

On January 10 Cody received word to have the task force in position to launch by the fourteenth. He was also informed by COMSOCCENT that the operation most likely would take place on the seventeenth. The need to make final preparations would surely invite speculation. In army terms, things were beginning to "tighten up."

On January 12, Cody assembled the task force members for their first full-scale mission briefing. Security was tight at the door. Identification cards were checked against access rosters. Once assured that all within the room were authorized to know, COMSOCCENT, Colonel Johnson, stepped forward and delivered the mission briefing. Tom Drew recalls the low and serious murmur that made its way around the room as Johnson revealed the mission and its targets. At the end, a somber and thoughtful group of pilots shuffled from the room. Cody began planning how to inform the rest of the 1-101st.

Believing that good units are built on mutual trust and professional respect, Cody knew that failure to inform all his soldiers would weaken, or perhaps destroy, their faith in him as their leader. He knew that he had to take the risk and brief them all. He could well imagine the gossip that the departure of the task force aircraft would create, just at the time that peace negotiations with Iraq were coming unraveled. The American soldier is too bright not to understand what that might mean.

Assembling the entire battalion in the center of King Khalid Military City airfield, well out of earshot of all others, Cody briefed all hands on the details of TF Normandy. Further, he spoke of his trust in each member to do his duty and cautioned them that, as of that moment, they held the lives of the entire task force in their hands. Events would show that Cody's trust was not misplaced; not a word was leaked, which certainly speaks well of the quality of the American soldier.

On January 14 Task Force Normandy departed for Al Jouf, 640 kilometers to the northwest of King Fahd International Airport. There the task force made their final preparations. The flight out consisted of the nine Apaches and a single Black Hawk from the 1-101st; the Pave Lows traveled separately. All flew low level and well back from the border to avoid being seen by Iraqi radar. Four Apache crew chiefs, their toolboxes and a few spare parts, the entire mission maintenance package—rode onboard the Black Hawk. Task Force Davis remained behind, anxiously watching in two directions, back to Al Jouf and directly across the border to their front.

Although the 101st Airborne Division (Air Assault) is lightly equipped for fighting armored forces, there is little doubt that it can damage an attacking force. Apache and Cobra aviators of the division have convinced themselves that they are responsible to play a primary role in destroying any armored threat to the division. However, with almost half the 1-101st Apaches 360 kilometers to the northwest, both Cody and Davis worried about an Iraqi retaliatory attack. By the time of the raid, however, the situation was not as dire as one might believe. In addition to the support from the 12th Aviation Group, the division had another Apache battalion, the 2d Battalion, 229th Aviation Regiment, available to fight within the division's sector. This battalion, normally stationed at Fort Rucker, Alabama, had been flown to Saudi Arabia and attached to the 101st Division for the duration of Operation Desert Shield and Operation Desert Storm.

These two Apache battalions, 1-101st and 2-229th, shared a common base airfield, mutual respect, and some rivalry. Though not informed of the details of Task Force Normandy, the 2-229th knew that something unusual was afoot with the 1-101st. With war close, the 2-229th was eager to demonstrate its prowess. This sense of duty might prove most important with half of the 1-101st now hundreds of miles away.

After Cody's TF Normandy arrived at Al Jouf, the aircraft were checked and then secured. Assembling the crews, Cody issued each his individual mission folder, complete with target diagrams and recent aerial photographs. Time was allocated for each crew to study these documents before the crews moved to two sand tables, one depicting each of the targeted sites. The topography and position of buildings and vehicles were carefully duplicated on the sand tables. Here the crews visualized and discussed how each target could be attacked. Using the sand tables, attack rehearsals lasted late into the dark night. Finally Cody realized that his crews were at their limit and ordered them to bed. It had been a long and full day. "Remember, we're here to start the war," he said as they filed out into the starless night.

At 2:00 P.M. on January 16, while the crews were preflighting their aircraft, Cody was visited by Col. Ben Orell, Johnson's deputy at COMSOCCENT. Arriving by car, Orell had come to deliver the news firsthand. He told Cody that President Bush, through the secretary of defense, had authorized General Schwarzkopf to commence hostilities the next day, January 17. Orell further informed Cody that he was to start the war at H hour, 2:38 the next morning—twelve hours away. Cody remembers a sense of relief at the news. The shortest way home is through Baghdad, he recalls thinking.

Their evening meal was MREs (meals ready to eat), food in a plastic pouch with such appetizing entrees as beef slices with barbecue sauce, pork patties, and frankfurters with beans. The Apache and Pave Low crews then conducted one last, meticulous sand table rehearsal. With all that could be done to ready themselves finished, Vincent, Drew, De Vito, and the others moved out into the unusually dark night and onto the pages of American military history. It was also to be a big night in the history of attack helicopters, a history that reaches all the way back to the early years of rotary-wing flight.

Chapter Three

In the Beginning

Army tribal lore holds that army aviation can trace its roots back to a professor named Thaddeus S. C. Lowe. A balloonist and super salesman, Lowe was able to convince President Lincoln that the Union army was in need of his talents. Before the war was over, Secretary of War Edwin M. Stanton directed the formation of the Balloon Corps of the Army of the Potomac, with the erstwhile professor as its chief. The Balloon Corps was soon placed in the Signal Corps, the branch charged with providing the army with its communications.

Like many army institutions, the original chapter of the United States Army Loyal Order Of the Nothing to Do With Aviation and Not Invented Here Club (USALOOTNTDWAANIHC) can trace its roots back to the 1860s and the Union army. The USALOOTNTDWAANIHC are folks who intensely dislike anyone eager and willing to defy gravity. They especially dislike those who receive extra pay (flight, hazardous duty, or incentive) for doing so. As soon after the Civil War as they could, the USALOOTNTDWAANIHC convinced the Signal Corps to disband the Balloon Corps.

By 1898, the year the United States went to war with Spain, balloons were once again included in the Signal Corps' Tables of Organization and Equipment (TO&E). Balloons saw some service in Cuba, but soon disappeared with the return of peace, victim once again of the jealous USALOOTNTDWAANIHC.

Once more the army's interest in flight waned and remained dormant until shortly after December 17, 1903, the day of great excitement at Kitty Hawk, on the outer banks of North Carolina. It would not take long before the army began to show some interest in the Wright brothers' flying machine.

In August 1907, as the result of his personal interest in flying machines, Brig. Gen. James Allen, the chief signal officer, established the Aeronautical Division within the Signal Corps.

In fall 1908, in response to an army advertisement for a "heavier than air flying machine," the Wright brothers, Orville and Wilbur, arrived in Washington with just such a machine.

In a letter to the author, Maj. Gen. Charles E. Saltzman (Ret.), West Point Class of 1925 and a Rhodes scholar, recalls witnessing some of the Wrights' activities.

The Chief Signal Officer appointed a board of officers, of whom my father was one, to look into the matter of the flying machine. The board told the Wright brothers to bring the machine to Fort Myer, across the Potomac from Washington, and demonstrate its ability to meet such requirements as ascending to at least a minimum number of feet, staying up for at least a while, flying away not less than a certain distance and returning within a given time. Although the Wrights somehow had managed to keep their experiments private, not generally known, this demonstration before the board was announced, and although hardly anybody had ever seen—or believed in—a heavier-than-air flying machine, everybody in Washington who could, including President Theodore Roosevelt, flocked out to the polo field at Fort Myer to see this nearly unbelievable phenomenon. Naturally my mother took me there as we had heard so much about the contraption from my father.

It was mid-September, a few days before my fifth birthday. I can remember the excitement of the crowd as the propeller-driven kite was catapulted down a monorail and actually took off and flew up like a bird.

The Board was not satisfied with a single satisfactory demonstration and in the following flights the Wrights began taking
members of the board, one by one, in the seat beside the Wright
brother piloting.

The day it was my father's turn they said to him when he arrived at the polo field: "Major Saltzman, do you mind terribly?
Lieutenant Selfridge is here but has to take a train tonight to St.
Joseph, Missouri. As you know, he is a balloon man but wants
very much to go up in the flying machine and would hate to miss
this opportunity. Would you be willing for him to go up today
and you go up tomorrow?" To which my father gladly gave his
consent. Selfridge took the seat beside Orville Wright and they
took off. Shortly afterwards something happened (Perhaps a wire
breaking loose and winding around one of the propellers), the
plane crashed, Selfridge was killed, and Orville Wright severely
injured. This was the first death in an air crash. I well remember
my mother's and my horror when my father came home and told
us this story. Orville Wrights injuries kept him hospitalized for
several weeks. In the meantime Wilbur repaired the airplane and
returned to Fort Myer. The tests showed the Wright brothers machine
exceeded the Army's stated requirements and soon, one by one,
flying machines and pilots were added to the Army's fledgling
air fleet.

As World War I approached, military aviation began to receive increased
interest. On July 18, 1914, Congress made army air activities legiti-
mate by creating the Aviation Section within the Signal Corps. By April
1917, when America entered the war on the Allied side, American pilots
had become veterans flying in British, Canadian, and French air squadrons.
So eager were some young Americans that they formed an American
squadron, the Lafayette Escadrille, within the French Air Service.

In May 1918, three months before the war ended, Congress, through
the Overman Act, removed all aviation assets from the Signal Corps,
created the position of director of Military Aeronautics, and named
the new flying organization the Air Service. Finally, men of vision,
few as there were, began to recognize the potential of armed men above
the battlefield. By November 11, 1918, the end of the war, the United

States had thirty-nine air squadrons engaged in some form of aerial combat. The majority were involved in reconnaissance, with "pursuit" taking second place. Only one squadron was allocated to bombardment. This allocation of assets to mission proved the complete opposite of that found in World War II. But even this meager force was doomed to suffer the effects of erosion. Over time, silent guns lessened the public's interest in things military.

Coming from World War I were two weapons systems destined to rule future battlefields—the tank and the airplane. Unfortunately, between the two world wars, these systems and the visionaries who understood their potential were relegated to brown pastures where they languished with just enough grass to prevent starvation. Both the tank and airplane suffered under the shortsightedness of postwar army leadership and a budget-induced hiatus (an early version of the "peace dividend"), which unwise American politicians rushed to impose.

Between World War I and World War II, army leadership insisted that both the tank and the airplane were but tools in the infantry's toolbox. But the champions of both systems refused to surrender, especially the airpower advocates. In time, the army would break up the Tank Corps and its tanks would be assigned to the infantry. The Air Service fared somewhat better. Veteran aviators of World War I, convinced that bombardment by airpower would be decisive in future wars, attempted to thrust their beliefs on an unconvinced Army Staff and Congress. The hypothesis put forth by this core of true believers was that by destroying an enemy's industrial infrastructure with aerial bombardment, America could win wars and save lives. As this doctrine spread through the Air Service, development of long-ranged bombers with greater payload became a primary goal, but for years remained only a dream.

Through the 1920s and into the 1930s, the Air Service, renamed the Air Corps on July 2, 1926, saw little in the way of research and development of new military aircraft. Although those who advocated pursuit aircraft as the proper role for the Air Corps made initial progress in aircraft design and development, bombardment enthusiasts saw little progress. Frustration finally reached such an extreme that Brig. Gen. William "Billy" Mitchell, wartime leader of all aviation units of the American Expeditionary Force, and himself a winner of the Distinguished Service Cross, the nation's second highest award for bravery, began to take actions that would eventually end in the destruction of his career.

After Mitchell made himself a severe pain in the military establishment's collective backside, the military decided to force Mitchell, the assistant chief of the Air Service, to prove his words. A test would be conducted during the summer of 1921 designed to put the upstart aviator in his place. The test was not complex. Two ships, a cruiser and a submarine, were anchored off Cape Henry on the Virginia coast. Mitchell attacked the hapless vessels with six army SE-5s, dropping twenty-five-pound bombs and scoring several hits. This was followed by a flight of MB-2 bombers dropping three-hundred-pound bombs and sending the vessels to the bottom. However, Mitchell's antagonists remained unassured. Convinced that Mitchell would fail, army leadership sent him against the former German battleship *Ostfriesland,* believed to be unsinkable. Once more the target ship would be anchored and General Mitchell's task was to attempt to bomb and sink her. Mitchell accepted the challenge with enthusiasm, and on July 21, 1921, before a large audience of generals, admirals, politicians, and members of the press, laid a spread of bombs across and on *Ostfriesland,* sending her to the bottom of the gray Virginia coastal waters.

Most of the distinguished observers departed unhappy with the results. They declared Mitchell's feat a lucky happenstance, and returned to Washington and other issues. Mitchell refused to accept the establishment's lack of interest and was soon acting as generals are not supposed to act, speaking out publicly. For his continued indiscretions, Mitchell was court-martialed under Article 96 of the Articles of War, "conduct prejudicial to good order and discipline." He resigned his commission on February 1, 1926. But even the events surrounding Mitchell's battleship bombing and subsequent court-martial failed to achieve his goal: the arousal of public and congressional interest in airpower, a separate Air Service, and acknowledgment of the potential of strategic bombardment, at least not immediately.

Over time aviation technology began to improve so much that army leadership found it difficult to ignore. Likewise there was no denying that Mitchell's message of the need for a separate air force and a single department of defense had been heard by some and would not go away. But for the time being, that would have to wait.

Leaders in both the Congress and army began contemplating use of the airplane in future warfare. By late 1926 Congress approved the establishment of the Army Air Corps, creating a split in the army's fabric.

In 1934 Maj. Gen. Benjamin D. Foulois, chief of the Air Corps, polled his officers asking for their views concerning the development of bombers. The consensus was for larger, multiengined, higher flying, longer ranged aircraft capable of carrying heavy payloads. At about the same time, instructors led by Lt. Col. Harold L. George began teaching General Mitchell's doctrine at the Air Corps Tactical Air School, Maxwell Air Base, Alabama. This instruction stated that bombers should be used to target and destroy the industrial heart of an enemy nation. Mitchell's beliefs dovetailed nicely with the theories espoused by the much-quoted Italian Col. Giulio Douhet. During the 1920s Douhet had written that future wars could be decided by fleets of bombers. Bombers could strike terror into the heart of an enemy by razing his cities and industries. Mitchell carried this even further. Airpower should not be squandered on attempts to influence tactical outcomes on the battlefield. Over time this dogma became ingrained in most of the Air Corps officers; it became Air Corps doctrine. In the meantime industry, sensing an opportunity, joined the Air Corps' struggle. Much to the Air Corps' dismay, technology lagged behind doctrine. But not everyone in the Air Corps signed up on the doctrine of bombers *uber alles.* Not even at the Air Corps Tactical School.

In 1931 Capt. Claire Lee Chennault, having just graduated from the Air Corps Tactical School (ACTS) and being considered the Air Corps' most experienced pursuit authority (his work in pursuit had established his reputation before he was selected for the school), was assigned to its faculty as the school's chief pursuit instructor.

For the next four years Chennault found himself embroiled in the ongoing debate over the roles of pursuit versus bombers. Soon everyone in the Air Corps found themselves forced to join one side or the other. Unfortunately, those standing with Chennault were few in number but great in devotion. Many saw this as a struggle for the future leadership of the Air Corps.

Popular thought at the ACTS held the belief that pursuit could not survive a toe-to-toe fight against large bombers, never mind the fact that at the time there were no large bombers. Pursuitists, on the other hand, held firmly to the belief that bombers would never reach their targets if not protected by friendly pursuit aircraft. Looking ahead,

Chennault and his small band of pursuit advocates saw a dark future for those destined to fly large bombers deep into enemy territory. Tactics developed and tested by Chennault had proven beyond question that small, fast, single-engine aircraft—fighters—could easily penetrate bomber formations and destroy the slower, heavily ladened aircraft. Additionally, Chennault felt strongly that pursuit aircraft should be capable of providing fire support, later called close air support, to ground forces. Neither of Chennault's concepts were well received by his Air Corps superiors.

History sadly records the winners of this argument. Not until bomber losses over Germany reached unacceptable numbers did the air force see the need for long-range fighter escorts, and it spent most of World War II trying to catch up, trying to develop fighter aircraft capable of escorting bombers to Berlin and back.

Finally, in 1937, after Chennault removed his name from the list of students selected to attend the army's Command and General Staff College at Fort Leavenworth, he retired and accepted a generous offer to help develop China's air force. But the army and the Army Air Corps had not seen nor heard the last of Claire Lee Chennault.

By the mid-1930s the Boeing Aircraft Corporation was engaged in developing a large bomber. This effort was company funded. The company was, so to speak, self-employed. Although persons within the Air Corps encouraged Boeing in its efforts to develop their Model 229, forerunner of the B-17, initially there were no government funds involved.

The Model 229 first took to the air in July 1935, capturing the imagination and hopes of the bomber-loving Army Air Corps leadership. The four-engine Model 229 was the fulfillment of the strategic bombardment advocates' dream, and it signaled the beginning of the big-bomber era. It also began the big-bomber advocates' control of the Air Corps. But for the time being and despite classroom instruction along strategic lines, the Air Corps remained divided into two camps: those who subscribed to the theories of long-range bombardment (strategic) and those who believed in pursuit (tactical) but were forced to hide in the closet.

The design of the Model 229 bolstered the idea of the bomber being a flying fortress bristling with machine guns. Now with hardware in hand, some in the air force could little understand the need for other types of aircraft. After all, heavily armed bombers would not need to be escorted and, besides, none of the existing fighters had the range to escort them. However, cooler heads prevailed, and the air force decided that a few pursuit planes would be required to defend the continental United States.

During the years between the world wars, the need for tactical air support for ground forces, although on the list of wartime requirements, was not seriously addressed. Writing of the army's organizational and combined arms employment concepts on the eve of World War II, Capt. Jonathan M. House stated:

> Finally, close air support was also lacking in the American combat team. Despite the efforts of a few aviators such as Frank Lackland, the U.S. Army Air Corps was preoccupied with strategic bombing to the neglect of close air support. As in France and Britain, American aviators argued that air power was best used in areas beyond the range of ground artillery.[1]

By the late 1930s civilian aircraft had made remarkable gains. But many air force fighter and pursuit squadrons were still mostly flying fabric-covered biplanes, aircraft vulnerable to small-arms fire.

By 1940, President Roosevelt, seeing war clouds bearing down on the world and understanding that America could not avoid becoming entangled, called up eleven army National Guard divisions and thousands of members of the reserves. The president wanted these forces available and trained in the event he needed to deploy regular divisions overseas. The National Guard and reserves would then take up the defense of the United States proper. With this decision it became clear to the world that a reluctant United States was moving to overcome years of military neglect. A large part of this effort would go to updating tanks and airpower.

By the time the Japanese bombed Pearl Harbor, the strategic bombing advocates were firmly in control of the air force. However, since they still came under the army, these strategic purists were not completely free to follow their beliefs. In respect to equals among army generals, army Chief of Staff George C. Marshall was most equal and in the position of having the final say. As America prepared for the inevitable, most efforts were directed toward managing and distributing shortages; there were just not enough aircraft to cover all requirements.

On March 9, 1942, the War Department established three separate and coequal commands within the army: Army Ground Forces, Army Air Forces, and Army Service Forces. The mission of the air forces was to support the army. It was how the air force interpreted the army's needs that caused friction between ground and air services. For many years this conflict would be about light airplanes and a new machine called the helicopter.

Linguists and historians agree that the word *helicopter* is derived from the combination of two words from the Greek language—*helix,* meaning spiral, and *pterone,* meaning wing. Although no one knows for sure, it is generally accepted by historians that the first rotary-wing, or helicopter, flight took place in November 1907 when Paul Cornu, a Frenchman, managed to get his "flying bicycle" off the ground long enough for someone to notice. Cornu's machine was twin rotored and uncontrollable. Cornu's flight identified one major problem, one that would persist for years and that would have to be mastered before the helicopter could become a practical means of flight. For the helicopter to be practical, to be a useful flying machine capable of vertical and forward flight, the forces of rotor-induced torque would have to be neutralized. This problem was created by the fact that, in a hover, wind resistance is greater on the rotor blades than on the machine's fuselage. Without some means of compensating for this, the fuselage tends to rotate, causing the blades to lose adequate lift.

Others followed Cornu, men determined to achieve controlled vertical flight. The Spaniard Juan de la Cieva's development of the autogyro brought rotary-wing flight even closer to realization. It was Cieva who developed the hinged rotor blade, which, as the blades rotate, allows the advancing blade to unload, to reduce lift, while the retreating blade loads, or produces lift. This discovery eliminated unequal lift between blades, improving flight by rotating wings. However, the problem of controlling torque remained.

Six years after the Wright brothers' first flight at Kitty Hawk, Igor Sikorsky, a young Russian flight enthusiast, managed to get his counterrotating, twin-blade helicopter into the air. Although his machine could carry no load, it was a first for Igor, and a workable helicopter was a quest he never abandoned.

The realities of World War I forced Sikorsky to put his work on the helicopter aside while he devoted himself to the design of large-load–carrying airplanes. By 1914 Sikorsky had progressed from single-engine to four-engine aircraft capable of carrying one-thousand-pound bombs.

Following the end of the "war to end all wars," and the Russian Revolution, Sikorsky came to the realization that Marxism, at that time, offered little opportunity for a serious scientist. He fled Russia in 1918 and by 1919 arrived in the United States, via Canada, flat broke. But like many immigrants of that era, Sikorsky, after four years of hard work and by holding part-time jobs, accumulated enough capital to found the Sikorsky Aero Engineering Corporation.

There is some evidence indicating that the United States Army first began to demonstrate an interest in helicopters and the advantages of vertical flight in the early 1920s. However, it was not until May 1941, after Igor Sikorsky managed to keep his V-300 in the air for an hour and thirty minutes, that enough interest was aroused for the Army Air Corps to award him a contract to build an experimental two-seat helicopter. His mastery of the forces of torque was the one development that turned the helicopter into a useful vehicle. On April 20, 1942, after a flight from the Sikorsky plant in Connecticut to what is today Wright-Patterson Air Force Base in Ohio, Mr. Sikorsky personally delivered the army's first Model XR-4.

Just as the contract had specified, this aircraft was a two-place, side-by-side design, adapted from Igor Sikorsky's production Model S-300. Sikorsky's earlier version, the VS-300, had been the first successful helicopter to use a changeable-pitch tail rotor in conjunction with the main rotor to control torque. By using foot pedals to adjust the pitch of the tail rotor blades, the pilot was able to maintain directional control and stability in vertical and forward flight.

During much of World War II, the helicopter was considered unproven technology, and only limited resources were devoted toward its testing and production. That notwithstanding, between 1942 and 1946, more than three hundred helicopters were purchased by the Army Air Force. Others were built for the U.S. Navy and the British. Not all purchases were solely from Sikorsky. Although Sikorsky teamed with the Vought Corporation, another conglomerate, the Nash-Kelvinator Company, also produced helicopters. This latter combination is interesting in that Nash primarily manufactured automobiles, whereas

Kelvinator's main suit was the manufacture of refrigeration equipment. But then, wartime needs forced industry to do whatever was required.

Both the air force and the British pressed the helicopter into combat service. In 1942 Britain, a maritime nation, was experiencing appalling losses to surface shipping from German submarines. She was dependent on her oceanic lifelines for supplies from the United States and others. Grasping for any solution, Britain came upon the idea of purchasing several American-made R-5 helicopters, equipping them with a fledgling radar, arming them with depth charges, and stationing them aboard merchant ships in the endangered convoys. The results of these early tests proved to be modest.

Combat employment of helicopters with American forces seems to have been limited. There was the first rescue of a downed and wounded airman by an American-piloted helicopter in Burma. This recovery, flown on May 3, 1943, by Col. Philip Cochran, 1st Air Commando Group, was a most remarkable feat for the little underpowered YR-4.[2] Burma, one of the most mountainous regions of the world, is known for poor-density altitude, a factor that has considerable effect on the performance of all types of aircraft, but especially on helicopters. This first rescue would prove to be the forerunner of events to come in the mountains of Korea and the jungles of Vietnam.

The small, frail, canvas-covered YR-4 looked much like a wingless, shrunken version of the army's World War II CG-4A Waco glider. But despite its low horsepower and frail appearance, the YR-4 proved its worth and was welcomed wherever it appeared.

With growing acceptance of helicopters, the army decided to acquire improved machines. The Sikorsky Company offered its R-5, which the army bought in some numbers. In designing the R-5, Igor Sikorsky must have turned to nature to determine the aircraft's appearance. The R-5 came off the drawing board looking much like a mechanical dragonfly. The R-5, also two-seated, was different from the YR-4 in that the seating was fore and aft, as opposed to the side-by-side arrangement of the YR-4. (This fore-and-aft seating would appear again when attack helicopters came into being.)

The R-5 was an early arrival in Korea and saw service there through much of the war with the army, navy, and air force. Like its older brother, the R-4, the R-5 may have inadvertently pioneered another helicopter capability.

There are as many versions of who was first to arm the helicopter as there are old aviators. Some believe it to have happened in Korea. Others claim that it was first done by the French during their war in Algeria. The truth may never be found. But the armed helicopter was destined to become an important system on future battlefields.

During World War II the ground fire encountered by the army liaison pilots, flying lightweight Piper Cub–type artillery spotter airplanes, caused these pilots to seek a means to defend themselves. No one seemed interested in providing suitable hardware to arm these frail aircraft, but the need was real. Authorities reasoned that with heavily armed aircraft available, why arm the small liaison aircraft? This argument gave little comfort to Grasshopper pilots, so pistols, rifles, and hand grenades—the weapons of choice of their World War I predecessors, were all too soon to see duty through the windows of frail L-4s. A few adventuresome pilots attempted to mount the shoulder-fired antitank rocket launcher, dubbed the Bazooka, under the wings of these machines. Reports indicate that this arrangement was not successful. In time word of the liaison pilots' plight spread across the army; however, it was left to each individual pilot to find a solution to his problem.

Although it was probably not driven by any particular combat experience, the decision was made in 1942 to test the feasibility of firing a 20mm cannon from the nose of one of the army's helicopters. This test died from lack of enthusiasm. After all, the sky was full of armed aircraft.

Three years later, another attempt was made to arm the helicopter. This test, conducted by Army Ground Forces Board Number 1, Fort Bragg, North Carolina, is worthy of mention. In the board's final report on project number XAB-296, dated December 14, 1945, one section reports on the attempt to fire a 75mm recoilless rifle from an R-6 helicopter. The report reads as follows:

Test Report No. 5.
a. Purpose:
   To determine if recoilless rifles can be mounted on helicopters and fired in flight.
b. Method:

A 75 MM Recoilless Rifle was mounted on the right-hand side of the aircraft; attached to the litter tubes. A temporary mechanism was then fabricated, which enabled the passenger in the co-pilot's seat to fire the piece. The aircraft hovered high enough to clear a slight defilade, and the piece was fired.

c. Results:

The aircraft hovered steadily enough to permit fairly accurate aiming. Firing of the weapon did not disturb the ship's equilibrium. However, the great difference between the high pressure of the blast wave and the interior pressure of the airplane caused the plexiglass to crack and break in five (5) places, and the metal surface of the tail cone to buckle slightly. Mounting the gun at right angles to the longitudinal axis of the airplane would obviate this weakness and prevent similar damage in the future. However, lacking an adequate means of sighting on the target for aimed shots, at right angles, the test personnel determined that the range safety regulations prevented further testing of this type. . . .

For the next few years, helicopter armament lay dormant, the result of the National Defense Act of 1947. This act, the divorce ending the stormy marriage between the army and the Army Air Force, gave the air force its independence and coequal status among the services. It also proved to be a watershed, a landmark for army aviation and subsequently the helicopter. For although the air force went about its pursuit of things fast and nuclear, the army began to study how to best harness light aviation and make it a more useful asset on the battlefield— but not without earning the disfavor of the new, junior service.

The day army aviation was truly born is difficult to establish. It might well have been Lowe's first ascent while employed by the Union army in 1861. Then again it might have been September 3, 1908, the day the Wright boys flew their Model 1905 for a group of army officers at Fort Myer. Perhaps it was the day Lt. Thomas M. Watson had the Piper Company come to Camp Beauregard, Louisiana, and demonstrate the Piper Cub's ability to fly from unimproved fields in support of the artillery. Although army aviation became a branch of the army on April 12, 1983, the United States Army Aviation Center and School holds June 6, 1942, the day the War Department authorized light airplanes to artillery battalions, to have been the official birthday. Whatever date, army aviation came into being to fill a need, a vacuum. The need was clear for light aviation capable of operating with the infantryman, artilleryman, and armored forces. This type of flying required not only special skills, it required a special mind-set, a willingness to endure hardship, a commitment to service. It required special soldiers. The army has always found pilots with these qualities; and although they are not always appreciated, they serve because they believe in their mission and in having a little fun. To understand it all requires a more detailed look.

Chapter Four

DAMNED IF YOU DO AND DAMNED IF YOU DON'T

On June 20, 1941, Congress, aware of the army's ongoing internal conflicts between its air and ground forces, changed the name of the Army Air Corps to the Army Air Force. The intent was to grant some degree of autonomy to the Army Air Force while requiring it to see to the ground army's needs. The following year, on March 9, 1942, General Marshall reorganized the army into three equal commands: the Army Air Forces, the Army Ground Forces, and the Army Service Forces. History shows that these changes only widened long-standing differences of opinion about the employment of air assets. The air forces, using their newfound autonomy, established priorities for the employment of aircraft that the ground forces viewed as doing little to support its requirements for air support.

To some this is perhaps a harsh indictment of the wartime leadership of the Army Air Force. But to discuss the history of army aviation without discussing the heated subsurface guerrilla warfare between the army's ground and air forces, which began in the 1920s and took on new meaning following the signing of the National Defense Act (NDA) of 1947, shows that one does not know history. This often-spirited, often-painful bureaucratic combat created scars that remain visible today. This collision of interests, which often had much the same effect as a midair collision between two aircraft, is as much a part of American military aviation history as is Thaddeus Lowe, Gen. Billy Mitchell, or the jet engine. Happily, over time, the two services reached an uneasy accord, allowing both to go about their nation's business of prosecuting the war against the Axis. However, much like a volcano, the heat of argument remained just below the surface, and to this day it occasionally comes bubbling up, blowing smoke and ash into the air.

In defense of the American air force, it must be remembered that the British Royal Air Force (RAF) set an extreme example for their American counterparts. Captain House, speaking of events between the wars, illustrates the problem:

> A related problem was that Great Britain was the first nation to create an independent air force. The Royal Air Force (RAF) was intent upon developing its own identity as a separate service and resisted any close relationship with the army. Like most other air services, the RAF was increasingly interested in interdiction and strategic bombing, not ground support.[1]

During the 1920s and 1930s and well into World War II, the RAF, much like the U.S. Army Air Force, was under the control of the big-bomber clique. For the most part, the RAF came close to absolutely refusing to provide support to British ground forces. Reluctantly, and when it suited the RAF, some support was given. However, even after witnessing the fall of Poland and France to the Nazi blitzkrieg, in which the German ground and air forces worked as one, the leaders of the RAF clung to their hidebound doctrine. The much-celebrated Battle of Britain, the successful defense of England by a handful of fighters, was considered an unusual blemish on Bomber Command's smooth skin. Importantly, the RAF's doctrine and the resulting internal struggles did not go unnoticed by American airmen who spent much of World War II in England, operating side by side with the RAF. The allegiance of the American Army Air Force to strategic bombing as the proper role of airpower remained unwavering and continued throughout the Cold War years.

Although it is probably too soon to tell, nearly fifty years after World War II, there have been faint yet encouraging signs that the quarrel between American air and ground forces may finally have ended in the warm deserts of Saudi Arabia and Iraq. Unfortunately, though, even that may not last; for while most of the world celebrates the end of Soviet communism and the defense budget shrinks, the current scarcity of defense dollars may well trigger a new struggle over roles and missions. Today, the United States Air Force is a service with a much smaller strategic mission than it enjoyed during the years of the Cold War. Budgetwise, it is no longer in the cockbird seat. But it is important to keep in mind that the history of distrust between airmen and ground soldiers is long and two sided.

It is difficult to determine the exact point in time when hard feelings began between Army Ground Forces and the Army Air Service (later the Army Air Corps, still later the Army Air Forces, and finally the United States Air Force). Technically the Army Air Force belonged to the army until 1947; but, in fact, it never was a good fit. It may well have begun after World War I with the struggles between the army establishment and rebel airmen like Gen. Billy Mitchell. Whenever it began, no one can deny that the volcano rumbled through most of World War II and beyond.

The gut issues centered on the employment of airpower and involved a fundamental disagreement over how airpower could and should be used in war. Ground leaders felt that they should be allowed the use of airpower to support ground tactical plans. Air leaders, on the other hand, felt that only they understood how to apply airpower, and they favored its use against strategic targets. In a television interview celebrating the anniversary of the founding of Headquarters, Eighth Air Force, at Hunter Air Field, Georgia, a retired air force major general spoke clearly to the issue. A wartime member of the Eighth Air Force and veteran of repeated bombing missions over Germany, the general capsulated the air advocates' position by stating that air leaders had "greater vision."

Between the world wars, aviation technology advanced so rapidly that the deep thinkers in the air force convinced themselves that future wars could be won solely through the application of strategic air power. They listened to people like the Italian theorist Col. Giulio Douhet, who viewed aerial warfare not in terms of defense but of offense. Douhet taught that the enemy's attacks must be ignored and he must be bombed with all available resources. It was hoped that this would inflict enough damage to cause him to quit. Said differently, we must bomb the enemy into submission, at the expense of all other missions.

In the early years, the differences between the ground army and Air Corps seemed to be most intense among staff officers assigned to the Army and the Air Staffs. Both of these Washington-based staffs were, and still are, crucibles of service opinion. (Generals are what their staffs allow them to be.)

The outset of World War II found American airmen of like mind with Douhet and the British, whose doctrine was one to which strategic airpower and big-bomber advocates could rally. This doctrine stated that if properly employed, strategic airpower (that is, big bombers) alone could bring the Axis to its collective knees. Carrying this doctrine to its prenuclear conclusion, air advocates maintained that bombing would make it unnecessary to commit large formations of ground forces. Therefore, they argued, the air force should have priority of resources.

On the other side of this dispute steadfastly stood the army's ground leaders who felt that airpower should be but another implement in the theater commander's toolbox. Initially, doctrine called for air assets to be parceled out and placed under the direct control of first the theater commander, and then the lowest level capable of ensuring quick response to ground-force needs—decentralized instead of centralized employment. (Centralized control meant that aircraft were assigned from Air Corps headquarters instead of ground commanders piecemealing them out to ground units.)

Additionally, the June 20, 1941, name change from Army Air Corps to Army Air Force and the subsequent reorganization of the elements of the army into three services appear to have come from negotiations that also included an unwritten agreement, perhaps a promise, that the air force would become a separate service soon after the successful end of the war. This "understanding" did little to improve cooperation. What is more, the leaders of Army Air Force commands deployed to overseas theaters were placed in the awkward position of trying to serve two masters: their immediate ground commander and Gen. Henry H. Arnold, chief of the Army Air Force. Although the War Department had its strategy for prosecution of the war, and the army had its assigned missions, the air force had an internal agenda of its own: Comply with the War Department's directives, but do it the air force way. This

was not openly sinister or insubordinate, but it certainly was not appreciated in the nonflying army. Clearly the sentiment among airmen was
that only the leaders imbued with the dogma of strategic airpower
understood its potential. Obviously the airmen felt that as long as they
belonged to the army, air assets stood a good chance of being ineptly
employed, and with some justification. But men on the ground also
held strong convictions.

It was natural for the ground commander to want to have all the
firepower available at his disposal. No competent commander enters
battle believing that he has enough firepower. He wants tactical air
support, Stuka-like aircraft, over his piece of the battle at all times.
But the ground army's neglect of airpower between the world wars
now came back to haunt it. Air leaders were initially faced with too
much war and too few airplanes. However, when the procurement and
production floodgates were finally opened, and new and improved aircraft
came off the assembly lines in number, the air force was caught in a
dilemma: Either employ assets tactically or go deep for strategic targets. The shadows of Mitchell and Douhet blotted out tactical use.

Air force doctrine said that airpower was best suited for strategic
purposes. In practical terms, air force leaders were convinced that airpower should be put to work destroying Stuka factories, tank factories, transportation and petroleum facilities, not necessarily Stukas, tanks,
railroads, and bridges. This doctrine was reflected in their initial plans
for prosecution of the air war. A strategic air offensive designed to
disrupt the enemy's capability and will to wage war received first priority.
Remaining assets went to providing air support of friendly ground forces.
Later on, ground support would be dropped to third priority by the
need for air superiority. Ground support was called "third phase," or
"priority three" mission.[2]

At the same time there was fear among the army's ground leadership, and with some justification, that as the result of air leaders' espoused
doctrine, bombers (strategic) would receive production priority at the
expense of the fighters (tactical). Compounding this concern was the
belief that the scarce funds allocated for air force fighters were being
spent to build fighters designed to protect bombers, not necessarily
to provide support for ground forces.

All of this distrust came to the fore during the North African campaign, the first major offensive operation involving American forces

in World War II. Ground commanders were clearly dissatisfied with
the results of the tactical air support they were receiving. This was
aptly demonstrated by the much-celebrated German air attack on General
Patton's headquarters during a conference between Patton, British Chief
Air Marshal Arthur Tedder, deputy theater air officer, and U.S. Army
Air Force Lt. Gen. Carl Spaatz. They had come to Patton as a result
of a message from Patton complaining that "total lack of air cover
for our ground units has allowed [the German] air force to operate at
will." In hindsight, the problem was numbers, not quality. During the
early days of the war (1942), the air force painfully discovered that
Claire Chennault's predictions about the vulnerability of bombers had
been prophetic. Flying Fortresses were not immune to defending fighter
aircraft, and friendly escorts were desperately needed. The air force
had come to war with too few fighter aircraft available to protect bombers
and provide close support to ground forces. In fact, there were too
few fighters to accomplish either mission. General Patton notwithstanding, these complaints ushered the air-ground argument to the fore.

The invasion of North Africa brought the army into a new phase
of warfare. Many American leaders, veterans of World War I, were
dumbstruck by the combined operations of the Germans during their
blitzkrieg conquest of Europe. The German use of close air support
had not escaped the attention of American ground commanders. (The
Ju-87 Stuka was a dive-bomber specially designed for ground support. German ground soldiers affectionately called it "flying artillery,"
and it soon became indispensable to German ground forces.) The advanced
technology of both ground and air weapons systems initially gave German
commanders weapons of new dimensions.

During the early planning for Operation Torch, the invasion of North
Africa, ground commanders insisted that many of the theater's scarce
air assets be employed in direct support of ground operations (decentralized employment). To make matters worse, they wanted aircraft
over them at all times. To the air force's way of thinking, and rightly
so, this was poor employment of an all-too-scarce asset. Sometime
after the invasion of North Africa and following several near disas-
ters caused by the Army Air Force's being compelled to spread its
scarce air assets too thin, the theater leadership decided to emulate
the British and "test" centralized control. Once the decision was made
to centralize, it stuck. As far as air leaders were concerned, there was

no going back. For the rest of World War II and until this day, with few exceptions, air leaders decided when, where, and how air assets would be employed.

Needless to say, this loss of control was unpopular with army ground commanders. They were resentful that these upstart "flyboys" had gotten their way. Even so, on rare occasions the air forces, strategic and tactical, were ordered to provide direct air support to ground operations. After the invasion of Europe, with more fighter assets available, army ground forces received much better support. However, long after the guns of World War II had fallen silent, the veterans of these early air-ground force skirmishes harbored hard feelings. Speaking with great passion to the students of the U.S. Air Force Air War College in 1977, thirty-two years after the end of World War II and thirty years after the air force had become a separate service, retired air force Gen. Hayward S. "Possum" Hansell, a member of General Mitchell's court-martial defense team, an early protégé of Chennault who later joined the strategic bombing advocates, and one of the wartime authors of Air War Plans Division I and II (AWPD I & II), expressed his continued dismay at General Eisenhower's "misuse" of the heavy bombers during the battle for Normandy. General Hansell's plans had been the keystone documents for the strategic employment of airpower in Europe. To the true believers of the power of strategic bombing, these plans became, and still remain, Holy Writ. When General Eisenhower diverted the Eighth Air Force's heavy bombers for D day and a few weeks later for Operation Cobra, he gained the everlasting disfavor of many of the air force's wartime leaders. So hidebound was the air force that Captain House states:

> Yet the Air Force was unwilling to provide aircraft even for major ground maneuvers, let alone small-unit training. Six months before the Normandy invasion, thirty-three U.S. divisions in England had experienced no joint air-ground training, and twenty-one had not even seen displays of friendly aircraft for purposes of recognition in battle.[3]

If the army was being subtly orphaned by the air force, then what about this thing we now call army aviation? What was it and what role did it play in World War II?

In 1940, the artillery decided that it had need of aircraft to locate targets for its guns and to help adjust the impact of artillery rounds onto targets, much as Lowe had done with his balloons. During the Louisiana maneuvers an artillery officer, Lt. Thomas M. Watson, decided that an aircraft like the then-famous Piper Cub would be good as an aerial spotter. Since high-speed fighters were neither suitable, available, nor cost-effective, the artillery requested that light airplanes be assigned to artillery battalions. Not waiting for the army bureaucracy to act, Watson asked the Piper Company if they would come to Camp Beauregard, Louisiana, and demonstrate their Cub.[4] Watson's efforts caused enough stir that a year later during the Louisiana maneuvers, three different manufacturers were invited to participate. Sixteen light aircraft were used in a test of their ability to meet the artillery's needs. It was left to the manufacturers to provide pilots and mechanics in addition to aircraft. By maneuvers' end, it was clear that the idea of using small aircraft to spot for the artillery was worthy, and the army declared the concept to be valid.[5]

Like most bureaucracies the army likes to do things slowly and formally. Therefore with the successful test results of light aircraft, it was decided to conduct a formal test of the feasibility of training pilots. A small cell of qualified flight instructors was assembled at Fort Sill, Oklahoma, and fourteen officers and noncommissioned officers were selected and assembled there for flight training. Known as "the Class Before One," these men graduated in September 1942, formally proving that the army needed and could sustain light aircraft.[6]

In November 1941 Gen. George C. Marshall, chief of staff of the army, approved the purchase of 617 commercial aircraft for use by the artillery. The secretary of war approved General Marshall's request on June 6, 1942 (now celebrated as army aviation's birthday). The basis for issue would be two aircraft, two pilots, and one mechanic for each artillery battalion in the army.

The Army Air Force was quick to distance itself from these "flying club" missions, and initially it stood on the sidelines muttering objections to the Army Ground Forces getting its own light aviation, an unfortunate precursor of frequent and heated arguments to come. However, for the time being General Marshall's and the secretary of war's approval of light aircraft in ground-force units carried enough weight that the Army Air Force reluctantly decided to do what it was told and oversaw the acquisition of the army's "liaison" aircraft and the training of liaison pilots.

Within the Army Ground Forces, it did not take long to recognize the value of these aircraft and to witness the expansion of their use to a host of tasks other than adjustment of artillery fires. In both the Pacific and European theaters, the L-4s built by the Piper Aircraft Corporation and L-5s manufactured by Vultee-Stinson became the workhorses of the liaison Grasshopper fleet. The ability of these light aircraft to take off and land on short, unimproved roads and grass strips near the front lines, and their ease of maintenance, placed them in continuous demand and made them special. These other missions— liaison, reconnaissance, column control, resupply of critical items to distant units, laying telephone wire, and dropping messages to isolated units—became common. Grasshoppers proved to be excellent airborne jeeps, good for whisking commanders and couriers about the battlefield. On many occasions liaison aircraft were adapted to evacuate seriously wounded soldiers, a mission that greatly enhanced their popularity with fighting soldiers.

In his book, *The Angels: A History of the 11th Airborne Division,* Lt. Gen. E. M. Flanagan, Jr., USA (Ret.), recounts that during the battle to recapture the Philippines, the 11th Airborne Division supplied several isolated battalions, deep in the jungles, using L-4s and L-5s. Likewise, the 11th Airborne used these Grasshoppers to parachute critical personnel replacements to isolated units, one parachutist at a time.[7]

On the other side of the world, L-4s, launched from a tank landing ship (LST), modified into a baby aircraft carrier by the addition of a makeshift flight deck, supported the assaulting units invading Sicily. Still later during fighting in the rugged terrain of Italy, Gen. Mark W. Clark, a supporter of liaison aircraft, signed multiple requisitions asking for more of these aerial jeeps. As Fifth Army, and later as 15th Army Group, commander, Clark himself made extensive use of L-4s to move about his command. On October 4, 1943, he landed in Naples to inspect the city soon after its capture by Allied forces.

Other invasions saw L-4s being partially disassembled, brought ashore in amphibious trucks and landing craft, quickly reassembled, and flown into combat. The versatility and multiple uses of these light "puddle jumpers," limited only by the ingenuity of those they were there to serve, made them indispensable tools of the rapidly advancing American forces in both Europe and the Pacific. It is safe to say that army liaison aircraft participated in most major battles of World War II.

A word about the men who flew in these little canvas-covered aircraft. Initially civilian pilots were recruited or drafted to meet wartime needs. However, demand soon outstripped supply, and the call went out for volunteers to learn to fly. Many adventurous young artillery lieutenants came forward, underwent training, and were quickly assigned to units. But learning to fly Cubs was only part of the liaison pilots' duties. Life in the world of the liaison pilots was far from easy. Most of them, by necessity, became self-trained mechanics and learned the arts of "rib stitching" and patching bullet holes. They were soldiers first, aviators second, a hallmark that army aviation proudly maintains to this day.

Discrimination was a large part of the liaison pilots' lives. It sometimes came from their fellow ground officers who viewed them as different. At other times it came from Army Air Force pilots who flew "real" airplanes. This discrimination was visibly manifested on the silver wings worn by liaison pilots. Their wings, designed like the standard air force pilots' wings, had a large *L* superimposed and centered on the shield. But despite all their travails, many of these early pioneers survived and went on to become tribal elders in what later became army aviation.

By August 1945, the popularity of these valued flying machines reached such heights that the War Department authorized the assignment of light aircraft to infantry, armor, cavalry, engineers, and tank destroyer battalions. However, this decision came late, and with the war soon ended, the inventory of liaison aircraft dropped from sixteen hundred to little more than two hundred; the balance were declared surplus and sold. But that was to be just the beginning of change for the army and its fleet of Grasshoppers.

The end of World War II brought major changes to America's overall military strategy. Just as the tank and airplane emerged from World War I to influence the future, two new and major technological developments from World War II would change future military thought and practices. The atomic bomb and the jet engine forever changed the face of war. Their existence forced the rethinking of the uses of airpower, and the air force quickly assumed responsibility of these awesome weapons. Mundane tasks like providing close air support to ground troops were easily set aside. Likewise, in the minds of air force leaders, these new responsibilities required new and different organizations—different service relationships. Something like a separate air force.

The passage of the National Defense Act of 1947 was a dream come true for the air force. Finally, it would become a separate and equal service, complete with a secretary of the air force and its own chief of staff operating under the new Department of Defense. The new chief would sit as a full-fledged member of the Joint Chiefs of Staff. The army would now have to negotiate as an equal for its air support.

The postwar nuclear era brought tough, lean years for the army. It was the time when the phrase "hollow army" first came into use. Trying to hang on to as much as possible, the army soon found itself with too many headquarters, too many units, manned by too few soldiers, with too small a budget. The lack of dollars made it difficult for the army to properly sustain the soldiers it did have, not to mention keeping them adequately trained. Sadly, the national leadership lulled itself into feeling that defense needs were being adequately met.

Not long before the surprise invasion of South Korea by the North Korean army, Secretary of Defense Louis Johnson, who had significantly reduced the strength of much of the defense establishment, stated: "Our defenses are in grand shape and are adequate to the needs of the hour."[8] Days later, using all the available airlift capacity of the Far East Command, General MacArthur would barely be able to airlift a task force of two infantry rifle companies and one artillery battery into the near disastrous defense of South Korea. This meager force, named Task Force Smith, was rushed into battle to face six tank-led North Korean divisions. It is important to keep in mind that in the Far East, TF Smith was all the force that America could immediately move just five years after the most powerful industrial nation in the world had led the defeat of the Axis powers.

As the war in Korea expanded, the army began receiving increased funding. However, for the understrength and undertrained units rushed from occupation duty in Japan into battle in Korea, these increases were too little and far too late. What is more, post–World War II lack of funding forced the army to enter Korea with equipment and munitions left over from battles with Germany and Japan.

Looking back, one might reasonably assume that such an experience would have carried a clear message to the American Congress.

Not so. After all, despite the 1945 publication of the U.S. strategic bombing survey, which clearly illustrated the shortcomings of massive bombing raids on Axis nations, the air force clung to its belief in the effectiveness of strategic bombing. Although Congress had been more generous to the air force than to the other services after World War II, the realities of fighting a ground war in Korea forced the air force to shift its priorities. North Korea had few strategic targets worthy of the name, and they were quickly destroyed or neutralized. This done, the B-29s joined B-26 medium bombers flying interdiction missions. (Interdiction missions were actions taken to prevent, delay, or destroy enemy movements of men and supplies to the battlefield.) At the same time, fighter aircraft, F-51s and later jets, arrived to establish air supremacy and assist in battlefield interdiction and close support.

Although close support to the army was not how the air force preferred to fight, the early days of the war in Korea saw air force close support prevent the Allied forces from being pushed into the Sea of Japan. Air support truly saved the day.

Luckily for the army in Korea, the Marine Corps had managed to keep its air arm intact and oriented to supporting ground warfare. Marines who fought in Korea recall that the army loved having their close air support come from marines flying Corsairs. The army understood that, unlike the air force, CAS was marine aviation's primary mission, not something they did when other missions allowed. Marine aviators are taught that when the enemy is killing their friends, they go and kill the enemy. Both the army and marines in Korea felt that air force pilots were capable, but they also believed that the air force lacked interest in being that close to the ground war. For a while the Fifth Air Force had control of all air assets in Korea. They scratched for places to run all their airpower, places where it would make a difference. As the fighting wore on, the marines and air force clashed over air tactics. The air force deemphasized close air support, promoting instead a policy of interdiction. (Interdiction attempts to isolate the battlefield by denying the enemy resupply or reinforcement. Close air support consists of air attacks designed to kill or destroy enemy forces in close proximity to friendly forces.) The interdiction campaign went on day after day. The Marine Corps, whose pilots trained in close air support, suffered 20 percent of its pilot losses during the air force's interdiction campaign.

Unlike the air force, marine aviation has preferred aircraft, some subsonic, like the Grumman A-6A Intruder, the A-4B Skyhawk, and the AV-SB Harrier II, designed for the close air support mission.

Following the Korean War, the army was once again relegated to nonessential status and returned to its prewar state of budgetary poverty. Although few in the army would have believed it possible, soon after President Eisenhower's inauguration, the army's budget and readiness posture grew worse. Eisenhower's New Look defense strategy was based on the belief that Congress would not support large peacetime forces and that nuclear war was much more probable than conventional war. At Eisenhower's direction, the Department of Defense returned to its doctrine of applying most funding to nuclear systems. With the capability for total annihilation with air-delivered nuclear weapons, what was the need for conventional ground forces? "More bang for the buck" became the Department of Defense's motto. Whoever delivered the nuclear mail got the lion's share of the defense budget. Antique items like infantry, armor, and artillery were relegated to "guard duty," relics of a day gone by. With the soil of Korea still red with their fellow soldiers' blood, the survivors found this difficult to comprehend. Denied in war, they would now be denied in peace. Awash in Defense Department dollars, the air force again called the plays.

The National Defense Act of 1947 is most remembered as the air force's emancipation document. However, the NDA of 1947 and the subsequent Key West Agreement, signed on April 21, 1948, had set forth clear obligations for both the army and air force. For the air force, the charge was to:

> furnish close combat and logistical air support to the Army, to include airlift, support, and resupply of Airborne operations, aerial photography, tactical reconnaissance, and interdiction of enemy land power and communications.[9]

Accordingly, the army was prevented from infringement upon those areas delegated to the air force. Army aviation's role on future battlefields was spelled out as:

> expediting and facilitating the conduct of operations on land; improving mobility, command, control, and logistics support of Army

forces; and facilitating greater battlefield dispersion and maneuverability under conditions of atomic warfare.[10]

Of necessity, army leaders would find themselves forced to view
this agreement as license to fill the voids created by lack of air force
support.

Two later memoranda, one in October 1952 and the second a month
later, restricted army fixed-wing aircraft to five thousand pounds. The
agreements allowed army aviation to transport army supplies, equipment, personnel, and small units within the combat zone, which was
defined as fifty to one hundred miles in depth. Added to the primary
functions for the air force would be:

> airlift of Army supplies, equipment, personnel, and units from
> outside to points within the combat zone; airlift for movement
> of troops, supplies and equipment in the assault and subsequent
> phases of Airborne operations; airlift for the evacuation of per-
> sonnel and material from the combat zone; and aeromedical
> evacuation of casualties to points outside the combat zone.[11]

Although the air force was the recipient of the lion's share of the
post–Korean War budget, multiple missions placed new pressures on
the air force aircraft procurements. With the experience gained in Korea
all too soon forgotten, and with no ongoing war, the Tactical Air Command
(TAC) soon saw its importance once again relegated to second place
behind the Strategic Air Command (SAC). Additionally air force leadership continued to cling to its belief that strategic bombing was the
best way to damage an enemy. This required establishing air supremacy
early. Deep interdiction was held as the second best way to inflict pain
and damage, while close air support was still deemed the least effective way to employ airpower. These multiple missions and the realization that Congress would not support too large an air force forced
the air force to design and procure multipurpose aircraft whenever
practical. Needless to say, aircraft designed to cover all contingencies
don't necessarily do them all well. Subsequently, the realities of life
in the nuclear age forced the army to begin thinking of how to fill its
aerial support needs on future battlefields.

Thankfully, back in 1947 when the air force departed from army
control to more lucrative fields, they forgot, intentionally or otherwise,

the army's light aircraft and pilots: the aviators with the unglamorous mission of living with and supporting soldiers on the forward edge of the battlefield. These little kernels were destined to become the seed corn from which today's army aviation would grow. These seeds sprouted in Korea and from their experiences came new convictions.

Korea proved that out of necessity the army was going to have to get back into the business of flying armed aircraft, a clear violation of earlier agreements hammered out with the air force. Realistically the army had much to gain and little to lose. It was clear that this was not going to be easy to accomplish, and understanding this, the army began to look about for the means to fill its aviation needs.

The helicopter, having come of age in Korea, appeared to be the army's best hope for future battlefield mobility. But full acceptance of the helicopter did not come without difficulty. Early on, the air force, acting as the army's aircraft purchasing agent, rejected the army's efforts to expand its helicopter fleet. The air force's attitude in this interservice disagreement is illustrated by an event reported by then Maj. Gen. James M. Gavin.

In 1948, Gavin, the wartime leader of the 82d Airborne Division, was appointed president of the army's Airborne Panel, which was charged with evaluating the army's present situation and proposing solutions to the problems of future airborne and airmobile needs. After modest testing of helicopters by the 82d Airborne, the panel and the army leadership decided that it should purchase additional helicopters. The air force refused to place the orders. In his book *War and Peace in the Space Age,* Gavin recalls a conversation with the air force director of requirements, during which he was informed that:

I am the Director of requirements and I will determine what is needed and what is not. The helicopter is aerodynamically unsound. It is like lifting oneself by one's boot straps. It is no good as an air vehicle and I am not going to procure any. No matter what the Army says, I know what it needs and what it does not need.[12]

So much for enlightened and progressive thought from air force leadership. This uncompromising attitude, illustrated by the remarks of the air force's director of requirements, convinced the army's leadership to force the procurement and size issues.

Although the helicopter was introduced into Korea in limited numbers, it became the one machine that captured the most attention. It was initially used to save thousands of lives by prompt medical evacuation of wounded. At the same time helicopters provided limited mobility to army and marine ground forces. Another memorandum of understanding was negotiated in 1952 by the secretary of defense. It freed the army to use more and larger helicopters. By 1953, the year the truce in Korea was signed, the reputation of the helicopter and its value to the army had reached such heights that the army struck out on its own. Within a few years army aviation had begun a pattern of growth that would see it become a vital force on the battlefields of Vietnam. All because of air force intransigence, the army, like the Chiricahua Apaches of 1881, gathered its braves and ponies (pilots and helicopters) and broke out of the air force's restrictive agreements reservation, declaring that, in the future, it would do its own aircraft procurement. With this defiant departure, the helicopter became a member of the army's family of weapons. Ironically, a few years later, a helicopter named Apache would become world famous for its exploits in another war.

Chapter Five

GROWING UP . . . AGAIN

While ground soldiers and airmen spent the better part of three de-cades (the 1920s through the 1940s) arguing over roles and missions for military aircraft, the helicopter was maturing into a machine of great potential value to the military. Like most fledgling and expen-sive technologies, the helicopter was slow to find sponsors. In the 1940s a few devotees brought it to the attention of the military and it saw modest service and success during World War II. However, during that war, the Army Air Corps, busy trying to pound the Axis forces into submission, spent little time or money on this unproven and fragile technology. Minor testing occasionally took place but was done with little immediate purpose or high-level enthusiasm.

By war's end the helicopter's military potential had reached the point where further government investment appeared worthwhile. Gaining acceptance with the military brought an infusion of some federal dollars, dollars that would allow expanded research, development, and pro-duction. Government purchase orders provided the capital needed to keep this infant industry alive and allow it to develop adequate pro-duction facilities.

In 1945 the Army Ground Forces began to give serious consider-ation to adding helicopters to a broadening range of missions being performed by the light fixed-wing L-4s and L-5s. Although the army continued to purchase fixed-wing aircraft, the need, and therefore the demand, for helicopters increased. How the army was able to acquire its first postwar helicopters makes an interesting story.

While a cadet at West Point in the 1920s, Gen. Bruce C. Clarke visited his brother, Dr. Elmer A. D. Clarke, in Buffalo, New York, and played golf with one of his brother's patients, Larry Bell. A former aircraft mechanic, Bell was founder and president of Bell Aircraft Company.[1]

During World War II Bell Aircraft Company designed and built several military aircraft for the Army Air Force, the most famous being the P-39 Bell Aircobra. However, Larry Bell foresaw hard times for the aviation industry during the immediate postwar years and constantly searched for that something special that would keep Bell Aircraft in business. Seeing a demonstration of Arthur Young's flying helicopter model convinced Bell that the helicopter was that something special— a flying machine with a future.

On November 24, 1941, Bell hired Arthur M. Young and his assistant, Bart Kelly. Bell moved them into an old automobile dealership garage in Gardensville, a suburb of Buffalo, New York. The garage was converted into a small plant where Young and Kelly built two prototype helicopters. With an assortment of fifteen craftsmen, Young and Kelly began work on what was to become the Bell Model 30. By the end of World War II, history had been made and the meager group in the garage in Buffalo had grown into the Bell Helicopter Company.[2]

In December 1946, Larry Bell and General Clarke met again. Clarke, by then a major general, was G-3 (operations officer) of Army Ground Forces at Fort Monroe, Virginia, when Bell visited his office. Bell, still president of Bell Aircraft, asked Clarke to arrange an appointment for him with Gen. Jacob L. Devers, commander of Army Ground Forces. Bell needed to sell helicopters to keep his company alive. Aware of the army's growing interest in helicopters, he hoped to convince the Army Ground Forces to purchase and test his machines. Clarke arranged the meeting, and afterward Devers wrote General Eisenhower, army chief of staff, recommending that the army purchase and test Bell's helicopters. Eisenhower approved Devers's request but told him that the shortage of funds within the army budget prevented him from providing the necessary money. Eisenhower, however, did authorize Devers to reprogram within the Army Ground Forces' budget, and by canceling other projects, Army Ground Forces made funds available.[3] In 1946, after some hassle in justifying Devers' requisition to the air force, the army placed an order for thirteen Bell YR-13s, later given the designation H-13 by the army. These were the aircraft that Major General Gavin received and tested in the 82d Airborne. The obvious battlefield utility of these helicopters gained them immediate acceptance wherever they went, and commanders began to clamor for more.

As the pace of helicopter production increased, so did the need for helicopter training. Initially, manufacturers conducted this training, but later it would be done under a loose agreement between the army and the Army Air Force. Captain Robert J. Ely, the first postwar army officer to complete helicopter transition training under this agreement, did so at Scott Field, Illinois, in 1945, and has gone into the history books as the army's first helicopter pilot.[4] Other army pilots underwent similar training at Sheppard and San Marcos fields, in Texas.

By 1947, the expanded use of helicopters and the need for more helicopter pilots and mechanics led the army to award a contract to the Bell Helicopter Company to provide training. Conducted in Buffalo, New York, this contractor, or factory, training produced some of army aviation's more famous helicopter pilots, one of whom was Lt. Col. Jack L. Marinelli, who graduated in the first class. Years later Colonel Marinelli served with great distinction as the president of the United States Army Aviation Test Board.[5]

By late 1949 the office of the chief of Army Field Forces had studied the army's helicopter needs and determined that the army required various short-haul transport helicopters. This effort led to an additional study conducted in Washington by the Department of the Army staff. The Washington study, released in May 1950, recommended that funding be sought in the 1952 budget for activation of five company-sized, helicopter-equipped aviation units. If approved, these helicopter units would be assigned to divisions stationed around the country. Their purpose was to expose a wider sector of the army to helicopters, and hopefully to solicit ideas for use in developing helicopter doctrine and tactics.

This army proposal came during the early months of President Harry S. Truman's second term. Truman was a veteran of World War I, with many years of service in the army reserve, from which he had retired as a colonel. Unfortunately Truman harbored great resentment and distrust for the regular military establishment. Inheriting the presidency upon Roosevelt's death months before the end of World War II, Truman reduced the military from twelve million to one and a half million men as fast as he could after V-J Day. Pentagon budget cuts followed. The army went from a wartime high of one hundred divisions to ten in a matter of months, prompting Gen. Omar Bradley to speculate that the army could "not fight its way out of a paper bag." It was in the face of this lack of interest in things military that the army tried to embrace the new helicopter technology. As far as the army was concerned, the helicopter unquestionably would become a viable vehicle on future battlefields. But as we shall see, the request for the five helicopter companies was delayed by yet another army–air force squabble.

KOREA

Early in his second term, President Truman was forced to replace Secretary of Defense James V. Forrestal. He chose Louis A. Johnson, a political hack from West Virginia with White House ambitions. Truman came to the presidency as a man with great distrust of the military. His instructions to Johnson called for him to further slash the Pentagon budget and to distribute what was left so that the air force received the most and the navy the second highest amount, while the army and Marine Corps, with no nuclear capability, were to have split the remainder and then be ignored. After all, in this, the nuclear age, when would there ever be a need for ground soldiers? Johnson was masterful in carrying out Truman's wishes.

Prior to June 1950, as the result of these additional deep troop and budget cuts, Gen. Douglas MacArthur, commander in chief Far East, had withdrawn the remaining American combat units from Korea, leaving behind the American Korean Military Advisory Group (KMAG) charged to advise the new and lightly armed Korean army.

The unexpected invasion of South Korea by the Communist forces of North Korea on June 25, 1950, saw the unprepared American army of occupation in Japan on its way to war in a part of the world it had not anticipated. Untrained, understrength, and poorly equipped units were collected and within hours were moving to Korea. All too soon after their arrival, these American soldiers found themselves fighting for their lives in the rugged Korean countryside while the American-advised Army of the Republic of Korea melted before the onslaught of hardened North Koreans. Much like General Custer and the 7th Cavalry at the Little Big Horn in Montana, the American troops were too few trying to hold off too many. Worse yet, many of their weapons and much of their ammunition, victims of age and neglect, were not up to standards.

At the war's outbreak, the tactical elements of the Far East Air Force (FEAF), also a victim of neglect, consisted of a few F-51s (formerly P-51s), B-26 medium bombers, a handful of B-29s, and a few transports. Since 1947, the air force had devoted most of its energies to courting the nuclear genie. Mundane missions like providing close air support were considered history. However, the meager forces of the FEAF were immediately committed to support the ground forces in Korea and deserve much credit for preventing the army from being pushed into the Sea of Japan. The presence of the F-51, a long-range fighter designed to escort B-17s from England to Berlin and back, turned out to be a blessing. At low speed these World War II leftovers could often fly under the weather and accurately deliver their ordnance. Later, when the F-51s were replaced by "fast movers"—F-80s and F-86 jets—close air support began to suffer. It would not be until the late 1970s that the air force would have another aircraft well suited for close air support. In the meantime, the air force found itself in an unexpected quandary.

Ignoring the results of the post–World War II strategic bombing survey, the big-bomber boys continued to follow the lure of strategic bombing doctrine. There was only one problem: Very soon all the strategic targets in North Korea were gone. It became clear that the FEAF was going to have to operate under conditions similar to those found in 1917: in support of the ground forces—full time.

On June 27, 1950, the United Nations Security Council passed a resolution asking its members to go to the aid of the Republic of Korea. On July 7, the United Nations Command, under American leadership, was created by the security council.

Slowly United Nations troops arrived to bolster the understrength American and Korean forces, taking up defensive positions to help hold on to what remained of South Korea. Grudgingly, United Nations forces had been forced to give ground and were slowly pushed down the Korean peninsula until, with their collective backs to the sea, they coalesced and held. But by now it was obvious that the war in Korea was going to be yet another conflict carried on the backs of the infantry.

The rugged Korean terrain lent itself to toe-to-toe fighting. But the country's sparse road network, mostly unpaved and poorly maintained, hampered military operations. For the most part, battles were fought either up or down steep hillsides in an effort to control the high ground. The most significant of these battles were for places called Heartbreak Ridge, Pork Chop Hill, or the Punch Bowl—high ground, all of them.

In 1950, the year the war began, army aviation's workhorse was the World War II–vintage Stinson L-5. Only a handful of these airplanes were in Korea on June 25 and they were immediately put to work. In one case an L-5 helped evacuate an American adviser from a South Korean unit, trapped by the North Koreans. On July 27, thirty-seven days into the war, Lt. Arvid O. Munson, a pilot flying for the 24th Infantry Division, became the first of many army aviators killed in action in Korea. Throughout this war, fixed-wing aircraft carried most of the army's aviation load. The L-5s and later the new Cessna L-19s, De Havilland L-20s, and North American L-17s were the most prominent army aircraft used in Korea. But this is a story about helicopters, and the Korean War was the stage upon which helicopters won their fame.

Included in the Emergency Supplemental Budget of 1951 was an accelerated request by the army for authorization and funding for the activation of five helicopter transport companies that had been recommended in its May 1950 study. The request asked that four companies be equipped with the Sikorsky H-19 Chickasaw helicopters and the remaining company with Piasecki H-21 Workhorse helicopters.

As this procurement request wound its way through the Pentagon, the air force, still charged with aircraft procurement for both services, once again refused to let the necessary contracts. Earlier the army had signed an agreement with the air force entitled "Joint Army and Air Force Adjustment Regulation 5-10-1, Combat Joint Operations, Etc.: Employment of Army and Air Force Aircraft for Performance of Certain Missions (JAAFAR 5-10-1)," a bureaucratic mouthful. This agreement placed weight restrictions on army fixed-wing aircraft at thirty-five hundred pounds and thirty-five hundred to four thousand pounds for rotary-wing aircraft. The limit of four thousand pounds is less than the lift limit allowed for some office-building elevators. Many in the army viewed this regulation as one to prohibit the army's return to serious battlefield aviation, and perhaps that was the intent. However, the proposed H-19 and H-21 both greatly exceeded these weight limits.

As part of the procurement process for the helicopters needed to equip the five companies, the army requested a waiver on the weight restrictions in JAAFAR 5-10-1. Unfortunately, that was not to be. In December 1950, Gen. Hoyt S. Vandenberg, air force chief of staff, denied the waiver request and declared the air force prepared to provide the necessary air transport support the army needed. The waiver denial put the final bullet through the head of the army's procurement request. In Korea soldiers and trucks continued struggling to move supplies and ammunition through the cold and mud. The air force had had its way.

In 1951, after more studies, tests, and requests, the interservice disagreement reached the secretarial level and, much to the army's surprise, resulted in a decision to lift most weight restrictions on army aircraft and replace them with new limits entitled "functional" restrictions. This was a return to limiting the types of missions army aircraft were allowed to perform.

Specifically what the memorandum of 1951 said was how the army could use its aircraft. For example, they could be used for "expediting and improving ground combat and improving logistical support within the combat zone."[6] Under this agreement army aircraft were prohibited from duplication of functions reserved by the air force, which included close air support, assault transport, photography, and reconnaissance.

Finally, army aviation had achieved a breakthrough, one equal in significance to the 1944 breakout at St.-Lô during the Normandy invasion. Clearly army aviation was moving on a course best suited to the army's needs. Although the interservice battle had turned in the army's favor, the war was far from over. Time and hindsight would prove this agreement to be hollow, a respite at best. A long, tough road lay ahead before the future of army aviation would be assured.

As the army and the air force drifted farther apart, many in the army felt that the air force either could not or was not inclined to place many of its assets in support of the army. Even in the midst of the Korean War, to the air force, the delivery of nuclear weapons remained their number one concern. Defense of the United States from aerial nuclear attack was number two on their list of priorities. Support of the army received leftovers. But there existed other critical battlefield issues driven by new technologies and resulting service attitudes.

Jet aircraft brought a whole new set of dynamics to warfare, dynamics that further affected the relationship between the army and the air force. In the early days, in World War I and to some extent in World War II, the Army Air Force lived and worked close to the front lines and the units they supported. By the end of World War II, the Army Air Corps was building airfields completely removed from sight or sound of their ground brothers and as far from the front as they could get. After 1947 and the coming of the jet, the physical distance between soldier and airman grew greater, and the old saw "out of sight out of mind" began to take on new meaning when applied to the relationship between the two "forces." Joint training in how to support ground operations and how to properly apply close air assets always lacked adequacy. After the separation of the services in 1947, joint training declined. The army came to feel ignored, and the air force seemed too busy with its own agenda to notice.

With the coming of the jet aircraft, which weighed more and required higher speeds for takeoff and landing, the air force sought added protection by operating from larger, fixed bases with hard-surfaced runways built well to the rear of the front lines. The greater physical distance between foxhole and flight line did little to enhance communication and understanding between the army and the air force. In addition, early jet fighters had "short legs" (insufficient fuel to travel far or loiter long once over the forward battlefield while carrying armament loads of any consequence), which further exacerbated differences between the services. The bureaucratic air request procedures, the procedures the army was required to follow in asking for air support, and a system that gave the air force decision power, combined with the distance from air base to the target, too often led to a dump-and-run style of close air support. Additionally, jet aircraft were less accurate in the close air support role. To the soldier who saw his marine counterpart able to obtain near-instant support by a dedicated marine air wing, the army–air force modus operandi left much to be desired. Again the complaint was with procedures and the institutional approach, not with the bravery of the air force pilots who, when allowed, gave grand support to the army.

All the while, light army aircraft, both rotary and fixed wing, were accomplishing astonishing feats in support of their ground brothers who were turning to them more and more for their needs. Aerial medical evacuation became routine. Resupply of units isolated in areas where terrain was difficult to negotiate became second nature. Although the army helicopter was still a rarity, it is important to recognize that air force rotary-wing aircraft were turning in impressive performances in support of the army. Envious army leaders, recognizing the tactical value of larger helicopters, began demanding more of these handy machines, but wearing army paint.

Soon after the start of the Korean War and in response to requests for additional aviation support, fifteen light, two-seat Bell H-13 observation helicopters were procured off the shelf and rushed to Korea. Throughout the war, as they became available, additional H-13s, pilots, and mechanics were obtained, trained, and shipped (some were sent by air) to Korea. The H-13 became the army's rotary-wing workhorse and caused the world to understand the contribution of the helicopter to modern warfare. Homemade kits were fabricated and attached to the H-13s' landing skids, allowing medical stretchers to be carried on each side. The image of the medical evacuation H-13, as portrayed in the television series *MASH* (mobile army surgical hospital), evacuating wounded soldiers from frontline positions, stuck in the public's mind and heart. Before the war ended, more than twenty-one thousand wounded were evacuated by H-13s. Perhaps more importantly, these small helicopters had proven themselves able to operate from, and be maintained in, the field right beside the ground soldier. Large cargo- and troop-carrying helicopters certainly would have been useful, but continued fighting in the trenches of the Pentagon kept them from being used until near the end.

In the quiet days after the end of hostilities, the army, and especially army aviation, found itself in a far better position than it had been in when it had arrived hurriedly and unprepared to fight in Korea. It possessed an expanding fleet of new and larger helicopters designed primarily to fill the light transport role. It had also developed a large stable of senior officers who believed in the helicopter's military future. More importantly, helicopter crewmen had gained experience in Korea that would go a long way in developing army aviation into the skilled force it would need to be during the early 1960s. The army would depend on the expertise of these veterans in the rapid post–Korean War expansion of army aviation. It would be the combat-tested pilots from Korea who would bring the army into the world of air mobility.

The Korean War, the first war since the separation of the army and the air force, turned out to be a watershed in the army's secret desire to own armed aircraft capable of living forward with the soldiers. Although the FEAF supported when it could, Korea proved that the army could not always depend on the air force for its around-the-clock close air support needs. Weather often grounded air force CAS aircraft, whereas low-and-slow helicopters were able to operate under the weather.

BETWEEN KOREA AND VIETNAM

With the truce in Korea, a world tired of war turned to containing the spread of Soviet-sponsored communism. America's monopoly of atomic weapons had come to an end in September 1949 when the Soviets surprised mankind by exploding their first atomic weapon five years ahead of predictions. By the end of the Korean War it was reasonable to assume that Soviet nuclear capability had advanced enough to be a serious threat to the Western world. After Korea, in some minds, America's nuclear-based doctrine of containment relegated the need for a large ground army to the nice-to-have category. Nuclear advocates believed that infantrymen, cavalrymen, and artillerymen should go the way of the cavalrymen's horses. While army generals publicly praised the air force for its support in Korea, both services, in fact, were privately trying to cut each other off at their budgetary knees.

Once again defense dollars became the root of fierce interservice competition. But unlike the years between World War II and Korea, not all the competition for dollars was between services. The expansion of army aviation created a new set of combatants within the army. Open intraarmy competition appeared for the first time since the departure of the air force. This time there was a new set of players, the big missileers.

The rationale of the army's big-missile gang was that if the army was to survive in the nuclear age, it must get into the nuclear business through its excellent family of missiles. Actions taken in the waning months of World War II provided the army with the assets needed to play in the nuclear arena.

During those last months of World War II, Capt. Robert Staver, an ordnance officer, was given the task of tracking and capturing Germany's foremost rocket scientists. Britain and Russia were equally determined to round up these men and their equipment. As the war drew to its close, Staver located and established contact with the noted German rocket scientist Dr. Werner von Braun and most of his colleagues. They, in turn, led Staver to eight tons of their most secret documents. Together, the scientist, documents, and several German V-2 rockets were brought out of occupied Germany and moved to what is today the army's Redstone Arsenal in Alabama for scientific exploitation.

Initially von Braun and his team were the best the United States had. When the air force separated from the army in 1947, von Braun's team remained with the army, much to the air force's chagrin. By the end of the Korean War, Dr. von Braun and his team had developed plans for several large heavy-payload missiles.

With von Braun's success, proponents within the army pressed for the army to produce and field a system of nuclear weapons delivered by surface-to-surface missiles. Despite the realization that the Eisenhower administration was cutting defense budgets, missile advocates felt that if the army moved boldly it might receive a sizable share of the dollars going to nuclear "defense." After all, these folks reasoned, firing medium- to long-range nuclear missiles was far more cost-effective than delivery by manned bombers. But the reality of dealing with the Department of Defense was that when it approved a new program, the requested dollars would then be refused and the service would be directed to cut other system procurements to fund new ones. To that end, army nuclear missile proponents viewed a growing army aviation (and all other army programs competing for scarce dollars) as a threat to funds they felt were needed to develop missiles.

If all that were not distraction enough for an army shrinking to peacetime requirements, army aviation found itself involved with others who viewed the expansion of army aviation as the wave of the future and were working diligently to corral and brand it. This faction was led by the army's Transportation Corps with artillery close on the transporters' heels. (The army is subdivided into functional branches, cannons in artillery, tanks in armor, and communications in the Signal Corps.)

None of this was life-threatening to army aviation, but it was real enough to require attention. The missile threat passed quickly, but the quest for control of aviation by the Transportation Corps and artillery would continue for several years.

The view of the Transportation Corps was parochial. Artillery, on the other hand, felt that possession was 100 percent of the law. After all, was it not the artillery that had given birth to army aviation? Transportation's premise was less sentimental. The transporters stated that if it flew and hauled things, then it was an aerial truck, and truck units marched under Transportation Corps guidons. Carrying this line of reasoning to its logical conclusion, army aviation units in the business of hauling things with aircraft also ought to follow Transportation Corps' guidons.

But not so, said the artillery. After all, artillery is the true mother of army aviation. It was artillery lieutenant Watson who bypassed the military bureaucracy and invited the Piper Aircraft Company to come to Louisiana and demonstrate their light aircraft in spotting for artillery units. It was Fort Sill, the home of the Artillery School, that in January 1942 was chosen as the site for the first fourteen students, destined to be known the rest of their lives as "the Class Before One." It was at Fort Sill that flight training for light fixed-wing aircraft would remain until after the Korean War. (During World War II, training for liaison pilots took place at other installations, but Fort Sill was the one most widely known.) Although after World War II students came from most branches of the army, artillery's influence in the army aviation hierarchy remained paramount.

It is important to keep in mind that the interest shown by the artillery and Transportation Corps was in many ways helpful. They cared and gave aviation advocates. But the army's internal struggles, especially among those wishing to become the proponent for army aviation, were mild when compared to the post–Korean War renewal of gunfights between the army and the air force over roles and missions. Although it was a war of little blood and low casualties, it was war all the same.

Internal study after internal study told the army that it had need for more and larger helicopters. By 1952, after the air force's refusal to let the necessary contracts to purchase what the army felt was required, the army decided that the bickering had lasted long enough and developed plans to cut the cord between army aviation and the air force. The first step was to establish army aviation's own aviation training program and to assume responsibility for army aircraft procurement.

The Department of the Air Force Air Staff quickly recognized the army's change in direction and called the army's hand. The result was yet another army–air force shootout inside the Pentagon. Once again, as the gunfire died and the smoke cleared, a new document of agreement was tacked on the wall. This "Memorandum of Understanding of 1952" was a temporary cease-fire at best; to some it was a step backward. Recall that the agreement of 1951 removed weight restrictions and delineated service aircraft missions. The "agreement" of 1952 returned weight restrictions to army fixed-wing aircraft, and it defined the helicopter's role strictly in terms of "performance of functions," whatever that meant.

In January 1953, the army, definitely serious about army aviation, took steps to establish its own aviation school. In the army's view, the air force, still officially responsible for aviation training, had drifted somewhat afield from training pilots and mechanics to operate and maintain aircraft in the field, the hallmark of army aviation. Therefore, on January 6, 1953, with little fanfare the Aviation School was formally established at Fort Sill, Oklahoma, already the home of the Artillery School. It was a brave move, but in the wrong location.

Within months, the army realized that Fort Sill was too small for two schools. If either required expansion, Fort Sill simply lacked capacity to accommodate growth. This revelation triggered yet another aviation study, this time conducted by the Department of the Army. After evaluating several options, the army decided to create an Army Aviation Center and School, commanded by a general officer and located where the majority of aviation training could be consolidated. Two segments of aviation training would remain where they were currently located: basic, or primary, helicopter flight training would remain at Camp Wolters, Texas; aircraft mechanic training would stay at the Transportation School and Center, Fort Eustis, Virginia.

Following several more weeks of study, Camp Rucker, Alabama, was selected to became the new home of army aviation. The official move from Fort Sill to Camp Rucker took place on September 1, 1954, and the Aviation School's first commandant, Brig. Gen. Carl I. Hutton, supervised the move, assuming command at Rucker on that date.

Events affecting army aviation now began to move at an accelerated pace. In the Pentagon, the Army Staff decided that since army aviation had become important to a large part of the army and was involved in spending a good share of the army's annual appropriations, it needed representation on the Department of the Army Staff. Thus a new division, the Aviation Staff Division, was established as an integral part of the Army Staff. Its first head, Maj. Gen. Hamilton H. Howze, saw to it that army aviation had a voice when major decisions were made.

TARGET FIXATION—THE TANK

Habits are easily acquired but tough to break. But in some cases that is not all bad. Soon after the creation of the Iron Curtain, the army began to fret, counting tanks in Eastern Europe. Through the post–World War II years, whenever danger from other hot spots subsided, the army's eyes automatically turned east and resumed the count.

The Soviet proliferation of armor (Soviet tank production would reach the astounding figure of nine thousand per month during the 1970s), not only in Eastern Europe but around the world, was recognized as a menace to the free world, but especially to Western Europe. There have been other areas—Korea, Lebanon, the Dominican Republic, and Vietnam to name a few—that have temporarily absorbed the army's attention. But for the most part, the army has spent the post–World War II years trying to divine methods of coping with Soviet armor. It would be the army's fixation on Soviet tanks that would become one of the reasons for today's attack helicopters.

From day one of the Cold War and the creation of the Warsaw Pact by the East European countries behind the Iron Curtain, the North Atlantic Treaty Organization (NATO) understood that it could never match the Warsaw Pact tank for tank. In fact, the sum of all NATO's tanks did not approach the sum of Warsaw Pact tanks. Finding a means of killing tanks became NATO's and the United States Army's primary concern. To the army the solution was to develop and field high-tech equipment capable of inflicting multiple kills, able to survive and participate in additional engagements. But what about the air force? What role could it play?

From 1947 until after Desert Storm, when the air force underwent a major reorganization, the United States Air Force was subdivided into three forces: Strategic Air Command (SAC), Military Airlift Command (MAC), and Tactical Air Command (TAC). Also from 1947 until after Desert Storm the air force's nuclear-carrying big-bomber club managed to keep TAC playing second fiddle to SAC. Even though TAC flies multipurpose aircraft labeled "fighter-bombers," support of the army has not been foremost in the air force's mind. From the air force perspective, the TAC mission is bomber protection, air supremacy, and battlefield interdiction; the remaining assets may be used for close air support. In fairness it must be said that interdiction and close air do provide assistance to the army.

For the army, the good news is that TAC has been the one subcommand of the air force that nourished the true warrior spirit. Unlike SAC's management, TAC and its fighter jocks maintained the élan that makes them special to ground soldiers. TAC has been the one command in the entire air force to which the soldiers, the grunts, could relate. Soldiers know that when TAC is released from its other missions and comes to their aid, fighter pilots will fly, fight, and die if need be, doing their best for the frontline soldier. Despite service differences at high levels, at the foxhole level fighter pilots are the ground soldier's stalwart kinsmen.

NATO, pondering the East-West tank imbalance, has for years wondered about the effectiveness of air force fighter aircraft in the antitank role. Could tanks be killed by high-speed fighter aircraft? If so, how many? What type of munitions must be developed and procured? How many enemy tanks would remain to be killed by ground antitank missiles or NATO tanks? How much could the army depend on the air force fighters when the weather turned bad? The answers to these questions were vital to NATO decision makers. If the combined efforts of fighter aircraft and ground antitank systems proved to be insufficient, what other means could be used? The armed helicopter?

As we have seen, army interest in arming helicopters first surfaced during and just after World War II. There was a slight resurgence of interest during the Korean War. Doubt about the air force's willingness and ability to provide close air support festered in the years following Korea. Initially the army limited its interest to the development of a flying tank destroyer. Later other roles were explored.

On February 1, 1955, the Department of the Army requested that the Continental Army Command (CONARC) conduct tests to:

> determine the desirability and feasibility of employing Army aircraft as tank destroyers. The tests were to establish requirements for doctrine, tactics, and techniques which, on confirmation of requirements and feasibility, would lead to the establishment of military characteristics for aircraft more suitable than currently available to the Army.[7]

CONARC envisioned that units of these antitank aircraft would be employed by regimental commanders, thus reducing the time it took to get aerial support.

The year-old Aviation Center at Fort Rucker was selected to conduct these experiments and was directed by its headquarters, the Continental Army Command, to conduct "Project Able Buster," tests and studies to determine the feasibility of arming army aircraft. Using an array of off-the-shelf, fixed-wing aircraft, and one specially built for the purpose, the "study" experimented with ways to arm aircraft and attack ground targets. There was conviction within the ranks of the army that since the air force appeared disinterested, some sort of army close support was needed. If the air force did arrive, the firepower of armed helicopters would still be a plus.

In the end, no one seemed happy with the results of these experiments. The idea died in Washington. The army chief of staff, Gen. Matthew B. Ridgeway, faced with severely reduced funding under the New Look strategy developed by the Eisenhower administration, was reluctant to confront the air force.

In June 1956 the CONARC issued Training Directive Number 13, instructing infantry divisions to create concepts and organizations for "mobile task force operations." About the same time, General Hutton, the Aviation School commandant, whom many would call the father of the armed helicopter, was dissatisfied with the lack of progress in the development of the army's air mobility. He was also aware of the army's search for new systems to kill Warsaw Pact tanks. Without letting the world know, General Hutton elected to use CONARC's Training Directive 13 as license to dedicate part of Fort Rucker's assets to examine how best to develop aerial fighting vehicles. To General Hutton, mobility was important, but armed aerial weapon platforms were more important.

With the air force concentrating on its strategic bomber fleet, many in the army felt the need for aerial weapons systems immediately available to the ground commander. The air force made it clear that it was not interested in providing low-and-slow aircraft for the close air support the army desired.

In war, army ground commanders need immediate close air firepower, something to complement artillery. Close air support, if available, fills that need. But too often, TAC air was not to be had. General Hutton reasoned that armed helicopters were more than capable of filling that need, making additional aerial firepower available. He also reasoned that the helicopter was one way of getting around the prohibition against the army's arming its aircraft.

In a telephone interview with the author, Col. Jay D. Vanderpool, the first director of combat developments for the Aviation School and Center, stated that part of the rationale for seeking to arm the helicopter turned on the word *support*. "Although the army received some support from the air force, it was not close support nor immediate," Vanderpool said. General Hutton felt strongly about the need for close support, and if the helicopter could be armed and live with army troops in the forward area, he knew that it could provide both close and immediate support. Hutton set out to make that happen.

After looking about Fort Rucker for the right officer, one with the experience and talent needed to head his experimental program, Hutton selected, Vanderpool to act as project director. Vanderpool, in turn, identified, selected, and organized some of the talented officers and noncommissioned officers at Fort Rucker into the Armed Helicopter Mobile Task Force. (Over time the task force would undergo several name changes.) It was charged to procure, or design and fabricate, and to test weapons suitable for arming helicopters. Vanderpool had come to Fort Rucker to command the 337th Field Artillery. Hutton recognized Vanderpool's talents and moved him to head the school's fledgling Combat Developments directorate. The assignment of Vanderpool, a nonflying officer, to head this key position was unusual. But much of Vanderpool's career could be considered unusual. When asked why he felt that Hutton had selected him to be the director of combat developments, a chuckling Vanderpool responded, "Probably because of my diversified background." Vanderpool had been trained in infantry, artillery, and intelligence. During the later part of World War II, and again in Korea, he found himself leading guerrilla forces deep behind enemy lines. Vanderpool was comfortable in the unconventional warfare arena. He was equally at home in the conventional army. The mission that General Hutton gave Vanderpool was almost too good to be true for an "unconventional conventional officer."

In his problem analysis, Vanderpool, who had helped author the National Security Act of 1947, made an astute discovery.

As potential enemy bombers flew higher and faster, U.S. fighters were developed for greater speeds and altitudes. As fighters improved, bombers were driven further aloft and to greater speeds. Each advancement our air force made, separated it further in speed and distance from the army. The necessary differences in mission of the air force and the army left a partial vacuum between ground and the fringes of outer space.

As a ground soldier, Vanderpool knew what the army required in the way of close air support. Starting with a few odd helicopters and a handpicked band of aggressive and smart young officers, warrant officers, and noncommissioned officers, organized in what was by then called the Sky Cavalry Platoon, Vanderpool commenced his experiments. The unit's name was soon changed again, this time to Aerial Combat Reconnaissance Company. However, its members began to call themselves Vanderpool's Team. (In defiance of Colonel Vanderpool's wishes, his team is still remembered by some as Vanderpool's fools.)

One of Vanderpool's first actions was to visit helicopter manufacturers to ask questions concerning the strengths and weaknesses of airframes and other qualities of their products. As word of Vanderpool's mission spread, representatives of the aviation industry began to come to Rucker offering help.

While Vanderpool established contacts within industry, his assistants scoured supply depots and salvage yards of other services, scrounging excess or usable "junk" weapons systems. Two of his team, Capt. Harold Hennington and Capt. Charles Jones, became self-trained machinists. Using an old, discarded lathe from a salvage yard, Hennington and Jones took scrap metal and built weapons mounts and parts needed to make weapons better suited for aerial use, items that the army's supply system did not have.

Hennington and Jones were ably backed by Capt. Stanley E. Ballentyne and a group of NCOs whose talents ranged from intricate design work to old-fashioned manual labor. The work went on around the clock, seven days a week. "Individual air force supply officers and armament personnel bent over backwards to help us," said Vanderpool. Personnel at Redstone Arsenal also lent their support. As an item of weaponry came out of the shop, it would be lovingly strapped onto a helicopter and tested in flight by Capt. James Montgomery, the team's chief test pilot. Knowing that time, equipment, and dollars were short, Vanderpool made every effort to ensure success. His team understood that their work would be of immeasurable worth to the future of the army and army aviation. But speed was of the essence. The goal was to finish and have systems in place before the air force hierarchy caught on.

Vanderpool selected the Bell H-13, by then common throughout the army, as his first test-bed aircraft. The first question he had to answer was whether or not these weapons would damage the aircraft when they were fired. (Perhaps he had read the 1945 report from Fort Bragg's Army Ground Forces Board Number 1.) During July 1956, the team test-fired Orlikon 80mm rockets and two .50-caliber machine guns mounted on an H-13. First attempts were made with the H-13 sitting atop an elevated platform of railroad cross ties to simulate the altitude of low-level flight. The guns were fired and no damage was incurred. Next came firing from a hover. Again there was no damage to aircraft or weapons system. Finally all systems were fired from forward flight at one hundred feet altitude. Again aircraft and weapons system were undamaged, and dispersion accuracy of the fired rounds was better than expected. The next step was to improve these home-made weapons kits.

In the meantime, Colonel Vanderpool was directed to study how to capitalize on his success, how to best put this new aerial weapons system to work for the ground army. He was to determine how armed helicopters should be organized and employed.

By March 1957, Vanderpool's program was going so well that the decision was made to export demonstrations to other posts. The Aerial Combat Reconnaissance Company (ACRC) traveled to Fort Knox, Kentucky, Fort Benning, Georgia, and Redstone Arsenal in Alabama, where they demonstrated equipment and tactics. By this time, the task force was using .30- and .50-caliber machine guns and 1.5- and 2.5-inch rockets.

About the same time, March 1957, the air force woke up and smelled the cordite. They were not ecstatic over learning of this new army activity and vehemently said so.

But all was not rosy within the army either. Once again internal squabbles bubbled between the aviators and those who resented the funds that aviation was taking from the army's too-small budget. The Transportation Corps did not initially concur with Rucker's experiments and once again insisted that "if it flies and carries stuff, it belongs in the Transportation Corps." After considerable argument, the transporters reluctantly conceded that low-flying helicopters might need protection. But at about the same time the deputy chief of logistics (DCSLOG) at the Department of the Army in Washington further compounded the problem by letting the world know that he, too, was opposed to arming helicopters, except for self-defense.

Soon thereafter, despite the DCSLOG's feelings, the army's senior leaders declared internal opposition to be ended. As far as they were concerned, the armament trigger had been pulled, and the projectile was moving downrange. After all, the army was not exactly being smothered by air force ideas for future close air support.

An unexpected boost came to the army after President John F. Kennedy and Secretary of Defense Robert S. McNamara witnessed one of Vanderpool's demonstrations at Fort Benning. The president praised the army's innovations and suggested it ought to have more "gunships." With this comment, open opposition faded, and the army turned its efforts to refining helicopter weapons systems and the employment of armed helicopters.

Vanderpool's legacy to army aviation and to the army is lasting and important. While he and his team worked on helicopter armaments and tactics, the army's commitment to Vietnam was growing, and the helicopter was already important to that war.

On September 24, 1962, toward the end of their work, the ACRC designation was changed to Troop D (Air), 17th Cavalry. Still later Troop D became the base troop for the activation of the 3d Squadron, 17th Cavalry, part of Fort Benning's 11th Air Assault Division (Test). Following the completion of the air assault tests in 1965, and after the redesignation of the 11th Division to the 1st Cavalry Division, the 3d of the 17th became the 1st Squadron, 9th Cavalry, and deployed to Vietnam, where it distinguished itself as the first air cavalry squadron committed to combat. Many of the officers who fought in Vietnam with the 1st of the 9th Air Cavalry were later involved in the development of the attack helicopter, men like Col. Bob Nevins, Maj. Gen. James "Jim" Patterson, Lt. Gen. James "Jim" Smith, and Gen. Robert M. Shoemaker.

But the real question remained unanswered: How many of those Soviet bloc tanks could be killed by helicopters carrying tank-killing missiles? The answer would be several years in coming. Vietnam, a war fought in the jungles of Asia, would hold the army's attention until it ended in 1975. Toward that sad war's end, the introduction of North Vietnamese tanks did cause the army to refocus its attention on aerial antitank systems. But no significant progress was made until the army's gaze returned to the Warsaw Pact. It was in Europe that the use of antitank helicopters was deemed important. And although the war in Vietnam demonstrated the need for fast gunships, it would be the Soviet tank threat to Europe that sustained attack helicopter development.

William T. Piper during the Louisiana maneuvers of 1941. Note the grass-hopper symbol on his aircraft. *U.S. Army Aviation Museum*

The model YR-13 Bell helicopter assigned for testing to the 82d Airborne Division in 1947. *Courtesy Benjamin M. Bradin*

Sikorsky R-4 helicopter, 1963. *U.S. Army Aviation Museum*

UH-1B armed with 2.75-inch rockets and NATO M60 7.62mm machine guns in Vietnam. *U.S. Army Aviation Museum*

AH-1G Cobra helicopter at Bien Hoa, Vietnam, 1968. *U.S. Army Aviation Museum*

UH-1B fitted with TOW in Vietnam. Note kills painted on fuselage. *U.S. Army Aviation Museum*

Early AH-64A with T tail. *Courtesy Summa Corporation*

Bell YAH-63A AAH prototype. *Courtesy Bell Helicopter*

Apache AV03 during test aboard navy helicopter carrier. *Courtesy McDonnell Douglas Corporation*

Apache AV04, which was involved in a midair collision on November 20, 1980. Note tail add-ons. *Courtesy McDonnell Douglas Corporation*

AH-1Q demonstrating NOE attack. *U.S. Army Aviation Museum*

AH-56 Cheyennes. *Courtesy John Burden*

1-24 AHB officers in front of Apache-destroyed ZSU23-4. *From left:* Capts. German and Clegg, Maj. Schnibben, Capt. Woods, and Lt. Col. Stewart. *Courtesy Tom Stewart*

1-101st TOC at Objective Viper in Iraq. *From left:* Maj. (Chap.) Moore, Maj. Gen. Peay, Lt. Col. Cody, Maj. Davis, Capts. Gabram and Shufflebarger. *Courtesy Dick Cody*

101st Airborne Division attack commanders at Objective Cobra. *From left:* Lt. Cols. Bill Bryan, Dick Cody, and Mark Curran. *Courtesy Dick Cody*

1-101st AH-64 in a sabkha (dry lake bed) north of Camp Eagle II. *U.S. Army photo*

Apaches of the 1-101st at forward area refuel/rearm point (FARRP). *U.S. Army photo*

1-101st AH-64 at King Fahd Airfield, Saudi Arabia. *U.S. Army photo*

1-101st Apache refueling at FOB Bastogne. *U.S. Army photo*

1-101st AH-64 patrolling along MSR Virginia. *U.S. Army photo*

Chapter Six

CLEAR AND UNTIED . . . BLADES ARE COMIN' THROUGH

Three years after the end of the Korean War, the eyes of the United States Army were again fixed on the threat posed by Russian and Warsaw Pact armor. The United States Seventh Army, headquartered in Heidelberg, West Germany, as part of the NATO forces, was responsible for the defense of a large part of central Germany. If war was to come to Europe, American soldiers in the Seventh Army would surely find themselves engaged by hundreds of armored vehicles. They could see their enemy daily.

Looking across the East-West border, no one in NATO mistook the seriousness of the threat they faced. Piles of threat documents amassed, all overflowing with large counts of eastern bloc tanks, armored personnel carriers, and self-propelled artillery.

To soldiers, 1956 was a year of rethinking the army's role. Eisenhower was still president and remained firmly committed to his New Look policy of reliance on nuclear weapons. Thinking soldiers within the army returned to contemplating how to fight a conventional war on the continent of Europe. NATO was seriously outnumbered by the Warsaw Pact, and the gap between the numbers widened with each passing month. NATO urgently needed to find an enhanced means to destroy tanks. The new U.S. M60 tank was nearing production. The German Leopard I was in the concept phase. Newly designed artillery weapons were being tested, and helicopters continued to be examined as possible platforms for antitank weapons systems.

But unlike most weapons programs carefully developed under the centralized control of the Army Materiel Command, the arming of helicopters became an armywide cottage industry. The cause of these homegrown weapons systems was that need outstripped the army's ability to produce gun kits.

As word of Vanderpool's success spread across the army, the fever for arming helicopters hopped both the Atlantic and Pacific oceans. No one who witnessed a demonstration of Fort Rucker's Aerial Combat Reconnaissance Company could miss the armed helicopter's potential for bringing increased combat power to the land battle. The helicopter's ability to rapidly move troops and weapons was being written into army doctrine. In the words of an unknown author: "There was a need for haste in perfecting this entirely new concept because an expanding vacuum existed in the vast area termed mobility." Even though today it is accepted that armed helicopters and air mobility are interrelated and interdependent, it was not always so.

In March 1957 (as the result of work accomplished by Vanderpool's team), the chief of Ordnance was ordered for the first time to develop machine-gun installation kits for H-13, H-21, and the H-34 helicopters.* It did not take long for the innovative energies of American industry to come into play. With this step, the army crossed a major internal and self-imposed barrier against doing anything to arouse the air force's opposition.

In Germany, Gen. Bruce C. Clarke had become the commander of the United States Seventh Army. He was the same officer who years before had helped Larry Bell interest the army in his OH-13 helicopters. Clarke recognized the potential benefits of adding armed helicopters to the Seventh Army's considerable arsenal. Clarke, an innovative soldier, hoped to find some means of having helicopters fight armor. However, the general's desire outstripped the army's ability to provide antitank weapons or mounting kits for machine guns; the supply

---

*The army added *O* for Observation and *C* for Cargo as prefixes to helicopter designations. H-13 became OH-13, H-34 became CH-34, and H-21 became CH-21.

system remained incapable of providing weapons mounting kits. Not willing to wait, General Clarke ordered the use of two proven assets: Gen. Carl Hutton, the former commander of Fort Rucker, who was then assigned to the 8th Infantry Division, and the Army Ordnance Depot at Mainz, Germany.

In August 1958, General Hutton was appointed president of a board convened by General Clarke to develop doctrine, tactics, and employment techniques for armed helicopters in Seventh Army. A second task for General Hutton was the fabrication of hardware needed to mount weapons on helicopters. General Hutton asked for and received permission to make use of Captain Hennington and other former members of Vanderpool's team who were by then serving in Germany. Hutton assembled his task force and started fabricating helicopter armament hardware.

Meanwhile, the Continental Army Command (CONARC), the new name of Army Ground Forces, was still trying to find a weapons system that would allow helicopters to kill armor. CONARC instructed Fort Rucker to obtain the French SS-10 antitank missile and test it from a helicopter. The SS-10, a first-generation antitank missile, was designed to be fired from either ground or air. The test at Fort Rucker also included tactics and organization for an SS-10–equipped unit.

Two OH-13 helicopters were selected for the test, and SS-10 airborne launching and guidance instruments were installed. Although the results indicated poor system performance, Vanderpool recalls their being better than any other existing antitank systems. But the SS-10 was not adopted, leaving the army still in need of a good helicopter antitank missile system.

One plus came from the SS-10 experience: The army believed it possible, and was seriously seeking ways, to use the helicopter to kill tanks. The SS-10 test also highlighted another shortcoming. The weight of an antitank system clearly demonstrated that the army needed a larger and more powerful helicopter than the Bell OH-13 in the antitank role. This discovery encouraged the army to evaluate its future aircraft needs against its existing aircraft capabilities.

THE ROGERS BOARD AND COMMITTEE

The Army Aircraft Requirements Board, hereafter referred to as the Rogers board, was named for its president, Lt. Gen. Gordon B. Rogers.

Convened in January 1960, the board explored ways to improve the army's aerial surveillance and transport capabilities. First priority went to determining the requirements for light observation aircraft for the years 1960–70. Secondary to the aircraft requirements was the need for plans for phasing these new aircraft into the army while phasing out older models.

The board's most important recommendation was to suggest that the army procure the Bell Helicopter turbine-powered UH-1 Huey utility helicopter.[1] As it turned out, the Huey was, and to some degree still is, the most important aircraft the army ever owned. More Hueys have been flown in combat than any other helicopter in the history of army aviation. Since the early 1960s, the Huey has been the backbone, the workhorse, of the army's helicopter fleet. Plans show that it will remain in the inventory for many more years.

The second army acquisition recommended by the Rogers board was the De Havilland AC-1 (later CV-2B, and still later the air force C-7A) Caribou. This Canadian-built twin-engine transport, a superb short take-off and landing (STOL) transport airplane, was capable of airlifting six thousand pounds of cargo or twenty-eight fully equipped troops from unimproved fields. The size, weight, and capabilities of the Caribou trampled all over the restrictions imposed on army fixed-wing aircraft by joint agreement with the air force. The Rogers board recommended that the Caribou, like the Huey, be procured as fast as production would allow. But unlike other aircraft procurements, the Huey and Caribou were off-the-shelf buys. The Huey had been flying several years, and the Caribou was already in use by Canadian forces. Both procurements would save development costs normally required in a new aircraft acquisition.

In the end, the Rogers board brought a sense of orderliness to the army's aircraft procurement program. Its recommendations pushed the army to fill voids long recognized but unfilled.

Although the Rogers board was tasked to address equipment needs, it received input from one general officer recommending organizational changes. Major General Hamilton H. Howze, chief, Military Advisory Group, Korea, a board member who would soon have great impact on army aviation, recommended the adoption of an organization he called air cavalry. These units would be specifically designed to perform classic cavalry missions but with helicopters instead of horses and armored vehicles. The Rogers board agreed in principle with General Howze, but elected to include Howze's recommendations as an addendum, with language suggesting that the Department of the Army study the "feasibility of the concept of air fighting units and their armament."[2]

Not necessarily as a result of the Rogers board, the first material requirement for arming helicopters was approved by the Department of the Army (DA) on May 16, 1960. In December DA approved a plan for distribution of machine guns and mounts for OH-13s. This was rapidly followed by approval of other weapons systems for army helicopters. A sign of the times, these requests no longer spoke only in terms of defense. In fact, language such as "to support offensive and defensive ground combat" became common in army writings. The hard work by Vanderpool and his team was beginning to reap dividends. The imagination and creativity of the team and its ability to avoid bureaucratic entanglements and structured development programs paved the way for the arming of army helicopters.

One result of the Rogers board was the concern for the adequacy of aviation training. In July 1960, Gen. Bruce C. Clarke, back from Europe and commanding CONARC, directed General Rogers to chair a committee to study aviation training. Convening on August 15, 1960, at Fort Monroe, the Rogers committee submitted many recommendations, the most important being that the Aviation School integrate helicopter gunnery and tactics into the advanced phase of the helicopter pilot qualification courses. Other recommendations addressed programming, budgeting, and the standardization of aviation instruction in all service schools.

THE IMPACT OF PRESIDENT JOHN F. KENNEDY

For the army, the election of President Kennedy was much like having the electrical power restored following a long blackout. Kennedy's initial impact was manifested most noticeably in the sudden availability of funds and materials. Somewhere a giant supply spigot opened. Tools that had been unavailable in the supply system suddenly appeared. Parts were delivered immediately for vehicles that had been sidelined for months awaiting them. Being a soldier became pleasant and once more seemed important. Life in the army took on new meaning as soldiers once again felt appreciated. It did not take long before the army understood why.

Early in his administration, President Kennedy was challenged by the Soviets over nuclear missiles in Cuba. The president, in turn, tasked an army recovering from too many years of neglect to provide the muscle for confronting the Russians and Cubans. The Russians had secretly introduced nuclear-tipped intercontinental ballistic missiles into Cuba and were caught red-handed by American intelligence. Kennedy was determined to do whatever would be required to force these missiles' removal.

From the beginning, Kennedy understood that this could not be handled by a single service. It would take the combined efforts of all services. Understanding that in this case reliance on nuclear weapons alone for strategic deterrence was flawed, even dangerous, Kennedy made it clear to Russia's Premier Nikita Khrushchev that he was prepared to use the total spectrum of force, including land forces, to see the missiles removed from Cuba.

For the first time since World War II, Korea notwithstanding, the United States' national security did not rely so heavily on nuclear response. Strategic forces of the air force, although still vital to national survival and kept at a high state of readiness, were not the tool needed for this confrontation. Suddenly the army's job was to hone its combat power and get ready for deployment and probable combat. Army aviation was now part of the power.

Like other army forces stationed within the United States, the 1st Armored Division was alerted for movement to East Coast ports of embarkation and possible further deployment. Located at Fort Hood, Texas, the 1st Armored and its commander, Maj. Gen. Ralph E. Haines (later to be the last commander of CONARC), prepared for war. It appeared that President Kennedy anticipated using the 1st Armored ("Old Ironsides") Division to spearhead an invasion of Cuba.

Prior to leaving Fort Hood, General Haines, another of the growing number of generals who recognized the potential of armed helicopters, made the arming of 1st Armored's helicopters a top priority. But, like everywhere else, the problem was the lack of armament kits. As yet, supply had not caught up with demand. Even so, General Haines had no intention of taking Old Ironsides' helicopters to war unarmed. He turned to the innovative aviators in the 1st Armored to ensure that this did not happen.

Major Charles E. Canedy, commander of Troop D, 1st Squadron, 1st Cavalry Regiment, the 1st Armored's cavalry squadron, responded to General Haines's instructions. Canedy did not bother to look to the supply system for a solution. He, of all people, knew that the necessary parts, kits, and systems were not there. He had checked earlier. Known as a go-getter, Canedy understood that if his aircraft were going to be armed, he was going to have to arm them.

To head his in-house armaments program, Canedy selected CWO Clemuel H. Womack, an experienced pilot and member of D Troop. Canedy provided Womack with a handpicked cell of workers and got them access to post maintenance shops, where they were soon designing and fabricating the much-needed armament kits.

After visiting navy facilities to scrounge anything from Navy armament systems that might be useful for fabricating mounting kits for helicopters, Womack and his troopers created the "Official Old Ironsides Machine Gun Kit." Produced in proper quantities, these kits allowed the installation of two .30-caliber machine guns on each of D Troop's Bell OH-13s.[3]

With all OH-13s armed, Chief Womack turned to arming the division's UH-1Bs. For B model Hueys, Womack elected to design kits for both the M2 .50-caliber and the .30-caliber machine guns. Enough kits were built to arm all the division's Hueys. Finally Womack dispatched scrounging parties to find launch pods for 2.75-inch folding fin aerial rockets (FFAR). These pods, hung on the Huey's skids, were wired to a homemade electrical firing apparatus, greatly increasing the UH-1B's firepower. More importantly, tests revealed that these hurriedly constructed systems worked.

By the time they were through, Womack and his ad hoc band of armament "experts" had exceeded expectations and forgone those last precious days and hours with their families. They were good soldiers— men who, in time of crisis, and for reasons not found in leadership manuals, rise to the occasion.

The Cuban missile crisis ended with the Russians dismantling and removing their missiles. Thankfully the 1st Armored Division made the long journey to East Coast ports and back without engaging in war. But all was not for naught, for the army now understood that the national leadership expected it to be ready at all times. More importantly, it understood that, in the future, it would be provided the means to stay ready. What the army could not know was that it was about to be challenged in ways never imagined.

Although Kennedy's strategy of massive retaliation replaced Eisenhower's New Look, the president urged the army to search for new and better ways to fight land wars, conventional and unconventional. For example, the ideas of Gen. Hamilton Howze (first put forth in the report of the Rogers board, but quickly squashed, sealed, and shelved by the DA staff for fear of raising air force hackles) were eagerly dusted off and reexamined. As it turned out, General Howze's ideas would have tremendous and lasting impact on the army. Upon learning of Howze's innovative concepts for war fighting, Secretary of Defense Robert S. McNamara encouraged the army to establish a board, later called the Howze board, to test General Howze's ideas.

THE HOWZE BOARD: A KICK START

In April 1962, Secretary McNamara popped a lethargic army, groggy from long slumber, with a high-voltage cattle prod. In two separate memoranda McNamara ordered the army to take a bold new look at "land warfare mobility." McNamara directed this examination to be conducted in an "open and free atmosphere." The second memorandum asked for examination of six specific areas and again ordered the army not to stifle new ideas. He further directed that all this be completed in five months, by September 1.

To comply, the Department of the Army convened the United States Army Tactical Mobility Requirements Board (hereafter referred to as the Howze board) and turned to one of its most innovative general officers, Lt. Gen. Hamilton H. Howze, commander of the XVIII Airborne Corps, Fort Bragg, North Carolina, to be its president.

Understanding that time was the most critical item in the test program, General Howze and the board secretary, Col. John Norton, both aviators, used the backward planning sequence to design schedules and establish test milestones. This completed, Howze and Norton discovered that their schedule could afford one month to assemble personnel and equipment, two months for the conduct of the tests, and the remaining time for analysis and report preparation.

The Howze board was charged to look to the future and determine army requirements for equipment and organization in the years 1963–75. The board understood that test outcomes would shape much of the army's future. Most of the handpicked members understood that it would be hard work but knew it would be fun and an opportunity to influence the future of their profession.

New ideas were solicited from across the army. Additionally, the board wrote letters to a wide sector of both industry and business asking their assistance. The air force was invited to be represented and sent a brigadier general who was given the freedom to move about and observe activities. Since part of the tests were designed to determine how and where the army would use air force support in future land battles, the air force brigadier's counsel proved valuable.

Testing aircraft weapons systems absorbed much of the board's efforts. One surprising and revolutionary recommendation surfaced. While most of the army was focused on arming helicopters, the Howze board recommended assigning twenty-four armed, twin-engine, fixed-wing OV-1 Mohawks in future air assault divisions. Their purpose would be to fill the void no one wanted to talk about—lack of responsive close air support (CAS).

The turbine-powered OV-1 Mohawk was the product of an earlier joint army–Marine Corps development venture. Although it was not an army requirement, the marines insisted on the Mohawk's being capable of bombing, resulting in the aircraft having built-in hard points under both wings for bomb shackles. The Howze board found the Mohawk's weapons very accurate. Since the Mohawk was a short takeoff and landing (STOL) aircraft capable of operating from unimproved airstrips, the Howze board felt that it should be integral to the army ground commander's fire-support team. Of equal importance, the Mohawk proved capable of being maintained in forward areas. No one intended to have OV-1s displace air force CAS, but the board felt that Mohawks could supplement when the air force could not provide support. In the board's view, this would assure the long-sought-after, dependable, and immediate support needed in forward areas.

The recommendation to arm the Mohawk, an open violation of army–air force agreements, sadly died from lack of high-level support. However, it sent a message that spoke loudly about army dissatisfaction with existing, one-sided, close air support arrangements and the need for immediately responsive close air support for ground commanders. More importantly, there was some indication that the air force had its radio receivers turned on for a change.

With all the impact of flying into a mountainside, the army's Mohawk recommendation gave a wake-up call to the air force's leadership. The news was received as a clear signal that army requests for CAS could no longer receive mere lip service. The announced results of the Howze board caused the air force to reexamine its CAS and airlift aircraft obligations. To soothe army complaints, the air force prepared and forwarded to Congress requests for additional fighter-bomber wings. It was no secret that over the years the air force had become equipment-limited and unwilling to operate in forward areas. Likewise, it was clear that in the past aircraft bought by the air force had not been procured with the army's CAS requirements in mind. It was also no secret that the air force did not want the army filling its own CAS or airlift needs.

One important Howze board finding impacted on armed helicopters. Fighting tanks has never been the infantry's favorite outdoor sport, even when tanks attack in small numbers. The Howze board reasoned that if future airmobile forces were going to have any usefulness across the spectrum of warfare, especially on armor-heavy, mid- or high-intensity battlefields, they needed aerial tank-killing weapons.

The Howze board examined the French SS-11 antitank missile, an improved version of the SS-10. Board tests, though certainly not scientific, once again showed the clear need for such weapons and, more importantly, antitank weapons mounted on helicopters. Although the SS-11's chances of hitting the target were improved over the SS-10's, they were still low. But the SS-11 was the best system available. As the result of Howze board recommendations, aerial SS-11 systems were eventually procured and issued to U.S. Army aviation units. All the while, a search for a more reliable antitank missile continued. To be prepared when such a system was finally found, the board recommended development of a specially designed armed helicopter. It was not long before test results from the 11th Air Assault Division and events in Vietnam would validate this recommendation.

In its final report, the Howze board offered other far-reaching recommendations. The scope of these recommendations was so extensive that the Department of the Army decided to conduct follow-on testing. With Secretary McNamara's support, DA elected to test two of the organizations recommended in the Howze board's report—an airmobile division and an air transport brigade.

To ensure that these follow-on tests would not be influenced by preconceived and biased organizational notions, DA created an entirely new and "extra" division. It also formed a separate aviation brigade.

In late 1962, the 11th Air Assault Division (Test) assembled at Fort Benning, Georgia. Led by Maj. Gen. Harry W. O. Kinnard, the veteran G-3 of the 101st Airborne Division's 1944 Christmas Battle of the Bulge, the 11th gathered up the loose strings left by the hurried Howze board. In theory, the 11th was to be a light division capable of movement by air force or army aircraft. Equipment authorizations were scrutinized and strict measures instituted to stay as lean as possible.

In addition to infantry, artillery, and other types of battalions, the 11th Air Assault Division included an extra multibattalion aviation group. This group, internal to the division, was designed to have enough aircraft to airlift one-third of the division's combat assets at one time. A typical lift might consist of a brigade with two infantry battalions and a supporting artillery battalion.

Another unit, the 10th Air Transport Brigade, composed of several battalions of both fixed- and rotary-wing aircraft, was activated and attached to the 11th Division. The mission of the 10th Brigade was to establish an air line of communications (ALOC) to move supplies to the 11th Division in the field.

For more than two years the 11th Air Assault Division's equipment, organization, and tactics were developed, tested, refined, and then tested again. Test sites were in Florida, Georgia, and the Carolinas. For participating personnel, times were exciting. No scheme was too wild to be considered. Much of the flying was dangerous and kept the pilots' adrenaline flowing. Lieutenants and captains found themselves making decisions that in other organizations would have been reserved for colonels. In hindsight, it was an early test of a decision process later known in the army as "power down," where decisions are made at the lowest appropriate level. What's more, those participating in the air assault tests had a lot of fun.

But unknown to most army observers, these tests turned out to be a precursor to large-scale airmobile operations in Vietnam. In the end, the efforts of the 11th Air Assault Division cemented airmobile doctrine into the soul and fiber of the army.

With tests ending and the war in Vietnam escalating, the Department of the Army decided to keep the experienced people of the 11th together and deploy an airmobile division to Vietnam. Someone in the Pentagon decided that the colors of the 11th should again be cased and the division renamed the 1st Cavalry Division (Airmobile). This done, the 1st Cavalry loaded for overseas shipment. Anyone who followed America's involvement in Vietnam knows the exploits of the 1st Cav and its years of distinguished combat. Time and again the 1st Cavalry and later the 101st Division proved the Howze board to be right about the usefulness of, and the army's need for, air mobility.

VIETNAM

The war in Vietnam is often described as a war of movement. The elusive soldiers of the Viet Cong and North Vietnamese Army enjoyed a freedom of movement not initially shared by the South Vietnamese Army. To call the terrain of Vietnam rugged is a gross understatement. Even when it is flat and open, as in the southern delta regions, rice paddies and canals make it a difficult place to fight a war of mounted, vehicular movement. In the early days, trying to guess where the Viet Cong might strike, and assembling government troops in position to defeat them, seemed impossible for the South Vietnamese Army.

As the involvement of American advisers grew to include American ground and air forces, the mobility differential between friendly and enemy forces narrowed. It did not take long for army leaders in Vietnam to recognize the need for helicopters. The helicopter, in adequate numbers, provided the mobility needed to carry the war to the Communist forces.

The question of which service first sent helicopters to Vietnam will not be answered here. However, in December 1961, the army's CH–21–equipped 8th Transportation Helicopter Company (THC) deployed to the Republic of Vietnam from Fort Bragg, becoming one of the earliest units there. Other helicopter units quickly followed. Almost from the moment of the first helicopter's arrival, helicopters became indispensable in day-to-day operations—a decisive tool, and the most visible tool, of the war. But as Americans and Vietnamese began to find tactical success through the use of helicopters, the Viet Cong and North Vietnamese gradually developed countermeasures against airmobile operations: nothing serious enough to stop air assaults, but enough to cause the Americans to pay a price. The large, slow, gangly, banana-shaped CH-21s carried a crew of four and could lift ten combat-equipped troops. Armed with machine guns in each door, the CH-21 was vulnerable during approach, landing, unloading, and departure from landing zones (LZs).

During the early days of American involvement, the vastness of South Vietnam and the paucity of artillery and tactical air support proved to be a serious shortcoming for airmobile operations. When TAC air support was made available, the lack of joint training lessened its effectiveness. Likewise, fighter aircraft, even the slower World War II models, lacked the accuracy needed for LZ suppression. The need for means to suppress enemy fires on and near landing zones became important. Helicopter damage increased as the Viet Cong and North Vietnamese riflemen and machine gunners learned to aim with adequate lead to shoot the slow-moving, ladened transports. Helicopter door gunners were too often unable to suppress enemy fire on landing zones (inadequate weapons). Heavily armed escort helicopters to protect troop-carrying helicopters became imperative.

THE UTILITY TACTICAL TRANSPORT HELICOPTER COMPANY

On July 25, 1962, the army activated its first armed helicopter company—on Okinawa of all places. Other units had armed themselves, but this was the first company-sized unit designed from the beginning to be an armed helicopter company (Vanderpool's Aerial Reconnaissance Company notwithstanding). Looking back, one might wonder if Okinawa was selected to avoid discovery by the air force's Air Staff. In any case, under the command of Lt. Col. Robert Runkle, the company soon moved to Thailand, where it trained for jungle combat.[4]

By October 1962, the Utility Tactical Transport Company (UTT) was in Vietnam and already combat wise. It did not take long for the UH-1B Huey–equipped company to achieve fame. Stories of their successes and exploits spread throughout the army. After all, the UTT was the army's only armed helicopter company, equipped with homemade weapons systems, in daily contact with an armed enemy. Names familiar from earlier homegrown weapons programs were prominent in the UTT. Chief Warrant Officer Clarence J. Carter, formerly a member of Vanderpool's team at Fort Rucker, joined with CWO Clem Womack, designer of 1st Armored Division's kits, to arm the UTT.

Not too long into their work, the army began delivery of the factory-built M6 quad machine-gun kits for UH-1Bs. Womack then shifted to developing a seven-tube launcher for 2.75-inch rockets. These launchers, suspended below the M6 system, significantly increased the UH-1B's firepower.

Lieutenant Colonel Runkle was replaced by Lt. Col. Ivan Slavich on November 21, 1962. Under Slavich's leadership, UTT's reputation continued to grow. It became the first army aviation unit to be awarded the Distinguished Unit Citation, and in 1962 the unit won the Army Aviation Association's Army Aviation Unit of the Year Award. The UTT also helped win a permanent place for gunships in army aviation.

As months turned into years and the UTT remained in Vietnam slugging it out with the Viet Cong, the need for more and better designed armed helicopters became apparent. Renumbered several times, the UTT ended the war as the 334th Aviation Company, the Playboys.[5] Meanwhile positive changes were occurring in other sectors of air mobility.

As the old, slow reciprocating-engine CH-21s were replaced by turbine-powered UH-1Bs and later UH-1Cs, UH-1B gunships found themselves increasingly "behind the power curve," underpowered for loads they were being asked to carry. With B model gunships having difficulty keeping up with troop-carrying Hueys (they were ten knots slower), the army understood that it seriously needed an aircraft designed purely as a gunship.

THE INDIAN AND THE SNAKE

For two years, from 1962 to 1964, the 11th Air Assault Division (Test) served the army as a test-bed division for development and refinement of the airmobile concepts recommended by the Howze board. At the conclusion of Air Assault II, the last and largest of the many tests conducted by the 11th Air Assault, the army's airmobile concept was considered proven and, for the most part, accepted. There were some dissidents, not all of whom wore blue uniforms, but for the most part everyone recognized that air mobility was now part of the army's doctrine.

However, two important questions were left undecided following the air assault tests: How many armed helicopters should the army have, and did it need specially designed gunships? Conclusions reached by the Howze board had pointed to the armed OV-1 Mohawk as the best candidate for escort of troop lifts. The later air assault tests leaned toward armed helicopters. The Mohawk's speed and ability to carry greater loads than armed helicopters gave it a big advantage over the overloaded UH-1Bs. However, the forceful, fervent, and stark rejection of the armed OV-1s by the air force forced the army to go to the helicopter as a less acceptable alternative to both the army and air force.

If the army could not arm the Mohawk and the air force did not have an aircraft suitable for escorting helicopter airmobile operations and landing zone preparation, then something was going to have to be built to fill this need—and built fast. As the air assault tests were analyzed, it became clear that strap-on, homemade gun systems for helicopters were not the answer. During the air assault tests and as in Vietnam, the UH-1B loaded with weapons and ammunition strained to stay up with troop-carrying Hueys. Dashing ahead or catching up was out of the question. The need for a faster armed helicopter designed from the skids up as a gunship was unquestioned.

But keep in mind the urgency of need in Vietnam. Costs also had to be considered. The quickest fix would have been the major modification of an existing airframe; however, after engineers examined all options, the concept of airframe modification was rejected. Instead, Cyrus Vance, then secretary of the army, directed a giant leap into the future, to press forward, to challenge technology. Secretary Vance insisted that the new advanced helicopter gunship must have a speed of at least two hundred knots. Although this did little to enhance fielding a system quickly, the decision drove the program to a new airframe and, subsequently, to long years of development and testing—not exactly what gunship pilots in Vietnam had in mind.

In June 1963 the army announced its intent to build its advanced aerial fire support system (AAFSS), later named Cheyenne. Almost a dozen aerospace companies responded to the army's request for proposal (RFP). A selection committee narrowed proposals to Sikorsky and Lockheed; they were contracted to proceed with further concept definition. Comparison of the two companies showed Sikorsky long on helicopter experience and short on armaments. Lockheed, on the other hand, was a company with less experience in helicopters, but with a strong history of fixed-wing aircraft production. In November 1965 the army made its final selection and awarded Lockheed the research and development contract for the AAFSS program.

Lockheed rolled out its first AH-56 Cheyenne prototype on May 3, 1967. In the area of challenging technology, Lockheed exceeded the army's wildest expectations. The appearance of the Cheyenne was a revolutionary departure from other helicopters. At rest, the Cheyenne was tall, yet it was most conspicuous for its narrow fuselage, made possible by seating the copilot-gunner in the nose and the pilot above and behind.

The Cheyenne was a "compound" helicopter, the result of Lockheed's unusual combination of stub wings, main rotor, and pusher propeller. Yet Cheyenne's most revolutionary feature was its rigid rotor system. Unlike other helicopter designs, Cheyenne's rotor blades were rigidly mounted to the rotor hub. Movement was controlled by a gyro system mounted above the rotor. Input for directional change was transmitted by the pilot to the gyro system, forcing the aircraft to change direction. Two additional and unusual features assisted the Cheyenne in reaching its 256-mile-per-hour maximum speed. The first was a set of stubby, cantilevered, fixed wings mounted amidships on each side of the fuselage. These wings gave the Cheyenne lift. The second feature was a Hamilton-Standard three-bladed pusher propeller, which provided forward thrust—the push needed to attain high forward speed.

It all worked something like this: As Cheyenne's forward airspeed exceeded one hundred knots, the stub wings began to fly, to provide lift. This lift allowed the main rotor to partially "unload," or discontinue acting as a wing and become more like a control surface, a means of changing direction. After the main rotor unloaded, the thrust provided by the pusher propeller allowed Cheyenne to accelerate to speeds never before attained by a helicopter.[6] A single engine—a General Electric T-64-GE-16 turbine engine—developing 3,435 shaft horsepower, powered the main rotor, antitorque rotor, and pusher propeller. This lone engine allowed the Cheyenne to reach 256 miles per hour, twice the speed of the UH-1B.

Designed to be an all-weather combat aircraft, the Cheyenne included the most comprehensive electronics package ever devised. It consisted of terrain-avoidance radar, Doppler inertial navigation systems, station-keeping radar, and an automatic flight control system to allow hands-off flying so the crew could use all the onboard technology.

Weapons added even more complex dimensions. The nose turret accepted either a 7.62mm machine gun or a 40mm grenade launcher. It could swivel, or traverse, 180 degrees side to side. A 30mm automatic cannon capable of 360 degrees of traverse was mounted under the copilot-gunner's station in a belly turret. The underside of each cantilevered wing had three pylons, each of which could carry a two-thousand-pound load.

The copilot-gunner's stabilized station with its advanced electro-optical sighting system was designed to traverse inside the cockpit, allowing the copilot-gunner to face his target. The nose and belly turrets could be slaved to either the pilot's or copilot's electro-optical helmet sight, allowing one or the other to aim and fire these weapons by merely a turn of the head. All of this was controlled by the integrated helicopter avionics system (IHAS), a system so advanced that it could engage two targets at once.

The Cheyenne was complex, to say the least, and complexity is expensive and difficult to perfect. By 1967, the year the first prototype was unveiled, cost and complexity were already damaging the Cheyenne program. Not all the problems associated with cost and complexity were Lockheed's fault. Many components slated to be installed in Cheyenne were provided by the army: Some arrived defective, late, or both.

Another millstone that hung on the Cheyenne program also came from the army. At the time of Cheyenne's development, the Army Materiel Command (AMC) had become a multifaceted, multilaboratory bureaucracy that sometimes was its own worst enemy. Perhaps the most startling example of this was AMC's insistence that Lockheed use the AMC's internally developed XM53 30mm cannon, which often did not work. In true bureaucratic form, defense of this decision was increasingly based on "sunk costs," meaning that since AMC had spent so much developing this cannon, it had to be used. The requirement to fix such problems ate away at time and increased expenses. Time was probably the dearer of the two.

In 1965, two years into the Cheyenne program, the urgent need for a quick fix to the ongoing situation in Vietnam ran smack into the reality that Cheyenne would not be ready anytime soon. In this crisis, the Department of the Army was forced to seek an alternative. A decision was made to go with an interim program, and requests for proposals went out to industry. One contractor was ready.

In the 1950s, long before the army ever mustered the courage to consider arming helicopters, Bell Helicopter had begun in-house work on design of a new, from-the-ground-up attack helicopter. By 1961, the program Bell called Project Warrior, showed promise, and the decision was made to take it into mock-up stage and build a full-scale model. The first mock-up, the D255, showed innovative thinking. Designed with a tandem, stepped-seat cockpit, with the pilot seated above and behind the copilot-gunner, the D255 had an unusually thin fuselage. These features would later appear in Cheyenne. To keep costs low, Bell planned to build this helicopter using as many of the UH-1 Huey components as possible. Although still confronted with air force opposition and internal conservatism, some of it within army aviation, Bell hoped that the attractiveness of commonality and low development costs would appeal to the army.

After learning that the Howze board looked with favor on the development of armed helicopters, Bell initiated work on a flyable gunship and began to "bend metal." To pad their bet, Bell decided to use a modified Model 47, or, by army designation, OH-13, as a test bed.

Calling it the Model 207 Sioux Scout, Bell got construction under way in 1962. Using the engine and rotor system of the OH-13, the Sioux Scout offered another notable feature: stub wings mounted high and behind the cockpit. At the time, it was the only helicopter to have these. The advertised purpose of these wings was for mounting external fuel tanks; however, testing showed that they improved climb and high-speed turning. Later the wings offered attachment, or "hard," points for mounting external weapons.

The cockpit, made of fiberglass, was completely enclosed and featured a narrow fuselage with stepped, tandem seating like that found in the D255 mock-up. The flight controls for the pilot in the rear seat were standard; the copilot-gunner flight controls were stunted and mounted to the side to allow operation of the weapon and sights. The aircraft's armament consisted of an Emerson Electric Model TAT-101 turret mounting twin M60C machine guns attached under the nose.

The Sioux Scout first flew in June 1963. Extensive company test flights continued until autumn, when Bell turned their one-of-a-kind over to the army's 11th Air Assault Division's Troop B, 3d Squadron, 17th Cavalry, at Fort Benning, for evaluation.

The air cavalry pilots were taken with this innovative machine and wrote fervent reports recommending army procurement. Seeing the skies of Fort Benning filled with turbine-powered UH-1Bs, the scout pilots suggested that, in the future, follow-on gunships like the Sioux Scout be powered by a turbine engine to ensure enhanced performance and commonality of engine types in aviation units. But the power of the turbine is what they really wanted.

Since the army was not officially interested, Bell took the results of the informal Benning test, reached deep into its corporate pockets one more time, and returned to the drawing board. Bell management believed that it was only a matter of time before the army would recognize the obvious—its need for a helicopter specifically designed for the attack role, and they made the bold decision to be ready when the army came looking.

Bell's new effort resulted in their Model 262, which they entered unsuccessfully in the army's advanced aerial fire support system (AAFSS) competition, losing out to Sikorsky and Lockheed in the first round.

Once more Bell walked that long, empty-pocketed road home. But they could see a faint glimmer of hope. Bell Helicopter maintained many technical representatives (tech reps) in support of aviation units in Vietnam. These "company men" kept Bell headquarters in Fort Worth informed of events and conditions in Vietnam. Based on what the tech reps were reporting, the need for a better gunship was immediate. In Bell's collective opinion, the AAFSS program was too far from bearing fruit to be much help in Vietnam. Events proved Bell correct. General Westmoreland's urgent and vigorous request for a better gunship would force the army to act sooner than it would have liked.

Once again Bell drank from its own funding bucket and moved ahead with in-house engineering and design refinement without an army requirement or even any encouragement. It was a brave position but, as it turned out, a wise one.

In December 1964, Bell President E. J. Ducayet approved initial design work for the Bell Model 209, a Huey-based gunship. In March 1965, at another confidential decision meeting, Ducayet approved the final plans for building a prototype Model 209 and directed that it be completed within six months. November 1965 was the target date selected for being ready to demonstrate the 209 to the military. Lastly, Ducayet directed that the project be kept secret; access to construction areas was to be limited. The prototype was assembled in a specially constructed room. To enhance security, this room was built inside an existing hangar. Only those directly involved with the project were allowed entrance.

Work began in March 1965. Plans for the Model 209 called for it to be powered by the new Lycoming T-53-L-13 gas-turbine engine, rated at fourteen hundred shaft horsepower (SHP), more than enough for the Model 209. In fact, when the production models, by then named Huey Cobra, began rolling off the production line, the power of the L-13 engines was reduced to eleven hundred SHP, a more compatible level for the Huey Cobra.

To obtain the major components for the 209's drivetrain, Bell simply took the transmission, the forty-four-foot, two-bladed, semirigid main rotor system (Bell 540), and the tail rotor system from the UH-1C and adapted them to the Cobra. The experiences gained with the Sioux Scout proved helpful in designing and placing flight controls in the Cobra cockpit. A set of full-sized controls was installed in the rear seat for the pilot, and the copilot-gunner again had the reduced-travel, stunted, side-mounted system.

Also capitalizing on Sioux Scout experience, designers outfitted the Cobra with stub wings. Although like those on the Sioux Scout, these miniwings provided some lift and assisted in control, but their real purpose was to serve as weapons mounts, each having two hard points with weapons shackles.

From the outset, velocity dominated Cobra's external design. Its slim, tandem-seated configuration enhanced the aircraft's speed. This crew arrangement allowed the designers to keep the first prototypes and production models at three feet seven inches in width. The AH-1G, or Vanilla Cobra, was fifty-three feet in length when the main rotor blades were stored fore and aft; one hung well forward of the cockpit. Drag was reduced by adding an aerodynamic doghouse enclosing much of the rotor mast, swash plate, and pitch-change links. Additionally, all screws and rivets were carefully flush mounted. External surfaces were to be as smooth as possible.

Initially E. J. Ducayet decided to produce the Cobra with retractable skids (his idea). He thought that this would further reduce drag and increase speed. Also, by flying with the skids up, weapons in the turret would be able to be fired while traversing 360 degrees. The idea was discarded when later flight tests showed that retractable skids added little but weight and cost.

As work in Bell's "room within a room" (called the Green Room) continued with company funds, the war in Vietnam took a new twist. As American pressure increased on the Viet Cong and the North Vietnamese regulars, they, in turn, found improved means to resist. To counter the effects of the ever-increasing numbers of UH-1D troop carriers, and UH-1B gunships, the Viet Cong and North Vietnamese forces introduced into South Vietnam the 12.7mm antiaircraft machine gun and limited numbers of their 37mm antiaircraft cannons. For airmobile operations, these formidable weapons brought a new set of challenges.

To quantify army aviation's changing needs in Vietnam, General Westmoreland directed Brig. Gen. John Norton (of Howze board fame) to conduct an in-country study. This study recommended that the army quickly find an escort gunship capable of flying considerably faster than the troop-carrying UH-1Ds. Although the army was near fielding UH-1H troop carriers and UH-1C gunships, both were more powerful than the D and B models, respectfully. Even with additional power, the UH-1C lacked the speed required for an escort gunship. Therefore, Norton concluded that the interim attack helicopter would need a speed of at least 150 knots.

With the scheduled fielding of Cheyenne still nowhere in sight, the Department of the Army agreed with Norton's study and Westmoreland's recommendations and announced that it would seek an interim gunship. With that, the corporate morale at Bell, especially inside the Green Room, where the Cobra prototype was taking shape, soared through the roof. But first, the bureaucrats would have to dance.

To assist army leadership in their decision, a selection board was formed at Headquarters, Aviation Systems Command, in St. Louis, Missouri. Bell was quick to offer its Model 209 as a capable, ready-to-go aircraft designed to make use of proven Bell components from existing aircraft.

The Model 209 flew for the first time in early September 1965 with Bell's chief test pilot, Bill Quinlan, at the controls. The next day, Quinlan flew the Cobra again, reaching a speed of 90 knots, and days later he reached 160 knots. Bell Helicopter continued flight testing through October. After modifications that reduced vibrations discovered during earlier speed tests, the 209 was eventually clocked at 174 knots, 24 knots faster than the army's stated requirement.

When the army's selection board finally spoke, it announced that the three finalists—Sikorsky's Model S-61 Sea King, Kaman's UH-2 Seasprite, and Bell's Cobra—would compete in a fly-off at Edwards Air Force Base, California, during November 1965. The flight test at

Edwards lasted from November 16 until December 1. Then in January 1966 the tests were moved to Fort Sill, Oklahoma, where weapons systems were tested.

On March 11, 1965, a month after testing at Fort Sill ended, the army announced its decision: The Bell Model 209 won. By April 13, Bell had a contract for two production models. These two aircraft were to be used for testing and crew training. As soon as a further contract could be written, Bell signed to deliver an additional 110 aircraft, which were scheduled to be issued directly to the field.

Bell's gamble had paid off. The first straight line production Cobra aircraft was rolled out in October 1966. On August 29, 1967, six Cobras plus the army's new-equipment training team (NETT) arrived in Vietnam to begin preparing pilots and crew chiefs to receive these long-awaited aircraft.

Cobra flew its first combat mission on October 9, 1967. Two aircraft from the 1st Platoon, 334th Aviation Company (formerly UTT), flew escort for UH-1Hs of the 118th Aviation Company. In time, the Viet Cong and North Vietnamese came to fear this aircraft and named the AH-1G Cobra Whispering Death.

With Cobra meeting the army's immediate needs, the pressure for hurried fielding of Cheyenne eased, perhaps fatally. Looking back, one might say that perhaps the snake, as the Cobra is often called, killed the Indian (Cheyenne).

Some speculate that the fielding of Cobra offered critics of Cheyenne the opportunity to muster forces and finally bring about its demise. No doubt the Cobra was "about right" for Vietnam and was a cheaper solution to the escort problem. But another question demanded an answer. In the post-Vietnam world, what contribution could either the Cheyenne or the Cobra make in fighting massed armored vehicles? Neither system addressed antitank warfare, a capability vital to Europe. Not surprisingly, in the post-Vietnam era, that one requirement would become *the* attack helicopter issue.

Birds of prey began to circle Cheyenne. After a long period of relative silence, the air force again flew into view. To the tribal elders of the air force, the existence of Cheyenne was evidence to support army claims of inadequate close air support, a shortcoming that the air force was not about to admit publicly. Said differently, the air force was not interested in close air support, but it was sure as hell not going to allow the army to fill the void.

Early in the Cheyenne development program, the air force launched into a new aircraft development program of its own, intended to show that the army did not need armed helicopters, especially not one as expensive and complex as the Cheyenne. Designed to compete against Cheyenne, this project, initially known as the "AX," would later become the A-10 Warthog, the first air force aircraft built for the close air support role.

Jet powered, the low-and-slow A-10 comes equipped with the GAU-8 30mm antitank cannon, and can carry bombs and Maverick antitank missiles. However, since day one, the Warthog has been unloved by the mainstream air force. No self-respecting fighter pilot from the "real" air force ever wants to be seen by colleagues flying a Warthog. Compounding this appearance problem were the results of tests where A-10s flew antitank missions against Soviet bloc air defense radars at the U.S. Army's Hunter Liggett Military Reservation. At low level, while attacking armored vehicles, A-10's losses were significant— suicidal in fact. However, when they were paired with army attack helicopters sent in early to neutralize enemy radar prior to the A-10s' exposing themselves, the A-10's effectiveness and survival rate were significantly improved. In fact, both aircraft benefited. More importantly, many more attacking enemy tanks died. Ironically, the much-maligned and politically incorrect Warthog went on to become the air force's deliberately unheralded hero of Operation Desert Storm.

The Achilles' heel for the AX-Cheyenne competition boiled down to dollars. The question was whether Congress would fund both. Whichever service could convince Congress that it had the best system for the lowest cost would win. It did not take long for the army to find itself in a funding corner.

Although the army was again nearly equal to the air force in the eyes of the Department of Defense, army decision makers knew that if the air force could entangle Cheyenne in enough controversy, the battle for funding would go the air force's way and close air support missions would remain in the air force's uninterested hands. Fate intervened on the air force's side. As Cheyenne's testing progressed, technical problems continued to surface. The most serious were unexplained vibrations in the main rotor system. On March 12, 1969, while undergoing tests to locate the cause of these vibrations, one of the prototype Cheyennes crashed, killing its Lockheed test pilot. Despite the human tragedy of this accident, the crash proved to be good news for Cheyenne's enemies.

On April 10, 1969, the army felt compelled to issue Lockheed a contractual "cure notice." It gave Lockheed fifteen days to explain how they would correct these technical difficulties. Following a short extension, Lockheed responded on April 28, 1969, asking for a six-month program slippage to find a solution for the mysterious vibrations. The army refused, and on May 19, 1969, Secretary of the Army Stanley R. Resor notified Lockheed that they were in default and that the army was canceling the Cheyenne production contract. The research and development contract was then renegotiated, requiring Lockheed to produce a new rotor control system.

With this much controversial publicity, it became likely that Congress would not continue to support the Cheyenne. That, in fact, turned out to be the case. From the time of cancellation of the production contract, the skies over Cheyenne became shadowed with bureaucratic vultures following the scent of sickness. Cheyenne became a victim of the sick chicken syndrome. Once its illness became known, all the other chickens in the yard gathered to peck it to death. Finally, on August 9, 1972, the Cheyenne program was officially laid to rest. Caught off guard by the army's unprecedented decision to end Cheyenne, the air force found itself boxed into continuing a program (AX) it really never wanted.

Speculation about why the Cheyenne program failed continues to this day. Certainly cost, complexity, and technical delays added to its problems. Interservice gunfights over roles, missions, and funding of close air support systems did not help. Sadly, from the time the army canceled the Cheyenne production contract until the program was terminated, Lockheed managed to correct the aircraft's serious technical deficiencies. Too late, Cheyenne met the army's original requirements for a high-speed attack helicopter. However, the decision to cancel would prove to be correct for the army. With the war in Vietnam winding down, the army's focus again turned to Europe, only to discover that a fast attack helicopter using diving fire tactics was the wrong aircraft for the European battlefield.

VIETNAM: IMPACT IN EUROPE

During the Vietnam War years, the Soviets watched and learned from the American experience. Responding to the NATO air threat, including helicopters, the Soviets developed and fielded a radar-controlled, antiaircraft blanket echeloned from forward of their frontline units all the way back to the "Motherland." Every Warsaw Pact tank was equipped with a 12.7mm heavy machine gun on a gun mount designed for fighting low-flying aircraft. The man-portable, shoulder-fired, low-altitude SA-7 Grail surface-to-air heat-seeking missile was issued to forward units in great numbers. A self-propelled, radar-directed, four-barreled 23mm antiaircraft gun, the ZSU-23-4, was liberally sprinkled throughout forward pact forces. The SA-9 Gaskin, with four short-ranged, surface-to-air missiles mounted on a scout car, reinforced the ZSU-23-4. Sophistication and capability increased further to the rear. For the NATO pilot all this meant that if he came within line of sight of pact forces radar, they would see him and he would be engaged. At about the same time all this was going on, the Soviets began development of a tank-killing attack helicopter of their own, the Mi-24 Hind.

Meanwhile, with the American army busy in Vietnam, and most of the training being Vietnam oriented, NATO aviators were developing flight tactics that increased the helicopter's chances for survival on the European mid- to high-intensity battlefield. These techniques, called nap of the earth (NOE), are best understood by visualizing the helicopter moving cross-country, hovering just above the ground, while selecting routes that reduce the aircraft's exposure to enemy observation, both electronic and human, and enemy fire. In flying NOE, the helicopter uses the ground and vegetation to hide from direct enemy observation and radar. American pilots assigned to the Seventh Army from Vietnam quickly learned these techniques from their NATO allies. Unfortunately, NOE was slow to be understood or appreciated back in the United States.

Extensive use of large numbers of attack helicopters, and helicopters in general, was a product of the Howze board and the Vietnam War. However, as the war in Vietnam ground down, there were many leaders elsewhere in the army who did not understand NOE flight techniques and remained unconvinced about using large numbers of helicopters in Europe against sophisticated Soviet forces.

There was one other concern not openly mentioned. Every military organization or facility has a specified ceiling of authorized personnel. Europe's Seventh Army was no exception. To many of the members of older branches, such as infantry, armor, and artillery, any increase in aviation units could dictate an equal reduction in their units. These proponents of other branches felt the necessity to defend their turf. Consequently the helicopter's survivability and usefulness on the European midintensity battlefield was frequently called into question. Some of those asking questions were senior general officers.

After listening to this continuous debate, Gen. James H. Polk, commander in chief, United States Army Europe and Seventh Army, and commander, Central Army Group, NATO, decided in 1970 to attempt to determine where the truth lay.

Polk, commissioned from West Point in 1933, was a distinguished soldier long on combat experience and leadership. He had come ashore at Normandy in 1944 with the 106th Cavalry Group and was later given command of the 3d Cavalry Group by none other than Gen. George S. Patton, Jr. Polk led the 3d Cavalry during its race across France and Germany and into Czechoslovakia, earning the reputation of a bold, aggressive, and innovative soldier.

Intent on determining the utility of helicopters, specifically the attack helicopter, Polk ordered a series of scientific tests to determine the effectiveness and survivability of the helicopter in the European environment. The first series of these exhaustive tests was called the air cavalry evaluations and took place between March 18 and April 30, 1970.

The air cavalry evaluations were designed to determine the usefulness of the Vietnam-proven air cavalry troop organization to European forces and to identify tactics and techniques of employing air cavalry in Europe. Although these tests were considered successful, doubt remained concerning the usefulness of attack helicopters as antitank weapons. Follow-on tests involving American, German, and Canadian aviators, entitled the joint attack helicopter instrumented evaluation, were held in April and May 1972 in southern Germany. These follow-on tests were to determine "the effectiveness of attack helicopter teams on anti-armor missions against attacking aggressor forces." Conducted from Ansbach, Germany, and using the U.S. 4th Armored Division, later renamed the 1st Armored Division, as the major support unit, these trials came to be known as the Ansbach trials.

THE ANSBACH TRIALS

In hindsight, the air cavalry evaluations and subsequent attack helicopter evaluations were an unheralded watershed for the army, army aviation, and thus for the attack helicopter. First and most importantly, these trials proved that helicopters, especially attack helicopters, would add combat power to NATO forces. Second, the tests graphically illustrated that NOE flight techniques would have to become integrated into all aviation training.

Part one of the air cavalry troop evaluations was designed to assess the suitability of the air cavalry troop and the AH-1G Cobra to the midintensity battlefield in the European combat environment.[7] Recall that the air cavalry was a product of the Howze board and had been tested by the 11th Air Assault Division. The air cavalry had become invaluable to American operations in Vietnam. Like all cavalry, air cavalry was intended to find the enemy. Once he was found, air cavalry was to then fix the enemy, holding him in place until the main body of the friendly force could position itself to handle the enemy force.

At different times during the years of American involvement in Vietnam, air cavalry units of varying sizes were deployed and engaged in combat. Each of the infantry divisions had one air cavalry troop in its divisional cavalry squadron. The author was privileged to command the regimental air cavalry troop in the 11th Armored Cavalry Regiment, the sole cavalry regiment in Vietnam. Several separate air cavalry squadrons were also deployed to Vietnam, adding to the numbers of armed helicopters operating with American forces.

In central Europe finding masses of attacking Warsaw Pact forces would not be a problem. Therefore the question begging answer in Europe was whether the air cavalry troop, equipped with Cobra, brought new capabilities to the battlefield and with adequate combat power to fight Warsaw Pact forces and survive.

At the time of the air cavalry troop evaluations, the AH-1G Cobra had no viable antiarmor capability. The Army Materiel Command (AMC) had been studying the problem since the 1960s. Colonel Edward M. Browne, program manager for the light observation helicopter, had test-fired a TOW from a Hughes OH-6A during the 1960s. Late in the Vietnam War, eight North Vietnamese tanks had been destroyed by TOW antitank missiles fired from B model Huey helicopters. However, history clearly showed that it was taking years for AMC products to reach the field. For Cobra to make a contribution to the antiarmor battle in Europe, a program to marry TOW with Cobra would have to be rushed through research, development, and testing by AMC.

As an aside, during the August 1971 siege of An Loc, South Vietnam, F Battery, 79th Artillery, the last aerial artillery battery remaining in Vietnam, which was equipped with AH-1G Cobras, flew 1,472 hours and fired 23,056 FFAR, destroying, among other things, six T-54 and four PT-76 Soviet tanks. These tank kills were with 2.75-inch FFAR, none of which were designed for attacking tanks. The air defense environment around An Loc was described as "intense," one of the worst encountered by helicopters during that war. Pilot courage and determination, not hardware, was what accounted for the tank kills.

The report of Seventh Army's air cavalry troop evaluations offered no surprises. Going into the tests, it was understood that the lightly armed AH-1G needed additional punch before it would be effective against armor. These tests validated the troop's organization and mission and conclusively proved that helicopters flying NOE could operate in weather that precluded air force aircraft from providing close air support—a major factor in Europe, where the survival of ground armies might well depend on air augmentation and where weather is often marginal or worse.

The air cavalry evaluations did not, however, answer the questions of the attack helicopter's ability, with adequate weapons systems, to attack and kill armor and survive. Follow-on testing was therefore ordered to provide answers to questions left unaddressed by earlier tests.

Part two of the air cavalry troop evaluations, entitled the joint attack helicopter instrumented evaluation, was designed to determine the effectiveness of attack helicopter teams on antiarmor missions against attacking aggressor armored forces.[8] The lack of a precise system for scientifically scoring engagements between attack helicopters and other weapons systems during the air cavalry troop evaluations left lingering doubts among skeptical senior NATO leaders.

These joint attack helicopter instrumented trials took place in April and May 1972 in a six-hundred-square-kilometer maneuver area made available by the German government. This maneuver area was composed of typical Bavarian terrain, consisting of rolling farmland interspersed with German villages and heavily forested woodlands. Weather ranged from bright sunny days to overcast to rain and fog.

Unlike the air cavalry troop evaluations, all players in part two were instrumented with a laser hit-kill system designed to produce scientifically recorded scoring data. The hit-kill systems were installed on all participating vehicles, ground and air, and provided near real-time data. The eye-safe laser guns were fired at special sensors mounted on all player vehicles. When these sensors received aimed laser energy from opposing vehicles, an orange smoke grenade on the target vehicle was ignited. No more "Bang! Bang! You're dead." A vehicle "killed" by laser emitted orange smoke for all to see, and the vehicle could not reenter play during that trial. This instrumentation provided realistic data, while giving instant feedback to the crews of both ground and air vehicles.

Dr. Harrison N. Hoppes, employed by Research Analysis Corporation and contracted to be the scientific adviser to the commander, United States Army Europe, proved to be invaluable to the trials. Responsible for formulating the detailed test plans for both the air cavalry and joint instrumented evaluations, Hoppes provided the objectivity needed to keep the test on track while analyzing test data.

For the joint instrumented evaluations, Hoppes, working with Lt. Col. Robert G. Downer, the test director, designed the trials to investigate three tactical scenarios: the delay, the defense, and the breakthrough attack. The results of these trials surprised everyone. German and Canadian flight crews killed 41.7 aggressor vehicles for each helicopter loss, an excellent ratio. But a startling finding dealt with the differences in flight crew training and skills. German and Canadian pilots and gunners were skilled at moving and fighting nap of the earth; U.S. attack helicopter crews were not. Results showed that U.S. pilots killed only 8.6 vehicles per helicopter loss, lowering the overall test average to 18 enemy vehicles to each attack helicopter loss.

The figures derived from U.S. crew performance sent shock waves through the U.S. Army aviation community. Clearly the difference was training. American attack pilots were trained to fight in Vietnam, employing the AH-1Gs in diving attacks to maximize the effectiveness of the 2.75-inch rocket and the 7.62mm machine gun. Prior to the air cavalry troop evaluations, American attack helicopter pilots had received little or no NOE training. Against Soviet antiaircraft systems, diving fire would surely see them killed. For the attack helicopter to reach its full potential, the American aviator would have to learn to fly and fight NOE and use hovering and standoff firing techniques.

When word of these new tactics reached the Cheyenne test pilots at Edwards Air Force Base, they were concerned enough that they decided to test Cheyenne using these new but proven tactics. Their concern was justified. Cheyenne's high-speed rigid rotor system would not allow it to safely hover out of ground effect (above the cushion of air created by the downward movement of air from the main rotor). In fact, testing in 1972 and again in 1973 found that Cheyenne suffered from "the inability to effectively perform low-speed, low-mission tasks below 120 knots . . ."[9]

In 1971 General Polk retired and was replaced by Gen. Michael S. Davison. Writing in the foreword of the final report of the joint attack helicopter instrumented evaluation, General Davison said:

Based on these trials, we have concluded that helicopters armed with missiles like TOW (tube-launched, optically-tracked [sic], wire-guided) can perform effectively in the defensive anti-armor role in Europe.[10]

The Ansbach trials proved that attack helicopters equipped to fire long-range, antiarmor missiles were too valuable an asset to ignore. Fielding hundreds of agile antiarmor attack helicopters would provide NATO its long-sought improvement in the ability to successfully defend itself against Warsaw Pact armor.

The results of these trials had a settling effect on the army's leadership. Equally important, the U.S. Congress, with few exceptions, seemed satisfied about the future of attack helicopters in Europe. This came at a time when the army was seeking funds to equip Cobra with the TOW antitank missile.

With the majority of the army leadership now in the attack helicopter's corner, Cobra with TOW became one of the army's top procurement priorities, especially now that Cheyenne was in its final death throes. Cobra had pinch-hit for the long-delayed Cheyenne in Vietnam. Now it was called upon to stand in once again, this time in Europe while the army looked for Cheyenne's replacement. Once more Bell Helicopter proved itself a worthy and capable contractor as it hastily upgraded and rushed what was by then being referred to as TOW Cobra to Europe.

Today the AH-1 Cobra, in its many variations, mounting a 20mm cannon, armed with TOW and Hellfire antitank missiles, and wearing either army or marine green, is still serving. Seven other countries—Jordan, Japan, Korea, Pakistan, Thailand, Spain, and Israel—have purchased and used this adaptable attack helicopter. Cobra has proven to be so versatile and dependable that the army expects to keep it in service well past the year 2020. The U.S. Marine Corps' twin-engine AH-1W version of the Cobra, capable of firing either TOW or Hellfire missiles and built for maritime use, will remain the Corps' primary attack helicopter for the foreseeable future.[11]

Over the years, Cobra has served the nation well. In such places as Vietnam, Grenada, Panama, and Iraq, Cobra performed better than expected. For many years it was the army's only attack helicopter. Many believe that the potential of Cobra has yet to be completely realized. In any case, once equipped with TOW, Cobra helped lessen the pressure on the army to hurriedly develop an advanced attack helicopter, (AAH).

Chapter Seven

Birth of a Brave

COBRA: THE STAND-IN

In war, timing is everything, even in a cold war. By 1974 it was clear to the army's leadership that while the army had focused on Vietnam, the rest of the world had experienced great and rapid change. The cancellation of the Cheyenne helicopter and the published results of the Ansbach trials gave the army reason to take the time necessary to regroup and take up a new heading.

Army aviation watched sadly as Cheyenne died, not fully understanding that this magnificent machine was incapable of survival against the sophisticated Russian air defense system installed all across the East-West border. Cheyenne had fallen victim to trying to please too many factions. Former Secretary of the Army Stanley Resor had pushed the army into new and untried technologies. Perhaps Lockheed had been too ambitious and tried too hard to accommodate the army. Whatever the reason, with its focus on Vietnam, the army had not responded to changes in Eastern Europe and failed to have its contractors make necessary adjustments. Cheyenne died and the army again found itself confronted with having to select an interim attack helicopter.

The results of the Ansbach trials left no doubt that tank-killing attack helicopters were a good, cost-effective solution to a very tough problem. For the most part, reactions to these findings were positive.

The majority of the army's leadership reacted affirmatively and sought to correct, fix, or improve. A small minority continued to resist and became defensive, trying to rationalize why things came to be as they were. Their voices were soon drowned out.

With acceptance of tank-killing attack helicopters as a viable force multiplier for the European battlefield, planning began on upgrading Bell Helicopter's Cobra to an antitank attack helicopter. Once before Cobra had been drafted to fill a critical void, and now Cobra again looked like the best solution. In the meantime Fort Rucker began to adjust its curriculum to teach pilots how to fly and survive in the European environment. The army also began moving toward finding a long-term solution to killing Soviet tanks.

On August 10, 1972, one day after giving Lockheed its final Cheyenne cancellation notice, Secretary of the Army Kenneth E. Belieu asked the Department of Defense to seek funds from Congress to begin the search for a Cheyenne replacement. Surprisingly, Congress was sympathetic and authorized funds for a development program that would become known as the advanced attack helicopter (AAH). No one argued the need. But since the new start with the AAH would take time, ten years being the average for the Army Materiel Command (AMC), the upgrade of Cobra became paramount.

Perhaps naively, the army believed that making Cobra over into a tank killer would be easily accomplished. On paper it looked simple. The belief was that by the addition of enhanced optics and the TOW missile, Cobra would become the army's interim antitank attack helicopter. The Department of the Army was determined to complete this integration as rapidly as possible. But events would prove that it would take longer than desired.

The practicality of firing the TOW missile from a helicopter had been demonstrated in the waning months of the war in Vietnam. Two UH-1B models equipped with specially developed TOW missile launch systems linked to handmade sights and guidance devices were rushed to Vietnam, where they engaged North Vietnamese tanks. It was a fragile first step but one that gave tank-killing helicopter enthusiasts confidence to go forward with plans for TOW Cobra.

As early as 1969, in response to events behind the Iron Curtain, AMC had been directed to examine options to improve the army's ability to kill armor in what was termed the midintensity battlefield—combat between massive armored forces supported by tactical aviation. With hundreds of helicopters soon to be returned from Vietnam, many of them AH-1G Cobras, and the success of the two TOW-firing B models, the decision by the army to upgrade the Cobra came easily.

However, before the Cobra upgrade could be implemented, AMC tasked the army's Combat Development Command, the agency charged to conduct studies of the army's future needs, to explore the feasibility of mounting the TOW or the Shillelagh antitank missile on Cobra. The 152mm Shillelagh missile was designed to be fired from tanks. The TOW had promise. The Shillelagh was another of AMC's bad ideas in search of a mission.

The Combat Development Command (CDC) study began in late 1969 and lasted into January 1970. Combat Development Command was also tasked to study the possibility of replacing the 7.62mm machine gun and 40mm grenade launcher mounted in the Cobra's chin turret with a 30mm cannon. If these two modifications, a missile and a cannon, could be made to work, Cobra's potential as an armor-fighting helicopter would be considerably enhanced. The decision of which missile to choose, TOW or Shillelagh, was easy: TOW was by far the best.[1] The cannon decision came a little harder.

Two 30mm cannon candidates were selected for testing as part of the TOW Cobra program. One was an AMC in-house–developed gun originally slated for Cheyenne; the other was a three-barreled Gatling-type gun developed by General Electric. However, early testing revealed that the 30mm was too much cannon for Cobra. When it was fired, vibrations caused Cobra's vertical stabilizer to come apart. Firing it ninety degrees to the main axis of Cobra would have probably destroyed the airframe. Another drawback of the 30mm was that its projectile traveled no faster than the TOW missile at two thousand meters. This weakness did what no one else had, as yet, been able to do: It caused AMC to finally shelve their less-than-successful 30mm cannon, at least for a while.[2]

A short time later, the advanced attack helicopter (AAH) task force assembled in the Washington, D.C., area and began defining the desired AAH characteristics. By November 1972 the task force issued requests for proposals (RFP) to the aviation industry. (An RFP is nothing more than an invitation to industry to submit a proposal, and, if the proposal is accepted, to compete in the development and building of a product for the government.) Not all ran smoothly, however. The problem was timing. How long would it take to field the AAH, and would the Cobra suffice as an antitank helicopter in the meantime?

Conservative opinion held that delivery of the AAH could not begin before 1980, an unheard-of eight-year development cycle. Even so, the armored threat to central Europe was deemed serious enough to demand a quick fix, one faster than eight years. Cobra with TOW was the only viable option.

The plan to field the AAH and an interim or alternate antitank helicopter became known as the high/low mix. Simply stated, the AAH, once developed, would be a high-cost, high-capability system. The modified Cobra with TOW would be a low-cost, medium-capability system. (TOW Cobra would lack AAH's night and all-weather capabilities.) This solution would allow the army to field a fleet of affordable antitank helicopters while removing some of the pressure from the more sophisticated AAH program.

In the meantime, Bell Helicopter had again begun in-house work with company money. Their first cut came to be known as the Model 309 King Cobra. Bell was intent on becoming the developer of both the interim and advanced attack helicopters. Although King Cobra was never put into production, the experience acquired from this program proved to be of great value to Bell and the army.

Bell Helicopter began work on TOW Cobra in March 1972, following the award of a $24 million contract. This contract called for Bell to initiate the improved Cobra armaments program (ICAP) and to modify eight AH-1G Cobras, the type being returned from Vietnam, with the XM65 TOW missile and the XM128 helmet directed fire control subsystem. The XM128 was a helmet sight that allowed the pilot or copilot to aim the weapons in the chin turret simply by moving his head.

Under the ICAP contract, Cobra, in addition to carrying eight TOW missiles, would continue to carry 2.75-inch FFARs and keep the chin turret with the 7.62mm machine gun and 40mm grenade launcher.

All military equipment is given a set or combination of letters and numbers known as the equipment's nomenclature. Changing an established nomenclature occurs whenever a significant modification is made to the item. For example, the Huey came into the army as the UH-1A Iroquois. The improved version was redesignated the UH-1B. Further improvements saw the C, D, and then H models. Cobra would follow a similar path. The Cobra with TOW would be labeled AH-1Q.

Early testing of the AH-1Q revealed that the tail boom and horizontal stabilizers needed to be reinforced to withstand the pressures generated by the TOW missile motor's back blast. Bell engineers developed and applied a fix, and by July 1974 eight test AH-1Qs were delivered to the army. Although not without tense moments, early testing of the AH-1Qs went well. However, later testing, operational tests II (OT II), discovered minor deficiencies, which were fixed while the program continued uninterrupted.[3] (The most serious was the discovery that the sight crosshairs were etched wider than the specifications called for, blotting out the target at extended ranges.)

In January 1974, months before the last of the eight test aircraft were delivered, the army made a most unusual decision and awarded Bell $59.2 million for a production contract, a clear violation of the Department of Defense's (DOD) "fly before you buy" policy. The army's excuse for disregarding the DOD policy turned on the point that this was but a simple marriage of two proven systems. Whatever the facts of the case, it was the army's story and they stuck to it. Congress acquiesced. The $59.2 million contract called for the conversion of 101 AH-1Gs to AH-1Qs before initial testing was complete. The need for AH-1Q in Europe was deemed so urgent that the army decided to take the gamble. After all, this was but a modification, and Bell Helicopter was a proven contractor. The first production AH-1Q returned to the army thirty-nine months after Bell received the go-ahead for the eight test aircraft.

The production contract awarded in January 1974 included an option allowing the army to modify additional aircraft. By December 1974, the army was so pleased with the AH-1Q conversion that it exercised that option and an additional 189 aircraft were scheduled for retrofit, bringing the total to 290 (test aircraft not included).

As testing continued on the first eight AH-1Qs, it became apparent that a stronger engine would be required. The existing engine was unable to adequately lift the additional weight of the TOW system. The army proposed that a product improvement program (PIP) be started to have Avco-Lycoming modify the Cobra's L-13 engine. This PIP succeeded in raising the shaft horsepower from fourteen hundred to eighteen hundred and the engine was redesignated T-53-L-703. This new power then required that Cobra's power train (transmissions and gearboxes) be modified to accept the increased forces. The program became known as the improved Cobra agility and maneuverability program (ICAM). Application of ICAM and other improvements triggered another change in model designation, this time from AH-1G to AH-1S, bypassing AH-1Q.

Initially the AH-1S came equipped with the M28 chin turret with the 7.62mm minigun and 40mm grenade launcher. With the "up-gunned" and modernized S models the M28 was discarded and replaced with a chin turret–mounted 20mm cannon.

Perhaps the most important non-power-train improvement in the AH-1S was the development of composite fiberglass main rotor blades. These blades, designated as K-747, were designed to withstand being struck by a 23mm high-explosive round and then allow the aircraft time to fly for a few minutes and land safely. (The 23mm is the most common air defense cannon in Warsaw Pact units.) The K-747 blades were made of composite materials, programmed to have a ten-thousand-hour life expectancy, and provided with patch kits so that damaged blades could be repaired in the field.

Two unexpected benefits came with the decision to use the K-747 blades. First, they were quieter. Second, they had far less radar reflectivity. (Rotating helicopter blades greatly increase the helicopter's radar signature.) Adaptation of composite blades eventually led to another Cobra designation, AH-1F.

As might have been expected, the first AH-1Qs or AH-1Ss available for issue to troop units went to attack helicopter units in Germany. By the end of 1977, 230 AH-1Qs or AH-1Ss were in the hands of soldiers in Germany. Finally the United States Seventh Army had antitank attack helicopters arrayed against the Warsaw Pact and could breathe a little easier.

The experience gained from the fielded TOW Cobras soon led to other refinements. In a short time the parade of different Cobra models became a blur to the average observer. For example, Bell developed a twin-engine model for the Marine Corps, designated the AH-1J. In December 1975 another study group, the army's priority aircraft subsystem suitability review committee (PASS in Review), reported its findings and recommendations. The committee reviewed Cobra's capabilities and configuration for the years 1975–85. Approved by the Department of the Army in April 1976, the report brought on three more Cobra model designations: AH-1P, AH-1E, and AH-1F. With the addition of the L-703 engine with new gearboxes and transmission, Cobra became the AH-1F. The F model is as far as the army has gone with Cobra.

The Cobra proved to be so adaptable that more than fifty improvements have kept it a viable low-cost, daylight attack helicopter. At its zenith, 1,081 Cobras were wearing army colors and designations, a sizable fleet of aircraft capable of adding significantly to NATO's tank-destroying combat power.[4] Once again Larry Bell's helicopter company served the army well.

Cobras continue serving in active army, Marine Corps, and reserve components. Nevertheless, the helicopter's future is now in doubt. During the fall of 1993 some Cobras were being withdrawn from units, stripped of much of their onboard equipment, and dumped into the ocean. Others were placed on firing ranges as targets. Nevertheless, with the army being held to a buy of 807 Apaches, it is reasonable to expect that some Cobras will remain in the inventory for the foreseeable future.

Many Cobras, both army and marine, were employed with great success during Operations Desert Shield and Desert Storm and still later in Somalia. During Desert Storm, some Cobras were equipped to fire Hellfire missiles. They were overshadowed by the "high mix" Apache but continued to give the deployed forces additional antiarmor capability and firepower.

THE ADVANCED ATTACK HELICOPTER

While the army rushed to field low-cost tank killers, the advanced attack helicopter task force began its work. Recall that the Cheyenne production contract had been canceled on May 19, 1969. Although the research and development portion of the contract remained in effect, most people knew that Cheyenne was dead.

From January to August 1972 the Marks board, chaired by Maj. Gen. Sidney M. Marks, assembled in Washington, D.C. Its mission was to conduct an in-depth study of the requirements for an attack helicopter in the 1975–85 time frame. The task force charter directed the board to: "Revalidate the Advanced Aerial Fire Support System QMR [qualitative material requirement, the document that outlines why the army needs a new piece of equipment] exemplified in the Cheyenne with its very accurate navigation, and its weapon complexity. . . . Computer simulations dealing with loss exchange ratios against a helicopter must show them to have a relatively small vulnerable area and a high degree of maneuverability in order to survive."[5] The task force was to further develop the operational requirements and draft the material need (MN) document for the advanced attack helicopter. Early in the process much of the work to be accomplished by the board was passed to Fort Knox.

In January 1972, the Marks board tasked the Combat Development Command's armor agency at Fort Knox to write the AAH material need documents complete with engineering development data. (In this document, the army details the tasks that the new equipment must perform and to what standard. In other words, how much mission improvement does the army desire from the new equipment above the performance of the item being replaced?) This requirement landed on the desk of Col. James R. "Ron" Hill. After a quick study, Hill determined the AAH MN to be beyond the capabilities of the armor agency, especially if engineering development data was required. The Marks board then formed a special task force of qualified people from other army agencies to augment and assist the armor agency. This task force was then assembled at Fort Knox to prepare the AAH MN. To Hill's great relief the requirement for preparation of engineering data was dropped.

Departing from normal practices, guidelines given to the AAH MN task force stipulated that the AAH should be in production by 1978, six years later. Initially, this target forced limits to the subsystems that could be considered for the AAH. For example, the Hellfire missile, showing great promise, was just beginning its firing tests and was still considered unproven, making it too chancy to be matched to AAH. The AAH MN task force was therefore limited to considering TOW as AAH's antitank missile. Additionally, the AAH MN task force was directed to consider AMC's in-house, Weapons Command (WECOM)–developed 30mm dual-purpose ammunition (another attempt to force use of the AMC WECOM cannon, which came complete with eight hundred moving parts). Lastly the AAH MN task force was told that AAH should be twin engined and use the same engine programmed for the UH-60 Black Hawk utility helicopter. Commonality of engines on two types of army aircraft, if it worked, was a smart move and could reduce overall program costs.

The AAH MN task force began its work by identifying mission

capabilities believed to be essential to AAH. At the top of the list was survivability. The expected price tag for AAH made it too precious to lose many aircraft or crews and made built-in survivability the most significant characteristic required in AAH. During the development of the UH-60, the army had also insisted on new, stringent survivability criteria. In AAH's case, the new airframe had to be capable of hitting the ground at a vertical rate of descent of forty-two feet per second with a forward speed of fifteen knots with 95 percent assurance of crew survival.

Another recommendation, considered by many as the most radical, was that AAH have wheels instead of skids. (Desert Storm would later prove this decision to have been correct.) Additionally, the task force insisted that AAH have adequate power to hover out of ground effect, at four thousand feet pressure altitude on a ninety-five-degree day, and initiate a five-hundred-foot-per-minute rate of climb. This would ensure that a fully loaded AAH would have adequate power to operate in most regions of the world. This requirement far exceeded those for the standard European day of two thousand feet pressure altitude and seventy degrees Fahrenheit.

The standard European day was a conceptual norm that came about almost by accident. In 1969 when the army first studied additional armament for TOW Cobra, an action officer at Fort Knox's armor agency grew concerned about the effects of temperature and altitude on the proposed TOW Cobra's ability to operate in many regions of the world. After some thought, this innovative officer divined that if a fully loaded TOW Cobra could hover at two thousand feet above sea level on a seventy-five-degree day, it should be able to accomplish most missions it might need to perform in Europe. Although these numbers proved to be about right, they had been pulled out of thin air with no real scientific research or basis. However, within weeks, the use of these numbers had spread from Fort Knox to Washington, where they were picked up by a congressional staffer who passed them to his boss. This congressperson then read them into the Congressional Record. From that moment on, they became Holy Writ and were known far and wide as the standard European day. Occasionally these figures are still used authoritatively. So much for scientific data.

Understanding that demands for air force airlift would be critical during the early days of a war in Europe, the AAH MN task force determined that AAH should be self-deployable, able to fly on its own to Europe across the North Atlantic. General Cockerham, the first AAH program manager, explained:

> Using the northern route, the shortest distance over water is 800 nautical miles (NM). Therefore the AAH engineering specifications required Bell and Hughes to design their aircraft to fly 800 NM against a 20 knot head wind with a 30 minute fuel reserve.

Although this requirement was later scaled back, AAH was fielded with the fittings required for external fuel tanks, the same used so successfully by the 1-101st and 2-229th during Operation Desert Storm.

The AAH MN task force asked for a minimum airspeed of 145 to 175 knots, vision systems capable of day-night NOE navigation, and target acquisition and designation at night as well as during periods of reduced visibility. AAH was also to be capable of withstanding hits from a 12.7mm heavy machine gun and flying for thirty minutes after being hit by a 23mm cannon projectile in a critical component like the main transmission or the tail rotor gearbox. There were many other requirements of lesser importance identified before the AAH MN was forwarded to General Marks and the AAH task force in Washington.[6]

In September 1972, the Department of the Army approved the AAH task force's material need. In November 1972 the office of the secretary of defense authorized release of requests for proposals (RFP). In January and February 1973, five companies—Sikorsky, Boeing-Vertol, Bell, Hughes, and Lockheed—responded. Each was highly qualified and experienced, and each presented interesting and innovative approaches.

In April 1973 the army named Brig. Gen. Samuel G. Cockerham, the deputy commander of the Aviation Systems Command (AVSCOM), as AAH's first program manager. Cockerham, a 1948 graduate of West Point, had an extensive background in aviation, command, operations, and maintenance, as well as research, development, and procurement. He was more than qualified to direct this important project.

Since work on AAH had been ongoing since 1970, General Cockerham had a large, informed pool of talent to draw from; however, he was under pressure to "eliminate the Cheyenne taint." In Cockerham's words: "There was tremendous animosity remaining against Lockheed or anyone dealing with Lockheed." At the time of the Cheyenne demise, Lockheed was in trouble with Congress, and indirectly with the air force, for cost overruns in the C-5 transport program. In addition Congress was arranging a bailout to save the entire Lockheed Corporation. As a result, during the early 1970s, at least in many government circles, Lockheed's corporate standing was at an all-time low.

Although the Cheyenne program had failed, many of the people involved were among the most technically qualified in the field of helicopter design and production. Cockerham knew that for AAH to succeed, he would have to ignore all this anti-Lockheed advice and make use of available talent, whether it had been involved with Cheyenne or not. Much of this talent had been assembled toward the end of the Cheyenne program and was still available.

After being given the opportunity to digest and adjust the RFP responses, the Department of Defense announced in June 1973 that the Hughes and Bell Helicopter companies had been selected to proceed to competitive development, phase I, eliminating the other companies from further involvement.

An office of the secretary of defense (OSD) cost analysis improvement group (CAIG) took the next thirty days to visit both Bell and Hughes to determine if the AAH could be built for the proposed $1.7 million design-to-unit-production cost in fiscal year 1972 dollars. The answer appeared to be yes, and OSD gave its go-ahead to the AAH program.

The contract awarded to Bell was for $44.7 million for design, development, and contractor testing of their proposed YAH-63A.* Hughes Helicopter, on the other hand, received $70.3 million to accomplish the same with their proposed YAH-64A. These figures were based on the bids submitted by the contractors. The contract directed that flyaway, or delivery, costs per aircraft should not exceed $1.65 million in 1972 dollars: The army planned to buy 472 aircraft. A deadline of March 1975 was established for the first flight of each prototype.[7]

Almost predictably the Bell YAH-63A featured a two-blade rotor design for both the main- and tail-rotor systems. Over the years the two-blade configuration had become Bell's unofficial corporate logo. Although twin engined, externally the YAH-63A resembled the Cobra. Internally Bell had reversed the positions of the pilot and copilot. In

---

*"Y" indicates prototype aircraft.

the YAH-63A the pilot would be in the front seat and the gunner in the rear. Bell had acted on the feelings of a small following within army aviation who believed that NOE flight required the pilot to have better visibility than was afforded in the backseat. Unlike Cobra, YAH-63A included a distinctive narrow-spaced tricycle landing gear. This arrangement had one set of small, dual wheels forward (nose wheels) and a larger main gear (wheels) set to the rear of and suspended from the fuselage below the stub wings. At rest, the Bell YAH-63A gave the appearance of being unstable. "This tricycle gear arrangement proved to be a most serious deficiency and was one of the primary reasons why the army failed the YAH-63A design," Cockerham recounts.

The Hughes candidate, designated the YAH-64A, came with four-bladed main-and tail-rotor systems. YAH-64A's forty-eight-foot rotor diameter was three feet smaller than that of the YAH-63A. The Hughes YAH-64A also had conventional landing gear—two main wheels forward and one on the end of the tail boom. The YAH-64A's twin T700-GE-700, 1,258-shaft-horsepower turbine engines were housed in large nacelles above and behind the aircraft's stub wings. Initially Hughes had planned to mount the horizontal stabilizer low near the end of the tail boom. The idea was that the low stabilizer would afford the tail rotor some protection in the NOE flight regimen. Test of a similar low-mounted system on a specially rigged OH-6A helicopter identified potential air-flow problems, causing Hughes to abandon the low horizontal stabilizer in favor of one mounted atop the vertical stabilizer. This decision would haunt Hughes during AAH's early development.

Prototypes were to be delivered in two batches. What would have been the first airframe (AV01) was designated as the ground test vehicle (GTV). By design, this aircraft was never to fly but was intended to be fully equipped with all systems and used for static testing, tests too hazardous to be conducted during flight. AV02 and AV03 would be the first flying prototypes.

On September 30, 1975, the Hughes AV02 was the first AAH to fly, beating Bell Helicopter by one day. The schedule allowed six months for contractors to conduct in-house testing before delivering the aircraft to the army.

The second increment of prototypes would be numbered AV04 through AV06 but would be required only of the winner of the phase I competition.[8]

While the AAH program gained momentum, interesting developments were taking place elsewhere that would impact on AAH and future warfare. Rockwell International's laser-guided Hellfire missile system had progressed enough for the army to view it as a feasible concept. In fact, some in the army believed that Hellfire should be the antitank weapon for AAH. Although TOW was lethal, Hellfire, if it worked when fired from the AAH, would have far greater potential. For one thing, Hellfire had a range of more than six thousand meters compared to TOW's four thousand meters. More importantly, its laser guidance system simplified the copilot-gunner duties. It offered near-fire-and-forget capability, or it could be guided by a laser designator either in another aircraft or on the ground. Additionally, Hellfire had the advantage of being capable of ripple-firing, or putting more than one rocket in the air at once, a capability frequently used during Operation Desert Storm.

Early in 1975, during phase I, both companies exceeded their budgets. To keep the program within allowable limits, Cockerham recommended, and the army leadership agreed to, a six-month extension of prototype deliveries. While both Bell and Hughes were reprogramming their expenditures, the army, on February 26, 1976, made the decision to proceed into engineering development with Hellfire and to arm AAH with Hellfire in lieu of the wire-guided TOW missile.

The decision to go with Hellfire was a brave step for the army, especially under the close scrutiny given by Congress and its staff to developing programs. Skeptics and the fainthearted might have called it reckless, but brave is a more accurate term. History further shows that it was a fortuitous act.

In June 1976 both companies delivered their candidate prototypes to Edwards Air Force Base (AFB) in California for the scheduled competitive fly-off. Prior to this, in April 1976, the army had assigned Maj. Gen. Edward M. Browne as AAH's second program manager.

Unfortunately, shortly before the scheduled delivery date at Edwards AFB, one Bell prototype crashed and was declared to be beyond repair. This forced a quick reaction by Bell, who refurbished their GTV and delivered it to Edwards in time to meet contract requirements for a full complement of test aircraft.

The fly-offs were limited to testing each contractor's AAH's flight characteristics. Armament, fire control, and other systems were to be built, integrated, and tested at varying intervals. To the casual observer it might appear that these systems were being designed and built off line, that is, somewhere else, not as part of the aircraft; they were not. In fact, to ensure quality control and proper fit once these systems were mounted on AAH, every facet of their development was closely monitored and coordinated by the project managers.

During early flight testing with Hughes prototypes it was discovered that when flying NOE the Hughes aircraft tended to fly with its nose slightly up, limiting forward visibility. If this were not corrected, it would hinder the gunner's ability to accurately aim his weapons. The problem appeared to be caused by the positioning of the horizontal stabilizer on top of the vertical stabilizer. In addition, during abrupt maneuvers the main rotor blades occasionally flexed down and struck the cockpit canopy roof. Hughes developed fixes known as mod 1 that it hoped would correct both problems. The rotor problem was corrected by extending the rotor mast nine and a half inches.* The horizontal stabilizer was redesigned, but it remained atop the vertical stabilizer. These fixes were applied to the GTV and both flying prototypes.

During the time the two companies were building their prototype aircraft, efforts were ongoing elsewhere to develop a cannon suitable for AAH. Originally the army's contract specifications required the AAH cannon candidate to be 30mm, mounted in a turret with eight hundred rounds of ammunition. AMC's policy was to get the army out of the development of small-caliber weapons (40mm and below) and make the 30mm gun development a contractor requirement. It was to be capable of firing the 30mm round of ammunition designed by AMC's Weapons Command. This stipulation was modified in 1976 when the additional requirement to fire the NATO ADEN/DEFA round was adopted. The ADEN round originated in Britain and the DEFA in France. Both had been adopted as standard within NATO, and it would be to AAH's advantage if its cannon could shoot "borrowed" NATO ammunition.[9]

The General Electric Corporation, one of America's most experienced companies in producing weaponry, offered their XM188, a three-barreled Gatling gun. The Gatling gun, invented by Richard J. Gatling in the 1800s, operates by having several barrels rotate around a cen-

---

*Mast extensions were required on both Bell and Hughes aircraft.

tral axis, automatically loading, firing, and extracting the empty cartridge casing from each barrel during one revolution. General Electric modernized the Gatling by adding an electric drive motor and improving the gun's moving parts.

Hughes Helicopter, one of the world's leading producers of automatic cannons, joined the competition and came forward with its own gun, the XM230, a single-barreled cannon. Hughes began work on what was to become the Hughes M230 Chain Gun in 1972. Initially it was designed to fire the 20mm ammunition common to both army and air force cannons already widely in use. The Hughes program received impetus from the army's earlier Bushmaster, a program to develop a cannon for use on the army's M2 and M3 Bradley fighting vehicles.

Single-barreled guns operate by taking energy either from the gun's recoil or from pressure of the gas bled from the barrel to a piston, which forces the bolt to the rear (blowback). In either case, the harnessed force opens the breech, extracts the spent cartridge casing, loads the next round, and closes and locks the breech.

Failure of a ground unit's single-barreled weapon to properly function can be corrected by simply grabbing a handle and manually pulling it to the rear. This action retracts the bolt, extracting the malfunctioning round. Releasing the handle allows the bolt to go forward, chambering a new round. However, for a gun distantly located on a wing or in a turret under the aircraft, a cannon stoppage cannot be cleared until the aircraft is landed and the gun is manually cleared, unless a mechanical system is substituted for the soldier's strong arm. Hughes engineers developed a unique method of coupling an electric motor and rotating bolt with a chain drive to replace the soldier.

In keeping with the AAH program to seek some subcomponents developed separately, industry proposals for the pilot's night vision sensor (PNVS) and the target acquisition and designation sight (TADS) arrived in November 1976. These were soon followed by a major announcement on December 10, 1976, a big day for Hughes. On this day the army announced that the Hughes AAH and cannon candidates had both won the competition over Bell and that the development would proceed to phase II.

Over the years, many observers have speculated why one company prevailed and the other failed. A number of army personnel not directly associated with the program have attributed Bell's loss to its corporate reluctance to give up its proven but dated two-bladed rotor system. Additionally, during phase I testing, Bell's long, wide blades (forty-two-inch chord) suffered from drag and separation problems. Perhaps a lack of confidence in the Bell candidate's ground stability, caused by the wobbly appearance of its tricycle landing gear, contributed to their prototype's failure. However, General Cockerham recalls:

> The Bell YH-63A weighed in sixteen hundred pounds heavier than the Hughes machine. But even so, Bell was reporting computer predictions of an 800-feet-per-minute rate of climb while Hughes predicted 600 against an AAH specification requirement of 450–500 feet per minute, vertical rate of climb. During developer/operational test I (DT/OT I), Bell failed to meet the vertical rate of climb.

The standard rate of climb sought was 450–500 feet per minute. As events turned out, Bell ran into technical problems with its rotor system. "Bell also had transmission problems," Cockerham recalls.

> They had over-engineered their transmission, making it much heavier than Hughes's. The links between the engines and the transmission were also a problem. The couplings Bell had used on the power shafts between the engines and the transmission had to be capable of deflecting 4.5 degrees to work. It was too much. Bell ran into a hell of a problem with this. Keep in mind that as a program manager, I could not have asked for two better contractors in calling for technical competition. There was competition across the board: different styles of management, organizations, approaches to design of aircraft, including space, weight, form, fit, and function. The army got its dollars' worth.
>
> In everything there was a contrast. For example Bell contracted 65 percent of their work in-house with 35 percent out-of-house [that is, with subcontractors]. Hughes, on the other hand, contracted 35 percent in-house and 65 percent out-of-house. Hughes put the pilot in the rear and the gunner up front. Bell put the gunner in the rear and the pilot up front.

In positioning the gunner in the rear,

Bell ran into one hell of a problem. For example, we had a day optics requirement. In the case of Bell's design, this required a 107-inch optical tube, running from the nose of the aircraft, where the day optics were in with the FLIR, underneath the pilot, back and coming up through and displayed in the rear seat. That killed them.

The difference in landing gear also played a significant role. Hughes had two main wheels suspended forward under the pilot and a tail wheel on the end of the tail boom.

In the case of the Bell design, Bell used a tricycle gear configuration, a nose wheel up front and two main gear in the rear . . . That was really what defeated the Bell design. The most precious real estate on any helicopter, especially an attack helicopter, is the chin and nose. We were putting a FLIR on the front and just behind it a 30mm gun. But Bell had its nose wheel there, causing the gun to be installed closer to the chin. With the nose wheel where the gun needed to go and the gun mounted too far forward and shooting out front, its bloom (muzzle flash) was blinding the FLIR. That is what defeated them.[10]

An interview with Maj. Gen. Edward M. Browne, who followed Cockerham as program manager, serving from April 1976 until December 1982, confirmed General Cockerham's analysis:

The YAH-63A had the pilot in front and gunner in back, a significant disadvantage because we had to run the optical relay tube back to the copilot/gunner's seat with all kinds of twisting, contortions, bending, and movements to the display tube. This caused it to be operationally unsuitable. The YAH-63A, as I recall, was substantially overweight, and in flight handling characteristics, it was substantially more sluggish than the YAH-64A, and its rate of climb was considerably less than the YAH-64A . . . All things considered, the Hughes machine was considered to be more agile, user-friendly (Pilot/copilot stationing), easier to maintain and had better overall flight handling qualities. Clearly the point spread of the source selection evaluation was in favor of the Hughes machine.[11]

Whatever the cause of Bell's failure, a longtime supplier of good, reliable army helicopters had lost two important contract competitions back-to-back, the UH-60 Black Hawk and the AAH.

About the time that Hughes was designated the winner, a significant event took place that impacted adversely on AAH, at least temporarily: Jimmy Carter became president of the United States.

The Carter administration, not too dissimilar from the Truman administration, arrived in Washington determined to reduce the Defense Department budget. AAH was not spared. During Carter's second week in office, his secretary of defense, Harold Brown, former secretary of the air force and godfather of the A-10 Warthog, cut the AAH funds by one-half. Originally the schedule for phase II was to last fifty months. With the Carter-mandated budget cuts, the plan was stretched an additional ten months. Based on the false theory that by stretching production time one saves money, this approach too often sees hoped-for savings eaten away by inflation. Only after Congress entered the fray on the army's side was a compromise reached and the program stretched to only fifty-six months. With timing finally settled, Hughes was awarded $390 million to begin producing aircraft.

In the decades following Eisenhower's warning of the dangers of an "American military-industrial complex," Congress has continually maintained a high degree of vigilance over high-cost Department of Defense programs. Certainly AAH was not excluded from this surveillance. Cost overruns brought increased congressional attention to AAH. These overruns were the result of program modifications and contract changes brought on by minor deficiencies identified during testing as well as the six-month phase I slippage. The increase in inflation caused by the 1973 Arab oil embargo indirectly harmed Apache. With time and higher costs, criticism became louder and more damaging. Recall that costs were to be below $1.7 million per aircraft in fiscal year 1972 dollars. By mid-1977 this ceiling had been exceeded with flyaway costs approaching $6.4 million in fiscal year 1977 dollars.

If all this were not enough, GAO released a report questioning AAH's ability to survive in the European midintensity battlefield. On Capitol Hill, memories of the stillborn Cheyenne remained fresh enough to cause congressmen to question continued support of a troubled program. Subsequently, fiscal year 1978's DOD appropriations bill contained half the funding the army requested for AAH engineering development.

General Browne said, "The program came damn near being cancelled." Even so, a determined army and program manager pressed on.

In March 1977, two contractors, Martin Marietta and Northrop, were selected to compete to produce the TADS and the PNVS, the systems that would give AAH the ability to navigate the battlefield, locate targets, and engage them with Hellfire at night or under reduced visibility. In time they would prove to be the heart of Apache's tank-killing capabilities.

By May 1978, all mod 1 changes had been applied and flight tested, and a second series, mod 2, was in the process of being applied.

By fall 1979, continued testing of both Hughes AAH candidates revealed that the attitude problem still existed during NOE flight. The "fixed" T tail had not corrected the low-speed, nose-high attitude problems. This condition hindered the gunner's ability to search for and engage targets. Additionally, strain on the tail boom created by airflow over the horizontal stabilizer promised to reduce the aircraft's overall life span. General Browne, realizing that the Hughes management seemed to be wedded to the T tail, became concerned enough that he assembled a team of outside experts to provide an opinion on the T tail concept. This blue ribbon committee consisted of experts from the Department of Aeronautics, Iowa State University, Princeton University, the Army Aviation Laboratories, and NASA. These highly respected engineers concluded that the T tail design was the cause of unacceptable vibrations and loads, and in their opinion it could not be redesigned to meet flight or contract specifications. Pressures generated by air flowing over the T tail located at the end of a long tail boom created vibrations, longitudinal and torsional loads, which they believed would eventually cause damage to the tail boom and considerably shorten the aircraft's life span. But Hughes Helicopter's top management refused to abandon their T tail. Browne, now convinced that the Hughes position would eventually cause the failure of the AAH program, took his case to the chairman of the Summa Corporation, the parent corporation of Hughes Helicopter. After he presented the results of his committee's inquiry, Browne informed Summa's chairman that this problem had to be resolved or he would take his case to the Department of the Army and recommend contract cancellation. Browne's position was convincing, and Summa made the necessary management changes to ensure that Hughes Helicopter Company would react to the army's and the AAH's specifications and requirements. Jack G. Real was appointed president of Hughes Helicopter, and the army and Hughes set out on a team effort to find a solution.

Once more Hughes engineers went back to their drawing boards. The fourth airframe was delivered with a redesigned tail assembly. The T tail was abandoned, and a new stabilator was installed on the lower portion of the vertical stabilizer according to a principle proven on the Black Hawk helicopter. General Browne recalls that the replacement stabilator was designed, approved, and successfully test flown within sixty days. In Browne's words, "all the problems went by the way, and the whole thing notwithstanding turned out well." Had Browne not stood his ground and nudged Hughes's management into abandoning its love affair with the T tail, there might never have been an Apache attack helicopter.

Also included in this same fix was the addition of three inches to the vertical stabilizer and the moving of the tail rotor thirty inches farther up to increase the clearance of obstacles while flying NOE. When AV06, the last prototype, was delivered, it came equipped with an even smaller stabilator and carried a tail rotor ten inches larger in diameter, both helpful in NOE flight.

The mod 2 program corrected other minor deficiencies discovered during earlier testing. Canopy glass was modified to reduce vibration. The addition of nine and a half inches to the rotor mast corrected the problem of the main rotor blades striking the canopy. However, the additional nine-and-a-half-inch height precluded the AAH from being loaded aboard air force C-141 transports without the main blades and rotor hub being removed first. Additionally, the main rotor blade tips were modified and swept back to reduce noise.

After the installation of navigational fire control and armament equipment, designers were forced to increase the size of the fairings located along the exterior of both sides of the forward fuselage. General Browne recalls that this additional space was needed to accommodate the increase of avionics equipment that made up the armament and fire control systems. With these modifications the fairings extended from the nose back to the forward edge of the stub wings. With Martin Marietta's and Northrop's TADS/PNVS systems mounted in prototype AAHs to ensure airframe compatibility, flight testing began in June 1979. The army's fly-off tests between the two TADS/PNVS systems began in January 1980 and lasted for approximately two months. In

April 1980 Martin Marietta was declared the winner. With this, AAH's schedule was back on track and test results were favorable. However, fate seeks opportunities to challenge the good.

On November 20, 1980, while filming tests of the latest tail configuration, an army T-28 chase plane carrying a photographer collided with AV04 and both aircraft crashed. The crews perished. Browne recalls this as a dark moment. Not only had the program lost key players, the accident renewed congressional concern with the AAH program.

Further escalation of costs gave program critics new reason to challenge the army's having the AAH. More intransigent opponents recalled that the army had developed the Cobra by simply using UH-1 components and wondered why they could not do the same using UH-60 Black Hawk components. Finally as the level of congressional carping crescendoed, the Department of Defense ordered the army to conduct a comparative evaluation of AAH and the Hellfire-equipped Black Hawk—the prizefighter versus the circus fat lady. AAH versus Black Hawk—the results were predictable. No contest.

By the time all the AH-64A Apache's systems were mounted and integrated, the T-700-GE-700 engine was at its upper limits of power output (sixteen hundred SHP). In the meantime, the navy's version of the UH-60 Black Hawk, the SH-60 Seahawk, had been issued to the fleet with T-700-401 engines. AV05 was tested with T-700-GE-701, an army version of the navy engine. The increase in performance gained with the T-700-GE-701 was so great that the army adapted it for Apache.

Operational test II (OT II) began in the summer of 1981. This test was the first in which Apache operated in a field environment with soldiers. Exercises with troops from the 7th Infantry Division (Light) from Fort Ord, California, were conducted at nearby Hunter Liggett Military Reservation, a subpost of Fort Ord that was once a cattle ranch owned by William Randolph Hearst.

Working the Apache with the 7th Division's ground soldiers allowed for practical tests. Flying more than four hundred hours in three months, the test aircraft were exposed to heat, dust, and mud while evaluators collected data on AAH reliability, availability, and maintainability (RAM). Analysis of RAM data provides the developer a glimpse of how the aircraft will do in the field when manned and maintained by operational crews. The results of OT II showed that the RAM features of Apache were going to meet and probably exceed initial expectations.

"Apache's performance during OT II exceeded expectation," Browne recalls. In fact, Apache performed so well that Browne persuaded the army to push for a decision to authorize full production. By April 1982, with testing on schedule and the Apache performing so well, full-scale production was approved. However, Apache still had its enemies.

Following additional attempts by a few unconvinced congressmen to kill or damage AAH, Congress relented and authorized $444.5 million in the fiscal year 1982 budget for construction of eleven aircraft. With this commitment by the government and some urging by General Browne, Hughes decided to gamble and began construction of a two-million-square-foot, $300 million AAH production complex. Looking beyond the immediate, General Browne decided that he would help Hughes in their site selection.

Browne feared that high contractor personnel and manufacturing expenses might hamper meeting the army's need for a sizable number of AAHs. Assembling a small team, Browne conducted a cost-analysis study of the California aerospace manufacturing corridor, which stretches from San Diego to Santa Barbara. Browne's study disclosed a turn-over rate of technical and manufacturing people at Hughes Helicopter of about 28 percent a year, fairly common in all companies operating in the corridor. It seemed that each time one of the corporations located in this corridor received a new contract, an auction was held for positions, and many of the best technicians moved to the highest salaries. The study concluded that the army would not be able to afford the quantities of AAHs needed if Hughes tried to manufacture the AAH in the corridor. In fact, Browne was convinced that if Hughes did not move, their personnel and manufacturing costs could reduce the army's total buy to about two hundred aircraft.

With his evidence in hand, Browne briefed his findings to the Summa board of directors and suggested that since they were going to build a new plant for production of AAH, they should relocate and build their plant away from the corridor. Once again Hughes responded to Browne's advice and selected Mesa, Arizona, as the site for their new plant. At the time of its completion in late 1982, this facility, which would employ two thousand workers, was touted as the most modern helicopter-production plant in the world.

Favorable publicity influences opinion. Air shows historically afforded aircraft manufacturers excellent forums for demonstrating their products. General Browne was convinced that the more people saw Apache, the more he could garner support for the program. The period from July to October 1982 saw AV02 on a European tour, including the Farborough air show in England. Wherever Apache went, crowds and officials were impressed by America's bold new attack helicopter. The tour included demonstrations for U.S. troops stationed in Germany, where U.S. commanders were provided detailed briefings on how Apache would increase American combat power on the European battlefield. All were impressed with this, the ultimate flying tank killer. Browne found nothing but supporters in Apache's wake.

With its European tour a success, AV02 returned to America, arriving just in time for the annual October convention of the Association of the United States Army in Washington. Once again Apache was seen by thousands of admiring visitors.

Even with this much success, life for AAH was not yet without a few bumps. Early in the program, army requirements had indicated the eventual need for 536 Apaches. Now, almost ten years after the AAH task force began its work, program costs forced that total number to be reduced to 446. It appeared that total AAH costs would be just shy of $6 billion. Grocery store math put the unit cost at more than $13 million.

Not surprisingly, as this information sank in, Congress went through the ceiling. Despite General Browne's constant briefings to congresspersons and staffers, few in or out of Congress understood the complexity of the navigational, target-acquisition, and firepower capabilities built into the Hellfire-equipped Apache. Weathering this wave of criticism, the army and Hughes renegotiated the production contract in November 1982 for an additional forty-eight aircraft at a cost of $106 million in fiscal year 1983 dollars.

September 30, 1983, saw Hughes roll out its first Mesa-produced AAH, now called Apache. The second soon followed, and as the new plant hit full stride, life began to look good for the Hughes family. The Mesa plant came fully on line just in time to meet their contract schedule, and the future for Apache looked good. However, an unexpected and unsettling event struck the Hughes corporate empire. Ownership of Hughes Helicopter was about to change.

Hughes Helicopter traces its roots back to February 14, 1934, when Howard Hughes, Jr., an American aviation pioneer, founded the Hughes

Tool Company Aircraft Division, later to become Hughes Helicopter, a company that prospered until Howard Hughes's death in 1976. Hughes is probably best remembered as the eccentric builder of the HK-1 Hercules flying boat, popularly known as the Spruce Goose. However, Hughes did far more as one of the best early aircraft designers in the United States and set records in transcontinental races piloting his H-1 Racer.

In December 1983, as part of the settlement of Hughes's estate, the Hughes Helicopter Company was sold to McDonnell Douglas Corporation. This transfer of ownership went through without interruption of Apache production, and after several years most of the Hughes management team was replaced. As McDonnell Douglas management assumed responsibility, they were eager to please their new army customer.

By then things were going so well for Apache that in spring 1984 another contract worth $841 million was signed for the production of 112 aircraft. In the meantime, the rate of production at Mesa reached three aircraft per month. Twelve years after the material need document had been written at Fort Knox, operational aircraft were being issued to troop units. The Apache had completed its ordeal, and it was now time for it to join the ranks of the warriors. Finally, after so many years and false starts, the army had its long-needed attack helicopter. Having survived many battles during its development and production, the Apache was fully tempered and capable of surviving other, real battles. Even so, doubters continued to hover close by, always ready to exploit any detected flaw. The ultimate test would be combat; when it came, Apache was ready.

Chapter Eight

RITES OF PASSAGE

The ultimate mission of a troop leader is to properly train his unit to fight. Nothing more, nothing less. In the world of short-notice, come-as-you-are wars, the importance of training and readiness has increased proportionally to the swiftness of the command authorities' ability to commit and move troops. Annually, millions of dollars are spent to keep soldiers proficient in their individual and collective duties. Unfortunately, placing the soldier and his equipment in the field, which is the best way to train, happens to be the most expensive. These high costs have forced the army to seek alternate, cheaper means for keeping soldiers professionally competent. Wherever appropriate, simulators are developed and used to maintain critical skills between field-training exercises. The combat mission simulator (CMS), to be discussed later in this chapter, is a good example. But first a look at enemies of good training.

Complexity of equipment has made the leadership of a modern army far more demanding than it was during the war in Vietnam. Not all complexity is equipment driven. Hundreds of conditions can and do arise to erode effective training, unexpected loss of funding in peacetime being but one. Within the army these disruptions are politely referred to as "training distracters."

A training distracter might be a soldier's visit to a doctor, taking earned leave, being selected to mow grass, or any other tasks that can keep soldiers from the preparation for war. Frustrated commanders have devised all manner of schemes to insulate their units from falling victim to the massive assaults on unit training all too common in most units.

With that in mind, add the complexity of equipment. The maintenance of skills required of an M1 Abrams tank gunner, loader, driver, or vehicle commander requires a great deal more time and practice than was required for the M1's predecessor, the M60 tank. (Crew duties for the M2 and M3 Bradley fighting vehicle approach those of the Abrams.) Many less complicated skills also require frequent attention. First aid, identification of friendly and enemy vehicles, map reading, qualification with individual weapons, land navigation, and survival on the nuclear, chemical, or biological (NBC) battlefield are but a few of the skills that require time, effort, and resources.

As the M1 Abrams reached the time for first deliveries to troop units, the army realized that complexity required new methods for issue and training. The system developed for the M1 tank provided the opportunity to acquire M1 skills unencumbered by the normal training distracters. Units scheduled to receive the M1 Abrams were relieved of all other duties, fenced from outside interference, and allowed the time to learn to operate and maintain this new system. A new-equipment training team (NETT) was sent out with the new equipment to assist in training the receiving unit.

APACHE ISSUE AND INITIAL TRAINING

Anticipating that Apache's complexity would require great effort for receiving units, army planners developed a logical, step-by-step sequence entitled single station unit fielding and training to ease receiving units through the process. The system calls for the receiving unit to physically pack up and move to Fort Hood, Texas, for delivery of aircraft and training of all unit members.

The process actually begins one year before the unit's planned E (for effective) date, this being the day the unit completes its conversion to the Apache table of organization and equipment (TO&E) and stands prepared to commence training with the Apache.

Two types of units go through this process. The first is an existing attack battalion converting from Cobra to Apache. The second is a newly created unit. The majority of units receiving the Apache are existing units being converted. The units being activated are units scheduled for assignment overseas.

For a battalion converting from Cobra, the process begins with turn-in of their AH-1 Cobras and all the special tools and equipment peculiar to the Cobra. This is accomplished while the converting battalion is still at its home station. The next step is the issue of non-Apache-related equipment authorized to an AH-64 Apache battalion. For example, the M16 rifle is not an Apache-peculiar item; however, the number of M16 rifles must be adjusted to coincide with the new personnel authorizations. The number of vehicles might also require increase or decrease depending on the number authorized for the Apache equipped unit. In the meantime, designated personnel, pilots, mechanics, and crew chiefs are sent to Apache-specific schools to learn new, Apache-related skills.

When all school training is complete, about three months prior to the unit's scheduled E date, the battalion packs and moves to Fort Hood, Texas, with all its on-hand equipment.

Soon after arrival at Fort Hood, the unit's Apaches arrive from the McDonnell Douglas plant at Mesa, Arizona. At the same time, representatives from the battalion travel to nearby Red River Army Depot in Texarkana, Texas, and receive all the other Apache-specific equipment, primarily the special tools needed to maintain and repair the Apache. Once the battalion is finally assembled at Fort Hood with all its equipment, it comes under the control of the Apache Training Brigade (ATB). The ATB is a small brigade, permanently assigned to Fort Hood, whose purpose is to teach the transitional unit how to employ, fight, and maintain this system known as Apache.

On E day the new Apache battalion begins ninety days of lock-step training under the supervision of the ATB. The first thirty days are spent in individual pilot and maintenance instruction. The second thirty days are devoted to company-level and aircraft weapons training. The culmination, the last thirty days, is dedicated to the battalion-level army training and evaluation program (ARTEP), an appraisement made under simulated combat conditions administered by the ATB. The purpose of the ARTEP at Fort Hood is to determine how well the transitional unit has done in acquiring its individual and collective Apache skills. A unit either passes or fails; there is no graded scale. A go leads to unit certification; and once certified, the unit is allowed to return home listed as combat ready. A no sends the unit back to correct those weaknesses identified during testing.

Again, the value of this approach is that it takes the unit off-line and protects it from all distracters, while providing the resources needed to return the battalion to its home station with its new equipment in combat-ready status and the personnel fully qualified to operate it.

Once the battalion is home, the emphasis shifts to skills maintenance. Again because of day-to-day training distractions and the added complexity of Apache's systems, staying ready is not easy.

The ARTEP, the same test used to measure progress by the ATB at Fort Hood, becomes the tool that the commander uses to keep his battalion combat ready and the standard he uses to evaluate its performance. In addition, since the battalion is an aviation unit, another tool, the army aircrew training manual (ATM), is also applied.

The ATM prescribes the annual minimum training requirements for individual aviators. For example, because of Apache's unique ability to operate at night, the ATM requires that 50 percent of all Apache training flights be flown during periods of darkness. (There are other considerations such as the availability and use of simulators, ammunition, and fuel.)

Apache's laser range finder and laser designator, capable of reaching out to extended distances, create a new and different set of problems. If not properly used, laser devices can cause harm to the eyes of man and beast; therefore, their use must be carefully controlled. Specially designated areas are selected and set aside for laser training. By necessity, firing ranges where lasers are allowed are limited, and this sometimes creates a scarcity that can further inhibit good training. Laser-related safety limitations, added to missile costs and the cost of other types of Apache ammunition, make Apache training expensive. To overcome these disadvantages, the army, over time, has discovered that simulation offers a cost-effective solution.

The Apache combat mission simulator (CMS) is an excellent training device carefully developed to duplicate the Apache's interior, weapons systems, and flight characteristics. It is understood that flying and shooting the Apache's weapons systems provide the best training and are a lot more fun for the aviators, but the costs of flying time and ammunition make the CMS the next best thing. To help achieve realism and to allow motion to be felt by the crew, these devices are mounted on six-degree freedom-of-motion platforms. The CMS uses video screens as the aircraft windshields to portray what is happening outside. Crewmen are able to simulate NOE flying in all types of weather, acquiring and engaging enemy targets and experiencing in-flight emergencies. With the CMS, crews are able to maintain an acceptable training edge that lack of funding and facilities might otherwise preclude. Unfortunately, for some aviators the CMS is not readily available.

The army aircrew training manual (ATM) requires Apache crews to log twenty-five to thirty hours per year in the CMS. However, as one might imagine, these simulators are so expensive that the army cannot afford to provide one to each Apache battalion. By placing the few CMSs it can afford at strategic sites across the United States and overseas, the army makes them accessible to Apache crews. For example, a CMS facility has been placed at Fort Bragg, North Carolina. In addition to servicing Apache crews stationed at Fort Bragg, this facility services all Apache crews, active and reserve, located in Florida, Georgia, South Carolina, and part of Virginia. The battalions must schedule time in the CMS for their aviators and periodically send crews to the CMS facility for several days of simulator use. As defense dollars become scarcer, Apache flight crews can expect to see the insides of a CMS more than an Apache cockpit. That may prove to be unfortunate in a world of quick-reaction wars.

PANAMA

The 82d Airborne Division remains the last army division trained to enter a conflict by parachute. First activated at Camp Gordon, Georgia, in August 1917, and composed of men from all of the then–forty-eight states, the division took the name All American and wore a shoulder patch of red, white, and blue with a large *AA* in its center.

Deployed to France in 1918, the 82d spent more time in the line during World War I than any other American division. Its most widely acclaimed soldier was Medal of Honor winner Sgt. Alvin C. York of Tennessee.

Reactivated for World War II on March 25, 1942, the 82d was selected on August 15, 1942, to become the first of the army's five wartime airborne divisions. The 82d participated in the North African campaign, the invasion of Sicily, and the invasion of Normandy; and it fought with distinction throughout the war, ending its tour on occupation duty in Berlin.

The division returned from Europe on January 3, 1946. (Legend has it that the Russian government requested the 82d be removed from Berlin. It seems that too many Russian soldiers were being injured in weekend bar brawls with the proud and cocky paratroopers.) Soon after its return to the United States and its settling in at Fort Bragg, North Carolina, the 82d became America's primary quick-reaction force and has remained on active duty as an airborne division ever since. Known nationwide as "America's Guard of Honor," the division, or elements of it, has on six occasions been sent overseas as part of rapid power-projection missions, either to show force or to fight.

Like other divisions composing the XVIII Airborne Corps (the 24th Infantry and the 101st Air Assault), the 82d must maintain a fixed percentage of its soldiers and equipment on alert status, available immediately to load onto air force aircraft bound for anywhere in the world. The key to the 82d's ability to accomplish its deployment missions is its frequent rehearsals. Called emergency deployment readiness exercises (EDREs), these tests require rapid assembly. Often they include loading personnel and equipment aboard air force aircraft at nearby Pope Air Force Base.

On November 14, 1989, 1st Battalion, 82d Aviation Regiment, 82d Airborne Division, the division's Apache battalion, was placed on alert. At first the alert was thought to be just another EDRE. However, once assembled the troopers were told to prepare for overseas deployment. Surprisingly, the 1-82d was told that for this deployment only six of the battalion's AH-64 Apaches, three OH-58C Scouts, and a limited number of maintenance personnel would be going and that they would depart after dark. Little else in the way of information was forthcoming. Puzzled, the remainder of the 1-82d returned home after being instructed to keep silent about the deploying task force. Elsewhere at Fort Bragg, clandestine plans were being made for other elements of the division to follow the 1-82d.

Operation plans are just that, a road map of how an operation is meant to be conducted. No prudent commander commits his forces without having gone through a thorough planning sequence, and no smart commander enters battle believing that events won't force his plan to be adjusted. As the small 1-82d task force packed, they did so believing that reinforcement would be quick in coming. Knowing this they were not too concerned when they discovered that there was room for only the bare essentials in the task force's allocated equipment-airlift aircraft.

That night (November 14), soon after dark, the unusually austere 1-82d task force secretly moved to the personnel holding area (PHA) near the loading ramps of Pope Air Force Base. There they were squeezed aboard two C-5 cargo aircraft and once aboard departed Pope on a nonstop flight to Howard Air Force Base, Panama. Arriving before dawn (Panama and Fort Bragg are both in the eastern time zone), the task force's Apaches and scout aircraft were carefully unloaded from the huge transports and quickly hidden in an air force hangar. By the time of the arrival, the 1-82d personnel had been told that their mission was secret and their presence in Panama was to remain secret until further notice. Mysteriously they were instructed to wear only civilian clothes, or uniforms without any trace of unit identity (divisional shoulder patches or regimental insignia). But why? the troopers wondered.

For several months, relations between the United States and the Republic of Panama had gone from poor to severely strained. For the past several weeks, Gen. Manuel Noriega, the belligerent and bombastic president of Panama, had been busy seizing every opportunity to denounce the United States and its presence in Panama. Finally Noriega's rhetoric approached the style of a frustrated dictator and serious threats began to become a normal part of his frequent inflammatory public speeches. It was not all one-sided. While Noriega was busy posturing and threatening the hated Yankees, members of the Bush administration began to speak of bringing criminal charges against Noriega for drug trafficking. This oratory peaked soon after a federal grand jury in Miami issued an indictment against Noriega, charging him with assisting in smuggling Colombian cocaine into the United States and laundering drug money through Panamanian banking facilities.

During all this, a democratic election was held in Panama, with new constitutional officers winning most seats from Noriega and his cronies. Noriega disallowed the election results, triggering an attempted revolution. Word soon leaked out that the revolution had been crushed and many of its leaders executed. (Some were allegedly executed by Noriega himself.)

This was soon followed by the death of an American officer at the hands of Panamanian police. Before the emotions of this tragedy could be calmed, another incident occurred involving the illegal apprehension of another American officer and his wife. The United States charged Panama with allowing improper "handling" of the officer's wife. Finally, right or wrong, the United States had had enough, and planning commenced for an invasion designed to topple Noriega and arrest him.

After off-loading the Apaches from the C-5s and concealing them inside a hangar, the 1-82d used the next two nights for reassembling the aircraft and conducting test flights to ensure that all was in proper working order. In the interest of keeping the Apaches' presence secret, orders were issued that all Apache flights were restricted to hours of darkness.

On November 19, Southern Command (SOUTHCOM), the United States' major headquarters for all military activity in Central and South America, was notified that all of 1-82d's equipment and personnel were ready to accept missions.

The need to maintain secrecy about the Apache's presence in Panama forced the task force to completely reverse its duty days. Empty family quarters were used to house the task force. The duty day began at dark and ended at daylight. The reversal of the duty day required crews to sleep during the day to be ready for missions at night. It did not take long before Lt. Col. Donald E. Vinson, commander of the 1-82d, began to refer to his small task force as "the Night Owls."

Soon after midnight on November 19, the Apaches flew their first in-country missions. These missions were three-hour flights designed to allow crews to become familiar with the terrain and topography of Panama. During the next two weeks, the Night Owls launched flights consisting of two Apaches and one OH-58C to reconnoiter three separate locations called *cuartels* or garrisons. The targets: Tinajitas, Panama Viejo, and Fort Cimmarron, the homes of heavily armed, company-sized (210 to 260 men) concentrations of the Panamanian Defense Force (PDF). The purpose of the Apaches visiting these facilities was reconnaissance—to locate and film each of them and especially their guard posts and fortifications. They were also to determine the best methods for attacking and neutralizing the *cuartels* during the invasion. Subsequently, night reconnaissance missions were flown against other known or suspected Panamanian military/police facilities, and the films were provided to SOUTHCOM intelligence officers.

Great care continued to be taken to maintain the secrecy of the Apaches' presence in Panama. This was done not only to avoid arousing Panamanian suspicions about the ongoing American buildup, but also to ensure that the Apaches could continue their clandestine intelligence-gathering missions free of indigenous interference.

Recall that operational requirements had forced the 1-82d task force to fit into two C-5 aircraft for their trip from Fort Bragg to Panama. With six Apaches, three OH-58s, two high mobility multipurpose wheeled vehicles (HMMWVs), and personal baggage, little room remained for spare parts. However, at the time of the departure from Fort Bragg, the task force fully expected to be quickly reinforced. The follow-on force was to be a reinforced brigade, complete with additional maintenance capability. Unfortunately, before all that could happen, it became clear that the few Apache spares brought by the task force would be gone before the scheduled arrival of the reinforcements. In an attempt to allay Panamanian suspicions, limits were imposed on the number of air force transports arriving and departing daily. Although several of these "normal" flights originated at Fort Bragg, they arrived filled to the limit with prescheduled loads needed for the buildup. Until the invasion began in earnest, the 1-82d task force was going to have to make do.

Flights by the Apaches continued to be scheduled and flown nightly. With each passing night the small reserve of high-use Apache parts was further depleted. The part shortage was becoming an operational problem. Within days of arrival, one Apache developed a fuel-cell leak that was beyond the task force's ability to repair locally. With little chance of receiving a replacement fuel cell, and with their parts supply rapidly drying up, the Night Owls exercised a long-standing tradition and turned to the unflyable Apache as their source of parts. Operational necessity forced controlled cannibalism, and the Apache force of six became five.

Limited space on the C-5s that brought the 1-82d to Panama had generated yet another maintenance problem. In addition to not being able to carry adequate spare parts, the task force had to leave its critical aviation ground power units (AGPUs) behind. The AGPU is a critical tool for Apache maintenance, especially when it must be performed indoors. Apache maintenance personnel equate the lack of an AGPU to having their hands amputated. The AGPU is a device that allows maintenance personnel to activate and check aircraft systems without having to start one or both main engines. The lack of an AGPU and the requirement for secrecy precluded taking the Apaches out of their hangars for engine run-up during daylight, when the aircraft were not flying and were available for maintenance. The AGPU would have allowed all this to be done inside without drawing undue attention. As a result, the Night Owls were forced to delay daily maintenance checks until after dark, eating into precious operational time.

Another unexpected complication for the Night Owls was the condensation that occurred after rolling the aircraft outside the air-conditioned hangars. When the cooled Apaches rolled into the warm, humid Panamanian night air, they immediately began to sweat. Sensitive electronics systems, such as the night vision equipment, fogged up and had to be dried before takeoff. (The Apache tool kit does not include an industrial-sized hair dryer.) None of these problems can be laid at Apache's or the 1-82d's feet. They resulted from rushed departure preparations done with insufficient information about what would be available in Panama, and were compounded by limited space on follow-on air force aircraft. In hindsight, the Night Owls managed to get a great deal accomplished in Panama under difficult circumstances.

With the approach of the invasion date, task force members began to have thoughts typical of soldiers about to go into battle. Chief Warrant Officer Two Charlie Dicker, a veteran of the division's Grenada invasion, recalled missing his family and being worried about the loose ends he might have overlooked before his hurried departure. Chief Warrant Officer Three Ron Ritter, Dicker's pilot, admits being apprehensive, perhaps a little scared. Even so, he recalls the excitement of the prospect of flying into battle.

As nightly missions continued, the crews became more and more familiar with their proposed operational areas. To avoid attracting attention, they carefully mimicked the flight patterns of army aviation units stationed in Panama as they flew in and out of the heliports and airfields scattered around the Canal Zone. Additionally, they learned the location of the local army training areas and made good use of them, all under the cover of darkness. By the time the invasion began, the crews of the 1-82d were prepared.

The invasion of Panama commenced at midnight, December 20, 1989. The Apache task force was briefed the previous day, and the aircraft were uploaded with Hellfire missiles, 70mm Hydra high-explosive rockets (FFAR), and 30mm cannon ammunition. For their first missions, the Apaches were to attack Tinajitas, Panama Viejo, and Fort Cimmarron, the three original sites reconnoitered on their first mission, and Rio Hato, which had been added later.

As it turned out, Rio Hato, Gen. Manuel Noriega's beach house and airfield, was to be attacked first. (The unit history shows that Warrant Officers Mark Welch and David F. Porter flew the first Apache combat mission.) Although Noriega's whereabouts remained unknown, his personal aircraft kept at the airfield at Rio Hato offered him an excellent means of escape, so it required early neutralization to prevent Noriega from taking flight. With that in mind, Rio Hato was scheduled to be hit precisely at midnight to coincide with the opening minutes of the invasion. The other three sites were changed to "on-call" missions.

Two Apaches were scheduled for Rio Hato; however, at the last minute a hydraulic leak forced one to abort. That Apache was grounded for the night; at the key moment the Night Owls were reduced to one Apache for the Rio Hato mission, and it was too late to train a replacement.

Even so, airborne soldiers are trained to anticipate the unexpected. Without registering any sign of concern, the remaining Apache crew took off for Rio Hato in company with their OH-58C Scout. En route they linked up with the remainder of the task force slated to assault and seize Noriega's suspected hideout. The mission went as planned, except that Noriega was not there. The assaulting soldiers were left with "liberating" a few Noriega souvenirs. Even so, the seizure of the nearby airfield did block Noriega's primary escape route. Apache had flown its first combat mission.

The loss of the second Apache to mechanical problems (the hydraulic leak) during the critical first hours forced the task force commander, Colonel Vinson, to quickly reallocate his assets. Each remaining target was reluctantly allotted only one Apache. Aviation doctrine says that, at a minimum, attack helicopters should be employed in pairs; however, tactical necessities during the early hours of the invasion forced Vinson to violate the two-aircraft rule, raising the level of danger for Apache crews. For Operation Just Cause (the invasion's code name), the OH-58s would have to be the attack helicopter crews' safety net in the event of a shoot-down, just as they had been in Vietnam. As soon as circumstances allowed, Vinson corrected this problem by doubling up his Apaches.

Overnight, air force maintenance personnel at Howard AFB volunteered their time and equipment, repaired the hydraulic leak, and had the fifth Apache back in service by morning. Even so, the shortage of Apaches was not the main problem hindering the invasion that first night.

Ice storms seldom invade the warm climes of the Piedmont region of North Carolina, where Fort Bragg sits sprawled across the Sand Hills. The evening of December 20, 1989, proved an exception. Unexpected icing conditions at Fort Bragg delayed the departure of the 82d paratroopers scheduled to parachute into Panama shortly after the midnight invasion start time. This delay forced other mission changes for the understrength Night Owls. (They had plenty to keep them busy until the troopers arrived.) Now with the security wraps gone, the Apache and Scout crews would be operating day and night. Missions for the Apaches were coming fast and furious. Crew rest for the too few Apache crewmen had the potential to become a problem.

In the early hours of December 21, CWO3 Ron Ritter and his co-pilot-gunner, CWO2 Charles Dicker, were one of the crews that received a last-minute mission change. Their new mission was to fly to an area where Panamanian mortars were reported to be firing on U.S. forces from a hilltop.

Just as daylight glowed in the eastern sky, Ritter and Dicker took off accompanied by a lone OH-58 Scout. Arriving at the objective, the Apache took a position to allow quick reaction if the unarmed Scout encountered fire. Both aircraft carefully searched for offending mortars but found no evidence of their presence. Mortars are high-angle-fire weapons that require open space for safe operation. The gun tube rests on a large base plate, which absorbs the recoil and prevents the recoil from driving the gun tube into the ground. The imprint left by the base plate and the disturbance of the surrounding area by the crew serving the mortar leave signs easily seen by Scout aircraft. Ritter and his team found no evidence of mortars or evidence that there had been any unusual activity. Convinced that there was no mortar at the reported location, Ritter climbed to an altitude high enough for his radios to reach Night Owl Operations Center and rendered a negative report concerning the reported Panamanian activity. Accepting the report, Night Owl Operations gave the Apache-Scout team a new mission. They were to move to Panama Viejo and join the support of U.S. ground forces attacking that installation.

After arriving at Panama Viejo, Ritter and his Scout remained on station until they ran low on fuel. Two Apaches arrived in time to allow Ritter's team to return to Howard AFB for fuel.

It was midmorning when Ritter and Dicker completed refueling. By then, heavy fighting had broken out in isolated pockets all around Panama. Checking in with Night Owl Operations, Ritter was teamed with another Apache and Scout. The crews received a detailed briefing to prepare them to go to Tinajitas, one of the three initial Apache targets. American forces there were experiencing considerable resistance and finding urban fighting difficult and confusing. Use of air support in such close quarters requires exceptional coordination, and the ongoing fighting in and around Tinajitas was taking place at extremely close quarters. To avoid accidental engagement of friendly forces, Ritter's team was instructed to be prepared to provide overwatch for the attacking American troops.

The low-level route of flight to Tinajitas required Ritter's team to fly through a pass between two large hills. After takeoff, with Scouts leading, Ritter's team headed for their objective. By now, the tactical situation all across Panama was so confused that it was nearly impossible to know which areas were in friendly hands and which were not.

Entering the pass between the two hills, the team's OH-58 Scout pilot reported receiving ground fire from a squad-sized unit believed to be deployed at the base of a large statue. Before he could react, Ritter's Apache flew into the gunfire. Dicker, believing the ground fire to be coming from the right, told Ritter to turn left. As they turned, Ritter and Dicker could feel rounds slamming into their Apache. Immediately lights on the emergency panels came to life, warning of damage to several of the aircraft's systems. A quick check of the warning lights and power gauges indicated serious damage to the number 2 engine.

Unsure of the extent of the damage and equally unsure how his fully loaded, heavy Apache might fly, Ritter decided not to shut down the number 2 engine completely. Reacting out of instinct, he reduced power to the damaged engine and brought it to idle. In the meantime, his wingman spotted the offending Panamanians and rolled in on them with his cannon spewing deadly 30mm rounds, killing several Panamanian soldiers and dispersing the rest. Once out of danger, the Scout and Apaches turned toward Howard. En route, smoke filled Ritter's cockpit, a situation that instantly strikes fear in the heart of an experienced airman. Ritter forced himself to remain calm and guided his battered and wounded aircraft to final approach at Howard. Because of the aircraft's weight (it was still fully loaded with fuel and ammunition), its unknown damage, the smoke-filled cockpit, and the fact that only one engine was operating, Ritter elected to make a running landing (like that of a normal airplane). A running landing would allow him to fly all the way to the ground while maintaining adequate speed. After touchdown, the aircraft would be allowed to roll to a stop, avoiding the need to hover the heavy Apache with one engine. Under the circumstances and at the time, it seemed a wise decision.

Ritter's approach was textbook. He maintained proper airspeed and lined up the wounded Apache with the runway centerline. At touchdown, Ritter discovered a surprise: His brakes were locked. If he hesitated for a split second to take the correct emergency action, the Apache could flip over on its nose. Again good training showed. Ritter reacted properly, preventing the Apache from rolling itself into a small metal ball. Instinctively, he slammed the fuel control of the damaged engine to full power while pulling up on the collective handle, executing go-around procedures. Ritter would make another landing approach. Struggling to see through the cockpit smoke, and using both engines, he executed a normal helicopter approach terminating in a low hover, and then gently lowered the heavy Apache safely to the ground.

Following a few minutes of public prayer, thanking the Creator for safe deliverance from gunfire and a nearly disastrous first landing, Ritter and Dicker dismounted to inspect their wounded bird. After their initial inspection, it is fair to assume that their prayers also included the McDonnell Douglas engineers who built the Apache to survive such damage.

The inspection revealed that the Apache had absorbed twenty-three hits from U.S.-manufactured 5.56mm M16 rifles, weapons that had been issued to the Panamanian Defense Force (PDF). The OH-58 had taken five hits.

The most serious damage to the Apache was in the nose gearbox of the number 2 engine. The design of the Apache's transmission and nose gearboxes is such that they have the robustness needed to run at full power for thirty minutes without oil.

In addition to the damaged nose gearbox, one round had passed through one of the Hellfire missiles without detonating either its warhead or its rocket motor. The locked brakes had been caused by a single round striking the brake system. Other rounds hit and damaged the 30mm ammunition storage magazine, or flat pack. Again there were no secondary explosions. Two push-pull tubes leading to the tail rotor had also been hit and one cut nearly in half, again testifying to the built-in robustness of Apache. Finally the tire on the left main gear had been shot flat. This too would have made the first running landing a dicey proposition.

Despite the damage, the Apache had held together, allowing Ritter and Dicker to enter the history books as the crew of the first Apache damaged in combat, a distinction that either crewman would probably have been most willing to forgo. To the credit of Apache's builders, this was accomplished without either crewman being injured.

Today, Apache's reputation is built around its ability to operate and fly day or night. In Panama, Apache had done both. However, from its inception, survivability was to be the top priority in Apache's design and construction. The waning months of the war in Vietnam clearly illustrated that if the helicopter was to survive on a midintensity battlefield, even with modest antiaircraft capabilities, it must possess increased robustness.

In Apache's design phase, engineers used redundancy and separation wherever possible to provide low-cost ballistic protection. Drive-train components were overengineered, and oversized parts were used to increase tolerance to battle damage. Kevlar and boron carbide are widely used throughout Apache to build in protection against 23mm high-explosive projectiles. A transparent ballistic shield, also capable of withstanding a 23mm hit, separates the pilot's and copilot-gunner's stations. Rotor blades were designed to operate thirty minutes after being struck by a 23mm shell. During high-speed impact with the ground, the main landing gear and tail wheel are designed to collapse to help absorb the forces of impact. As of this writing, several aviators in addition to Ritter and Dicker have either crashed or taken large-caliber hits in Apache. Most lived to walk away.

Twenty-four hours after their unscheduled landing, Ritter and Dicker were back in action in their patched but serviceable Apache.

As the campaign in Panama progressed, the fighting became increasingly urban, complicating the Apache's work. Overflying highly populated areas, Apache crews might encounter women and children waving American flags in one block and take ground fire from the next. In that situation, Apache crewmen began to feel that the 30mm cannon was too large for urban warfare. Several crewmen spoke of having to hunt for unoccupied spaces so they could fire a few rounds of 30mm as a show of force. This usually was adequate to discourage further potshots from Noriega's "Dignity Brigade" dummies.

By January 10, with the war ended and their mission accomplished, the troopers of the 82d Airborne Division returned to Fort Bragg. Apache had seen its first combat. But in seven short months, America's Guard of Honor would again find itself on the loading ramps of Pope Air Force Base, out-loading to America's next crisis, Operation Desert Shield/Desert Storm. Once again Apache was destined to be the key to the army's success.

Chapter Nine

Get Ready

In August 1990 the 1st Battalion, the Vipers, of the 24th Aviation Regiment, 24th Infantry ("Victory") Division (Mechanized), was commanded by Lt. Col. Thomas F. "Tom" Stewart. Stewart is typical of today's army leaders. He is trim and fit and looks the part of a leader. His manner is pleasant, and it's obvious that he loves his work—leading soldiers. Stewart conveys the impression of being studious and deliberate; he weighs his words carefully, not to mislead or to deceive, but to ensure that he is correct, clear, and understood.

The appearance of an office tells much about its occupant. Tom Stewart's office contains the usual baggage of a modern, busy army leader: map boards, clipboards, rows of notebooks, and many telephones—the scourge of all army leaders—all neatly arranged on his desktop. A wall locker for field equipment stands in one corner, camouflaged Kevlar helmet centered on top. Video equipment is arranged on a bookcase against one wall. A computer terminal sits on a table against the opposite wall. All these are additional badges of office for the modern, high-tech army leader.

Tom Stewart speaks with an accent defying geographic identification. He was born and raised in Kings Park, Long Island, New York; however, his quest for adventure caused him to leave home after high school. After a short stint wandering cross-country, Stewart landed in

Las Cruces, New Mexico, where he enrolled and graduated from New Mexico State University, something he accomplished by hard work, luck, and an army Reserve Officers' Training Corps (ROTC) scholarship. Stewart also won a spot in ROTC's flight-training program. Graduating from college in 1972, he was commissioned in Air Defense Artillery and soon thereafter entered the army.

Stewart originally had no intention of becoming a professional soldier; however, once in the army, he never looked back. Stewart discovered his future; he would become a regular army officer, a soldier.

In college a daring courtship gave early indication of Stewart's being a man of unusual courage, bordering on recklessness. Tom Stewart met his wife-to-be at her engagement party to his ROTC commanding officer.

Stewart applied for and was accepted for army flight training, which he completed in 1975. Today he has more than sixteen years as an army aviator and sixteen hundred hours of flying time, most in attack helicopters.

With great pride and feeling Stewart recounts the 1-24th's part of Operation Desert Storm. He speaks as if recalling some notable achievement of one of his children. He is proud of his soldiers and quick to give them credit for the battalion's success. Likewise, the soldiers of the 1-24th speak of Stewart with respect, admiration, and affection.

The 1-24th Battalion is organized along the same lines as other attack battalions, consisting of five companies, a Headquarters and Headquarters Company, three attack companies, and an aviation maintenance company. The battalion has an allotment of thirty-four aircraft.

Although the Apache is the battalion's primary fighting aircraft, it is complemented by two other models, the OH-58C Kiowa Scout and the UH-60 Black Hawk utility helicopter.

Headquarters and Headquarters Company (HHC) takes care of the battalion's housekeeping chores and provides supplies and administration to the battalion's other companies. Four staff sections internal to the headquarters assist the company commanders to accomplish their missions while helping the battalion commander to command, control, and supply the battalion. Two UH-60s assist HHC do its job.

The three attack companies are the fighting elements of the battalion and the reason for its being. Each attack company has a scout platoon and one attack platoon. The company is assigned six AH-64s and four OH-58s.

The role of the Scout helicopter is to move ahead of the Apaches, locate enemy forces, and assist the Apaches in selecting positions from which they can engage targets. Although the Scout helicopter spends much of its time in danger, it is not equipped to fight and lacks built-in night vision equipment to make it compatible with Apache.

The UH-60, with some radio augmentation, provides the attack battalion with the necessary communications needed for command and control of the battalion's companies. It also provides troop or cargo airlift. The aviation maintenance company provides the mechanics, communications, and electronics specialists needed to keep the battalion's aircraft ready to fly and fight. Two UH-60s round out the maintenance company's equipment. These Black Hawks are used to move mechanics and spare parts to grounded aircraft and can sling-lift small, nonflyable aircraft to the battalion's maintenance facilities.

With its thirty-four aircraft, the attack battalion brings immense combat power to the battlefield. It can fight day or night, and can do so with speed and flexibility over great distances. If the division commander needs to add combat power to some danger spot in his part of the battle, he can quickly shift his attack battalion. More importantly, he can do this at speeds never before available.

After watching diplomacy fail to resolve conflicts between Iraq and Kuwait, and closely following the actions of the United Nations, the soldiers of the 24th Division were not surprised when they were alerted for possible overseas deployment on August 7, 1990. Within hours the word "possible" was dropped, and the Vipers of the 1-24th began packing their equipment, vehicles, and aircraft. When all was ready, trains and convoys took it all to nearby docks in Savannah. There the Vipers loaded their equipment aboard the Military Sealift Command's transport ship *Antares,* one of several required to move the mechanized 24th Infantry Division to Saudi Arabia.

The equipment went aboard ship as near combat ready as possible. Air defense and chemical decontamination teams were included on each outbound ship. Major General Barry McCaffrey, commanding general of the 24th, watching events unfold in Southwest Asia, felt that there was a strong possibility that the troops might have to fight during off-loading in Saudi Arabia. He insisted that they arrive prepared to do just that.

On August 16, the *Antares* slipped her lines and moved down the

Savannah River to the Atlantic. This done, all that remained was to wait for the airplanes that would take the men of the 24th to Saudi Arabia. In the meantime, they went home to spend what time remained with family and friends. On August 29 the Vipers boarded chartered airliners and flew outbound to Saudi Arabia . . . and the unknown.

Chief Warrant Officer Two Robert G. "Bob" Glover is a United States Army aviator and an Apache pilot. A soft-spoken man with a quick, infectious smile, he belongs to an exclusive group of soldiers, combat veterans, and he became one in the cockpit of an Apache.

Bob Glover recalls thinking how lucky the soldiers of the 1-24th were as they winged their way to an early dawn. The battalion still had almost 90 percent of the personnel who had gone through the Apache fielding training at Fort Hood. With only one aviator missing in his company (B Company), Glover felt that the unit was "well trained and very cohesive."

The *Antares,* after several midocean breakdowns, was taken in tow and slowly inched into the harbor of the U.S. Navy base at Rota, Spain. Members of the 1-24th flew back from Saudi Arabia aboard a "hijacked" air force C-141 that Stewart had "procured" from the flight line at Dhahran airport and met the unlucky *Antares.* (Stewart had talked the pilot of the empty C-141, which had been en route to England, into dropping his men at Rota.) The 1-24th soldiers helped unload their equipment from the *Antares* and reload it aboard another ship, the *Altair.* On September 26, the *Altair* and the 1-24th's equipment finally arrived in Saudi Arabia.

On September 28, with everything off-loaded and in working order, the Vipers moved to Assembly Area (AA) Viper, a barren desert site near the small, ancient village of Thadj. The word *austere* is the only way to describe the living and working conditions the Vipers found at Thadj.

The landscape at AA Viper shocked soldiers accustomed to the thick pine woods of southern Georgia. The desert site was hostile and forbidding, like a barren moonscape.

The deserts of the Arabian peninsula are some of the harshest on the face of the earth, where for centuries men and animals have struggled to survive. The Vipers' arrival was the beginning of a seven-month ordeal of heat and sand.

Training and preparing equipment consumed the next three and a half months. The training was basic: how to maintain, fight, and win under the harsh conditions of the desert. For one young leader, this preparation period brought the fulfillment of a soldier's dreams, the chance to command, perhaps in combat.

Captain Kevin Woods, the thirty-year-old son of a career naval aviator, graduated from Auburn University in 1983 and completed flight school at Fort Rucker in 1984. Trained as a Scout pilot, Woods spent three years flying the German-Czechoslovakian border for the 2d Armored Cavalry Regiment.

By 1990 Woods was back in the United States, had completed several service schools, including Apache transition, and was in the process of assuming command of an attack company in the 1-24th when Iraq invaded Kuwait. His plans were shelved as the division prepared to ship out. Tom Stewart, the battalion commander, unsure of what his unit might face once in Saudi Arabia, elected to delay Woods's assumption of command, a prudent decision but a disappointment for Woods. Instead of commanding, Woods found himself flying to Saudi Arabia as part of the 24th Division's advanced party. He was to act as Apache adviser to General McCaffrey. However, once settled in Saudi Arabia, Stewart decided that if Woods were to assume command straightaway, there would be adequate time for him to meld with his company before the war began. The change of command took place on December 7, 1990, and Woods and B Company proved to be a big part of the 1-24th's success.

While the preparation for war continued, soldiers of the 1-24th kept sneaking glances at the calendar and clock, watching as days and hours ticked away, moving ever closer to January 15, the United Nations deadline for Saddam Hussein to withdraw his troops from Kuwait. The Vipers understood what the deadline meant. They knew that the decision between peace or war rested in the hands of a man not known for rational behavior. Secretly the Vipers wished time to hurry. The leaders should either go to war or call it off. As far as the Vipers were concerned, they were ready to go home. Finally, with the deadline near, the Vipers became resigned to the fact that they were going to war; they would have to fight to get back to Georgia.

Allied war plans called for an intense air campaign prior to the Allied ground attack. With the air campaign complete, massed tanks, armored personnel carriers, artillery, and attack helicopters would be told to move forward to "close with and destroy the enemy" in accordance with the time-honored and proven doctrine of ground soldiers.

When the division's operations order arrived with details of the invasion of Iraq, the Vipers and the remainder of the 24th Division were steeled to the inevitable. Their mission was to drive swiftly and decisively 190 kilometers across the enemy's rear to the banks of the Euphrates River, blocking the escape of the now ill-famed Iraqi Republican Guard.

At 8:00 A.M. on January 14, 1991, the 1-24th packed their dusty equipment and meager personal belongings and began to move toward war. Three hours later, the 1-24th arrived at its staging area near the Saudi Arabian village of Jelady. There they were to prepare to move west to the division's tactical assembly area (TAA) and the final assault into Iraq.

The Victory Division was to be part of the far left flank force of General Schwarzkopf's "Hail Mary," the great sweeping envelopment of Hussein's Republican Guard. By means of deception, Schwarzkopf kept the Republican Guard oriented to the southeast to defend against a UN attack they believed to be coming from the south and from the sea. By January 21, 1991, the 1-24th had closed into their forward assembly area (FAA). They had moved 260 nautical miles and were situated far to the northwest of Thadj in FAA Ginger. Although the assembly area was near the Saudi-Iraqi border, the 24th Infantry and other divisions making the long, dusty march remained well back from the border to preclude discovery by the Iraqis. The air war, now six days old, left no doubt in the 24th soldiers' minds that the Victory Division would fight.

The heralded threats of Hussein to use chemical and biological weapons added to the agony of the troopers of the 24th. Although they had been issued protective clothing and equipment, soldiers fear the unknown, things that cannot be seen or touched. Once in FAA Ginger, the Vipers began to take the necessary antidotes for nerve agents. Reality sank in.

The long march from Jelady to FAA Ginger took a toll on vehicles and aircraft. For the first two weeks at FAA Ginger, the 1-24th worked hard to put back all its equipment in top order. In the meantime, the soldiers watched air force fighters fly in and out of Iraq to pound Hussein's army, long since abandoned by its leadership.

Since the Vipers were close to an enemy border, conducting reconnaissance made good sense. Initially the Vipers were assigned to conduct flights close to and along the border. For Kevin Woods this was déjà vu. Except for the difference in terrain, these flights were like 2d Cavalry missions along the wooded German border.

Soon the border flights became cross-border. Intelligence information seemed to be suffering an acute case of constipation. By the time something was seen or heard, processed by the intelligence bureaucrats, and dispatched to the battalions in need of the information, it often arrived too late to be of much use. To gain useful tactical intelligence, army aviation assets were pressed into service. Attack/Scout helicopter teams were sent out to conduct reconnaissance. But these teams had much better capabilities than the teams used in Vietnam.

Commanders like Stewart, Bryan of the 2-229th, and Cody of the 1-101st knew that the Apache could fly day or night, videotape what it saw, and turn over cassettes at either division or brigade headquarters minutes after landing. By the time the ground war began, attacking infantry unit commanders in most divisions possessed recent videotapes of their expected border crossing points and unit objectives. The information acquired by Apache reconnaissance flights often made the difference for attacking units.

Apparently the flow of intelligence was an army problem. Months after the war, Kevin Woods learned that the air force flight crews had access to timely information not available to frontline army units. While participating in a joint training exercise at Fort Stewart with an air force A-10 squadron, one that had supported the 1-24th in Iraq, Woods was surprised to learn that during their deep reconnaissance missions into Iraq, the A-10 pilots had forty-eight-hour-old photographs and current information on the location of all radar sites in the proposed reconnaissance area. The Apache pilots had been provided little or nothing.

However, Captain Woods concedes that the Apache crews at first felt that reconnaissance by Apache, like many changes in the army, was a waste of a tank killer. Since the use of Apache systems for reconnaissance had never been discussed in training, much less practiced, crews had little idea of the value of the videotapes they collected. It did not take long for the Vipers to understand the value of their work to ground commanders, and they came to understand that Apache brought not only additional war-fighting means to the battlefield, but also an excellent means of collecting intelligence.

The OH-58C Scout was built as the reconnaissance companion to Apache. However, events in the desert highlighted two significant shortcomings that prevented it from being an adequate member of the Apache/Scout team. First, the OH-58C lacked the night flying ability of Apache, limiting Scout pilots to ANVIS-6 goggles. Second, the C model had no weapons for self-defense except for a few equipped with the air-to-air Stinger missile.

Initially, 1-24th attempted to follow doctrine and use the time-tested Scout/gunship team. All too soon, they tragically discovered that the failure to make the Scout as night capable as Apache limited the Scout's ability to operate at night. With much of the reconnaissance being performed at night, Apaches, of necessity, became the scouts.

Despite these reconnaissance flights by Apaches, CWO2 Bob Glover recalls that blade time, another term for flying time, was closely controlled. Maintenance was increased and closely checked. No Viper aviator wanted to be left behind when the ground war finally started.

Captain Raymond "Scott" Hanling had much to do with keeping the Apaches airborne. Hanling grew up in a suburb of Philadelphia and graduated from the Citadel in 1984. Initially enrolled in naval ROTC, Hanling was determined to fly helicopters, so he switched to the army ROTC program and set his sights on Fort Rucker. Commissioned in the regular army, he graduated from the Infantry Officers' Basic Course, Airborne School, and then went on to Fort Rucker. Graduating from flight school in 1985, Hanling initially piloted for a medical evacuation company at Fort Carson in Colorado. While at Carson, he managed to get reassigned to a Cobra unit and flew gunships the rest of his time at Carson. After completing the aviation advanced course, Hanling was schooled as an aviation maintenance officer and assigned to Korea. He had just completed a year in Korea and reported to the 24th Division when the alert for Desert Shield arrived. By the time the division shipped out, Hanling had been back in the United States less than thirty days.

In the aftermath of Desert Storm, Apache critics complained that Apache's success was made possible only by flooding Apache units with technical representatives (tech reps) from McDonnell Douglas and its subcontractors. Hanling, assigned as a shops officer in F Company of the 24th Aviation Maintenance Battalion, smiles when he is asked about the allegations of wall-to-wall tech reps. There had been eight with the brigade before Desert Shield/Desert Storm, and the same eight traveled to Saudi Arabia with the brigade. In Hanling's words: "The

Apache's success was due to good soldiers supported by a good maintenance system."

On reflection, Hanling believes that the basic load of parts brought from Hunter initially kept the 1-24th combat ready. Over time, the supply system caught up, took hold, and filled the growing need for parts.

Not surprisingly, sand was the helicopter's biggest enemy. It ate away at rotor blades and engines. The 3-M Corporation developed an early fix for the rotor blades. Tape strips were added to the leading edges of all blades, extending blade life. Unfortunately, rain would loosen the strips. Hanling recounts that later a special paint replaced the tape.

To extend engine life in the rugged desert conditions, hover time was limited to reduce dust ingestion. Engine filters and particle separators were carefully cleaned at the end of each day; and when adequate water was available, the engines were flushed.

Once the ground war began and the division moved into Iraq, maintenance contact teams followed the speeding ground units in helicopters, repairing and maintaining aircraft on the spot. Interestingly, the war ended before there was a need to move the maintenance base forward. Scott Hanling came away from Desert Storm impressed by the army's maintenance and supply system. "Overall it worked," he says. However, his most lasting impression is of the American soldier. Like many soldiers before him, Hanling discovered that, "if you take care of him, he will do anything you ask."

While Hanling was concerned with total Apache systems maintenance management, Bob Glover found his maintenance responsibilities to be somewhat less consuming. As company armaments officer, Glover's duties were to ensure that all weapons systems were ready. By G day, February 24, the first day of the ground war, his armament crews "were pretty well worn out" from checking, cleaning, and making final adjustments. But for these tired weapons specialists, the real test had just begun. Looking back, Glover is proud that his company experienced only one Apache weapons malfunction, which was quickly corrected. But even during the period of preparation for the invasion, probing operations, designed to gain intelligence, were going on.

Soon after the 1-24th's arrival "out west," in FAA Ginger, intelligence reports trickled in describing an electronic listening/radar site directly across the border from the 24th Division, fifteen kilometers inside Iraq. If the reports were true, the presence of such a facility threatened the 24th Division. This enemy eavesdropping site might discover the 24th hiding in the desert. It was decided that the Iraqi facility had to be destroyed, and B Company was given the mission of conducting a raid to shut it down.

Carefully planning their moves, Kevin Woods prepared B Company to fly the mission at 4:00 A.M. on February 17. At 2:00 A.M., a weather check showed twenty-knot winds, enough to pick up sand and dust, thus lowering visibility. Woods remembers that the visibility at take-off was poor. Even so, the threat of discovery by the Iraqis was reason enough for Tom Stewart to order the mission to go.

The operation was to be commanded from an accompanying Black Hawk command-and-control (C&C) aircraft. The C&C took off twenty minutes ahead of the Apaches. Finding weather conditions beyond his capabilities, the C&C pilot returned to FAA Ginger and landed. Believing that the Apache's night systems would allow safe flight, Woods pressed on, leading his attacking Apaches across the border to the electronic warfare (EW) site. Arriving at their predetermined attack positions, Woods ordered his aircraft to prepare to attack. However B Company found visibility so poor that some aircraft were never able to identify their targets. Visibility proved to be too poor to use Hellfire. A thirty-day-old satellite photo of the target showed the presence of antiaircraft weapons in the area. Woods, well aware that this was the 24th Infantry Division's first offensive operation of the war, did not want to screw it up. Rather than return without having done some damage, Woods ordered the gunners who could identify targets to fire 70mm MPSM rockets. Thirty-eight MPSM rockets roared from their launchers toward the Iraqi EW facility. Once again dust hindered the Apache crews' ability to assess the damage their ordnance inflicted; however, no one missed seeing the large secondary explosion in the target area. Although the crews felt cheated by the weather and wished they could have reported complete target destruction, the mission did have its pluses. The Vipers were sure they caused some damage and had proved that Apache could inflict damage in spite of bad weather.

A few nights before G day, "sometime around the 20th," and after several conflicting intelligence reports about what lay in the division's intended path, Bob Glover and his new backseater, CWO3 James "JD" Douglas, were alerted to fly "to within a few miles of the Euphrates River and back." They were to confirm or deny the presence of Iraqi forces in the division's way. Douglas, a former enlisted marine and brand-new Apache pilot, was B Company's first in-country replacement. (Recall that B Company had deployed one pilot short.) This mission was about to provide the new pilot an evening of excitement.

On cross-border flights it had become normal practice to establish communications with the air force airborne warning and control system (AWACS) aircraft constantly orbiting high overhead. For reasons never understood, Glover and Douglas were unable to contact the AWACS on this flight. After several attempts to talk to the AWACS, Glover decided to follow his instructions to push into Iraq, to the Euphrates River, and return to report Iraqi activity.

Nearing the midpoint of the inbound leg, Glover caught sight of a hot spot on his FLIR. Seconds later he saw, heard, and felt a high-speed jet flash across the front of his aircraft, extremely close to him. Although he is still not certain, Glover thinks that AWACS, not sure who or what it was watching, sent a jet to intercept. The near miss was enough for Glover to make a mental note that, in the future, he would always find a way to say hello to AWACS.

Days later the electronic listening and radar site attacked by B Company was reported to be once more intact and operational. On February 21, C Company was briefed to prepare for a follow-up attack to destroy the site and capture Iraqi prisoners if possible. The C Company Apaches departed TAA Ginger at 9:30 A.M. and minutes later reported that the site, including two Soviet-built BTR 60 vehicles, had been attacked and destroyed—again.

The day before G day, February 23, Glover and his backseater, JD Douglas, accompanied by another Apache, were assigned to provide gun cover (act as escort and provide suppressive fire if required) for a UH-60 Black Hawk belonging to 3d Battalion, 24th Aviation Regiment. The 3-24th Black Hawk was to cross the border to drop off several of the division's long-range surveillance detachments (LRSDs) at sites in the Euphrates River valley. (LRSDs are small teams of soldiers, specially trained to operate deep behind enemy lines to conduct reconnaissance and report enemy activity by radio.) Although Glover's Apache team was not scheduled to enter Iraq, they were to stand by in case the Black Hawk ran into trouble.

By dark Glover and his team had departed Ginger and were in their standby position. However, a dust storm, which had been blowing all day, made visibility unusually poor. Even so, the Black Hawk departed, and the LRSD missions went without difficulty. Glover and JD spent the night in their cockpits prepared for a quick start if needed by the Black Hawk. The insertion of the LRSDs was yet another indication that the start time for the ground war was now close.

The early hours of February 18 found C Company across the Iraqi border conducting reconnaissances of Routes Yankee and X-ray, the two primary axes of advance designated for use by the 24th Division's attacking brigades. The 1-24th Battalion tactical command post (TAC) and a forward area refueling point (FARP) had been carefully moved forward, close to the border to support C Company's operations, yet not so close as to be discovered by passing Iraqi patrols. Requested air force A-10s arrived overhead on time to accompany the Apaches. During missions where Apaches were sent deep into Iraq, A-10s were used to provide additional security and to act as radio relay for the low-level Apaches. Early experience had shown that the Apache radio package lacked adequate range for long-distance, low-level operations.

The plan for the mission on the night of February 18 called for half of one axis to be reconnoitered inbound and half of the other axis checked outbound. The second half of each axis would be reconnoitered as the division moved closer to the Euphrates.

Initially the mission seemed to go well, although the weather was getting worse. On the return flight, following a new track, the Apaches encountered unexpected dense fog. However, by using their FLIRs, they were able to work their way back across the border.

By now, reconnaissance flights along and across the border were routine. Two missions were flown on February 19 and another on the twentieth. Unfortunately, the mission flown on the twentieth proved to be tragically different.

At 8:00 P.M., A Company entered Iraq in the 2d Brigade's proposed zone of attack. Its mission was to see if Iraqi forces had occupied the division's route of advance since the last flights flown the day before. Additionally, A Company was authorized to engage and destroy any enemy forces encountered. One OH-58C Scout accompanied the two Apaches. Fifty kilometers short of their limit of advance (LOA), weather forced the team to abort the mission and start back to TAA Ginger. During the return flight and without warning, the team encountered a fog bank, which had formed after the team had passed inbound. The

FLIR-equipped Apaches were able to penetrate the fog with little concern; however, once in the fog, the accompanying Scout pilot, flying with ANVIS-6 goggles, lost his ability to navigate, became separated from his Apaches, and disappeared.

By 11:30 P.M. the Scout was declared missing. A combat search and rescue (CSAR) team of one Black Hawk and two Apaches set out to find the missing Scout. The fog proved to be too much for the goggle-using Black Hawk crew, forcing it to turn back. Much to the anguish of the Vipers, the search was called off until the weather improved. By 6:00 A.M. another CSAR crossed into Iraq. Daylight found the weather adequate to allow additional aircraft, including OH-58 Scouts, to join the search. It took only minutes to discover the downed OH-58C and its dead crew. With sadness Viper soldiers removed the bodies of CWO2 Hal Reichle and his scout/observer, Sp4 Michael Daniels. They were brought to Log Base Charlie to begin the long journey home. The 1-24th Battalion was later able to honor its fallen comrades, but only briefly. The rapidly escalating pace of war preparations forced the grieving soldiers to mourn quietly and individually. With the ground war just forty-eight hours away, there was much left to be done, and all along the Saudi-Iraqi border, units were busy making final preparations.

Chapter Ten

The Eagle's Talons

Following the return of TF Normandy from the raid that destroyed the radar sites, the 101st Division braced itself for Iraqi retaliation. Surely Saddam Hussein, commander of the world's fourth largest army, would not allow such an indignity to pass unchallenged. After all, saving face is a large part of Eastern culture. It was a given that the men of the 101st were not afraid. In fact, they were confident and prepared to make Hussein's army bleed for every inch it tried to take. They were, however, unsure of just how the irrational Saddam Hussein might respond.

But first things first. The major task facing the reassembled 1-101st was to get TF Normandy's men and equipment back to combat-ready status. Getting the equipment back in shape was the easier of the two. The exhausted crews were another matter. While others inspected, rearmed, refueled, and in a few cases repaired the task force's aircraft, the crews were allowed to catch up on much-needed sleep. Major Mike Davis, battalion S-3 of the 1-101st, recalls that Cody and his triumphant but weary band "zonked out" for several hours. By the time they awoke rested, everything else was ready. More importantly, during their slumber, Hussein had done nothing. But their reason for being in the deserts of the Saudi Arabian peninsula was not ended.

For their part of General Schwarzkopf's ground battle, the 101st Airborne Division was required to move nine hundred kilometers west to TAA Campbell, seventy-five kilometers southeast of Rafha. Using ground convoys and air force C-130 transports, the Screaming Eagles took seven days to complete the move. Secrecy of their movement was most important. Once in position at TAA Campbell, the 101st Division was to be prepared to attack north on the left flank or west of the 24th Division to the Euphrates River. The only friendly forces farther west were the U.S. 82d Airborne Division and the 6th French Armored Division. It was a situation reminiscent of the days of Cadet William S. Carpenter, Class of 1960, West Point football's "Lonesome End."

January 20 saw the 1-101st's convoys begin their hot and dusty two-day road march west to TAA Eddy, the assembly area set to receive the battalion. The battalion's aircraft departed the following day, and all elements had arrived by the evening of the twenty-third.

A corps, even a light corps like the XVIII Airborne Corps, is composed of thousands of soldiers, vehicles, and pieces of equipment. To move something as large as a corps across the open desert without discovery is nearly impossible. The movement of the XVIII Corps Headquarters, Corps Artillery, the Corps Support Command, the 82d Airborne Division, the 101st Airborne Division (Air Assault), the 24th Infantry Division (Mechanized), and the 6th French Armored Division was carefully planned to reduce the chances of discovery by the Iraqis. Even though what was left of the Iraqi air force was by then grounded, dust could be seen for miles and Iraq still had many units scattered about. Keep in mind that General Schwarzkopf's strategic plan was to keep the Iraqis believing that the main thrust would come from the sea, led by United States Marines.

Measures had to be taken to prevent Hussein's soldiers from detecting the XVIII Corps move. The dust signature created by moving the corps' vehicles over poor roads would and did give telltale signs of something unusual taking place. To lessen chances of detection, everything was moved parallel to, but well back from the Saudi-Iraqi border. Unknown to the Allied forces, and perhaps making these precautions unnecessary, was the extent of the damage done by air force bombing to the Iraqi army and its ability to see into Saudi Arabia. If not blinded by the Allied bombing campaign, Iraq's ability to see the battlefield had been severely blurred.

The corps' plan for the westward move saw logistical units moved first to establish support bases. This done, the remainder of the forces arrived and were assisted by the logistical forces in preparing for the pending invasion.

In modern high-tech warfare, logistics (supplies and maintenance) are not just important, they are absolutely essential, and they are even more so in a harsh desert environment. In the desert, the importance of a good logistical system increases tenfold. Had the Allies not been capable of establishing an adequate logistics base and transportation system, no invasion of Iraq could have taken place. The logisticians from XVIII Corps and its divisions proved to be magicians, and the divisions moved to well-stocked forward bases. In the 101st's case it was TAA Campbell.

Arriving in their western assembly areas, the lead units of XVIII Corps were at a loss for information about Iraqi forces in their area. Like the 24th Division, the 101st was not willing to wait for outside sources to provide intelligence. What little information they received came from outside the division and showed few Iraqi troops in the western regions of Iraq.

The first attack helicopter battalion to arrive in the division's western area of operations was the 1-101st. Until other divisional units arrived, it fell to 1-101st to provide advanced warning and local security. As the other divisional attack battalions arrived, responsibility for a share of the division's sector was shifted to them.

Although there was now no real chance of a concerted attack by the Iraqis, in the opinion of the division staff the 101st might be vulnerable to sneak attacks by infiltrating terrorists or Iraqi reconnaissance patrols. To detect such activities, Cody, with the division commander's permission, initiated local patrols with his Apaches and OH-58Ds along the Saudi-Iraqi border. Just to be safe, Cody elected to patrol both at dawn and at dusk. Infiltrators, of necessity, begin moving just prior to dusk and are often discovered racing for home just prior to dawn.

The 101st's plan of attack for G day, the first day of the ground war, was to launch brigade-sized helicopter combat assaults eighty kilometers into Iraq and to establish a forward operating base (FOB), which would be called FOB Cobra. Again logistics drove tactics. A forward operating base is an austere forward logistics site, a convenience store, so to speak.

From Cobra, the division's infantry brigades would then launch attacks farther to the north and into the Euphrates River valley. There they would establish bases across the highway network to cut the Iraqi

Republican Guard's avenues of retreat. But before such airmobile assaults could take place, every participant would have to be drilled to perfection.

Once the division was assembled in TAA Campbell, rehearsals for the combat assaults by infantry and utility helicopter units began. Brigade by brigade the division rehearsed each planned air assault. Meanwhile, the two Apache battalions, the 1-101st and the attached 2-229th, continued their protective screening flights along the Iraqi-Saudi border.

Major Davis, executive officer of the 1-101st, recalls that on January 26, three days after the division's arrival in TAA Campbell, the infantry units received permission to conduct patrols to the vicinity of the Iraqi outposts along the border. During one of these patrols, the 1st Battalion, 187th Infantry, part of the 3d Brigade, reported being in a gunfight with Iraqi troops. With Cody and Col. Thomas Garrett, the aviation brigade commander away at division headquarters, Davis found himself in charge of the 1-101st. He immediately diverted his patrol aircraft to the site of the 1-187th's contact with the Iraqis, and for the next five hours played a game of cat and mouse with frightened Iraqi soldiers. Soon after the Apaches arrived in the 1-187th area, Davis requested permission to open fire if the need arose. Still hoping not to draw Iraqi attention to this area, HQ denied permission. It was still not time to make the division's presence known. In retrospect, whether the Apaches fired or not didn't really matter, because the infantrymen of the 1-187th reported that at first sight of the Apaches, the Iraqis "took to their feet and disappeared behind the nearest hill," Davis said.

The 1-101st's first cross-border mission since their January 17 raid was flown on February 14. Other missions soon followed. These flights were deemed necessary to gather additional intelligence on the Iraqi forces arrayed to the division's immediate front and deeper in its proposed sector of operations.

The 1-101st Apaches conducted their recons at night and in phases. The first were conducted close in and became progressively deeper with each passing day. Their mission was to conduct zone reconnaissance and report any observed enemy activity, but under no conditions were they to reveal the 101st Division's positions. During the first night, the division's intended zone of operations was carefully reconnoitered from the border to half the distance to the proposed site of FOB Cobra (it being the division's first-day objective). OH-58D Scouts, supported by Apaches, breached the Iraqi border and performed close-in reconnaissance. A second Apache company followed and conducted a zone reconnaissance while the third Apache company remained on strip alert. Cody instructed all his aircraft commanders to be as unobtrusive as possible, to avoid detection; but if discovered, they were not to become decisively engaged with enemy forces.

These recon flights soon became routine daily events. Most were flown between 8:00 P.M. and 3:00 A.M. Immediately after each landing, Cody reviewed the Apache's videotape of the zone or specific objective. Then the tape was rushed to the brigade headquarters in whose sector the reconnaissance was flown. As the days passed, TV film was made of all critical areas and suspected enemy positions. Superimposed on the film was information giving the azimuth and distance from the helicopter to the target, and the grid coordinate of the Apache. At brigade headquarters the film would be reviewed on VCRs by the brigade commander and his staff. Cody ensured that the Apache crew that had flown the mission accompanied the film and was available to answer questions. Using the Apache for reconnaissance was a mission never dreamed of during its development. Now, of necessity, Apache had became indispensable to the division's preparation for the invasion of Iraq.

Speaking of the first night of cross-border operations, February 14, Mike Davis recalls, "It was the darkest night I can remember. There were no lights anywhere, on the ground or on the aircraft." As part of their reconnaissance, elements of the 1-101st landed in what was to be FOB Cobra to determine if the area met the needs of an FOB. No enemy were encountered the first night, and that, in itself, was valuable intelligence. The night mission was followed by a day recon; still later, personnel landed in Cobra during daylight. No Iraqi presence was detected day or night, and after all this careful and detailed reconnaissance, FOB Cobra was determined to be satisfactory for future operations.

During operations the second night, 1-101st Apaches discovered a battalion-sized bunker complex, which was exploited the following day by the 2-229th, an Apache battalion attached to the 101st from XVIII Corps. This attachment deserves explanation.

When the army was first developing its plan for issuing the Apache to operate against Warsaw Pact units, some thought was given to assigning two crews per aircraft to allow round-the-clock operations. Later, maintenance considerations caused this idea to be discarded, and instead, some divisions, the 101st being one, were selected to have an additional Apache battalion assigned. However, in August 1990, the 101st's second attack battalion, the 3-101st, had not as yet received its Apaches and was still equipped with AH-1S Cobras. To add the necessary Apache depth to the 101st Division for Desert Shield/Desert Storm, another battalion, the 2d Battalion, 229th Attack Helicopter Regiment, stationed at Fort Rucker, Alabama, was designated to join the 101st Division in Saudi Arabia.

Normally the 2-229th is assigned to the 18th Aviation Brigade, XVIII Airborne Corps, but lives at the U.S. Army Aviation Center, Fort Rucker, Alabama. The 229th Attack Helicopter Regiment is officially designated the Flying Tigers by the Department of the Army, tracing its lineage from 1937 and Maj. Gen. Claire L. Chennault's famous pre–World War II American Volunteer Group (AVG). Chennault's AVG, supplied with American P-40 planes that were flown by 90 volunteer American pilots and maintained by 150 volunteer mechanics, formed the backbone of Allied fighter strength in China until 1942, when it was absorbed into the Army Air Force. Proud of this heritage, 2-229th has adopted Bengal as their radio identification, or call sign. Today the 2-229th acts as the Apache test and evaluation unit for attack helicopter doctrine and tactics. However, like all the other units belonging to XVIII Corps, the 2-229th must stay ready for rapid deployment. It was this latter mission that caused the battalion to find itself suddenly packing, loading, and shipping its equipment.

In August 1990, the time of the initial alert for Desert Shield, the 2-229th was commanded by Lt. Col. William H. "Bill" Bryan, a quiet man with a low-key leadership style. In addition to responding to a short-notice overseas movement, Bryan was forced to contend with another problem. Due to one of those unforeseen circumstances that sometimes happens in a busy army, Bryan, his executive officer, and the battalion sergeant major were all brand-new to the battalion. The sudden press of events caused by the battalion's unexpected deployment forced them to immerse themselves in planning and leading. Initially their newness placed them at a disadvantage. Soldiers like to know the men they are expected to follow and fight beside. The qualities of the new command group quickly became evident; the soldiers accepted them, and the battalion went about its business of preparation for war.

With the urgent need for the 101st Airborne Division (Air Assault) to reinforce the already deployed 82d Airborne Division, the attachment of the 2-229th to the 101st Division gave it high priority for air movement. Within hours of the battalion's first alert notification, Maj. Gen. Rudolph "Rudy" Ostovich III, the commanding general of the Aviation Center and School, reoriented all of Fort Rucker's assets and focused them on getting the 2-229th and other deploying units' personnel and equipment into top order and shipped to Saudi Arabia.

Most of the 2-229th's equipment was driven to the port of Jacksonville, Florida, by nondeploying personnel from Fort Rucker and loaded aboard ship. Personnel from the 2-229th and a minimum number of HMMWVs were driven to Lawson Army Airfield, Fort Benning, Georgia, and loaded aboard air force transport aircraft for the flight to Saudi Arabia. The written orders covering the 2-229th's deployment stated that upon arrival in-country, the battalion would be attached to the 101st Division. For all intents and purposes, during Operations Desert Shield and Desert Storm, the 2-229th became an integral part of that division.

After reviewing the division's tactical requirements, Maj. Gen. J. H. Binford Peay III, commanding general of the 101st, instructed his aviation brigade commander, Col. Tom Garrett, to ensure that the division had Apache coverage around the clock. Garrett, more familiar with 1-101st, designated it the division's night battalion, while assigning the 2-229th the day mission. The AH-1S Cobra-equipped 3-101st Attack Battalion was also given day missions. Additionally, the 1-101st was given responsibility for providing escort for all air assault missions—day or night. Needless to say, this caused the 2-229th to feel, at least for a while, like victims of parochialism. However, within days, they came to realize that perhaps they had been dealt the better cards.

Major George E. Hodge, executive officer of the 2-229th, remembers Bryan saying, "You know, George, I don't think the Iraqis (a) have a capability to fight at night and (b) plan to fight at night. Let's don't say anything about us having the day missions since I have a feeling that most of the action may take place during daylight." Events would prove Bryan correct. During the ground war, most action involving Apaches did take place during the day—so much so that the day-night arrangement prescribed by General Peay was, in time, abandoned.

Early on the morning of February 17, seven days before the start of the ground war, the 2-229th was across the border deep inside Iraq, revisiting areas covered the night before by the 1-101st. It did not take long for A Company of the 2-229th to discover an enemy encampment complete with vehicles. Opening fire with their 30mm cannons, they destroyed the Iraqi vehicles, which were the bunker occupants' only means of escape. Almost immediately ten Iraqi soldiers indicated their willingness to surrender. An accompanying 2-229th Black Hawk, there to provide C&C communications and to act as emergency combat search and rescue (CSAR) aircraft, landed to collect the Iraqis. With no infantry unit available, the Black Hawk carried two infantry soldiers trained as pathfinders. The threatening presence of the Apaches, which kept their cannons pointed at the Iraqi soldiers and filmed the entire encounter, made the task of rounding up the prisoners much easier for the pathfinders. One at a time, each prisoner was searched and then loaded aboard the Black Hawk for the flight to TAA Campbell and intelligence exploitation.

Later the same day, B Company of the 2-229th discovered that additional Iraqis remained in the bunker complex. When they again fired their 30mm cannon at the bunkers and nearby vehicles, forty-one more Iraqis climbed out of their bunkers and surrendered. This time the number was too great for the 2-229th's lone Black Hawk and its two pathfinders. Bryan requested and quickly received a platoon of infantry and additional aircraft from the 2d Brigade.

For the 2-229th, February 17 was a big day for prisoners of war: Fifty-one were captured. But in days to come, even larger catches awaited the Flying Tigers from Rucker.

While conducting reconnaissance flights deep in Iraq on the night of February 19, the 1-101st reported scattered sightings of what appeared to be Bedouin tribesmen. The following afternoon, while operating in the same area, B Company, 2-229th, videotaped "numerous soldiers in the area."[1] The film of the Iraqi troops was rushed to division headquarters, where it was viewed by the division chief of staff and operations officer (G-3). Planning began immediately for an artillery raid (moving artillery pieces by helicopter to a location close enough to allow for fire to be placed on the reported enemy soldiers). As the last artillery round fell, infantry would be air assaulted in to mop up. When this plan was later reviewed by Major General Peay, the division commander, it was rejected. Instead the Cobra-equipped 3d Battalion, 101st Aviation Regiment, was ordered to attack the enemy found and filmed by the 2-229th. The 2-229th was again placed in division reserve.

At 5:00 A.M. on February 20, Lt. Col. Mark Curran, commander of the 3-101st, briefed Col. Tom Garrett, commander of the 101st Aviation Brigade, on his concept for locating and attacking the Iraqi soldiers seen on the 2-229th videotape. Garrett approved Curran's plan, and the Cobras of 3-101st took off and were en route by 6:30 A.M. With this mission the combat tempo began to build.

Curran and his Cobras returned a few hours later having expended their ammunition. Garrett turned to Bryan and ordered him to "continue the armed reconnaissance." Bryan immediately ordered Capt. Joe Mudd to take his B Company back into Iraq to the site of his earlier encounter with the Iraqi soldiers and "find and shoot them."[2] Mudd, a good soldier, did what he was told. Returning to the place videotaped the day before, B Company, 2-229th, discovered a sizable bunker complex, this one much larger than either of the earlier discoveries and located where it could be a problem to future 101st operations. Mudd approached the enemy bunkers to determine if they were occupied. They were. This time there was no sign from the occupants of a willingness to surrender. Using the Apache's 30mm cannon, B Company opened several bunkers, revealing Iraqi troops. Unlike their dealings with other complexes, Mudd's helicopter force began to receive heavy fire from the bunkers. With that, Mudd sought and received assistance from air force A-10 Warthogs. The complex was pounded until noon with the full fury of the Apache/A 10 joint air attack team (JAAT). Bryan next requested a psychological operations (PSYOPS) team. A loudspeaker-equipped Black Hawk was then flown over the complex, broadcasting surrender messages and dropping leaflets in Arabic, encouraging the Iraqis to give up. With this, white and near-white flags broke out all over the pummeled desert floor. Bryan recalls:

> That did the trick. They began coming out of the ground everywhere. We had no idea that there were so many. The Apaches hovered over them and herded them into one area. It took almost an hour for an infantry company to arrive with CH-47 Chinooks to take possession of the EPWs.

The 1st Battalion, 187th Infantry, was tasked to assist in the roundup of prisoners. B Company of the 1-187th, was first on the ground, and it did not take them long to realize that the complex was too large for a single rifle company. Two additional companies were then airlifted in. Although most of the dazed Iraqi soldiers had little fight remaining, a few had to be coaxed out by direct American rifle fire. By day's end, a total of 476 prisoners had been collected, so many that CH-47D Chinook (medium) helicopters were used to haul them to EPW holding areas in Saudi Arabia. This complex became known as Objective Toad—"a toad on the road to FOB Cobra." The number of prisoners (476) is probably a record for EPWs captured by a helicopter unit.

Chapter Eleven

G Day

Dick Cody remembers G day, not because of the clashing of two great armies, but because of the weather, the kind of weather that causes months of careful planning to go for naught, with no one able to do anything about it. Bad weather causes opportunities to be missed.

Few of the troopers of the 1-101st got much sleep the night of February 23. Preinvasion tension, although kept in check, was almost overpowering. Fear of the unknown filled soldiers' minds. The knowledge that in a few hours, after months of waiting and training, they would go into battle made rest difficult.

The 101st's divisional operations order for G day called for a night combat assault to seize FOB Cobra. The operation would begin by having Apache-supported OH-58Ds move to the border to check for enemy forces that might have slipped up to the border near the division's preselected border-crossing points. If an enemy were detected, the OH-58Ds were to call for artillery fire and destroy or neutralize them.

Once freedom of movement was assured at the border-crossing points, an Apache company would cross and conduct zone recon along the air routes to FOB Cobra. Black Hawk helicopters bearing pathfinder teams would follow the reconnoitering Apaches. These pathfinder teams were to be inserted at two sites along the air assault routes. At each site the pathfinders would erect nondirectional aircraft navigational

1-101st AVIATION REGIMENT OPERATIONS
20 January - 8 March 1991

beacons to assist in guiding the troop-carrying helicopters (UH-60s and CH-47Ds) to FAA Cobra. One beacon would mark the midpoint and the second the release point (RP) closer to Cobra.

With this accomplished, Cody was to move one of his Apache companies to Cobra to soften up the area prior to the arrival of the first helicopter assault. The leading wave of assault helicopters would arrive at Cobra escorted by the remaining 1-101st Apache company. Once the first air assault force had been landed, the 1-101st was to be prepared to fight for three hours, until daylight, and then hand off the battle to 2-229th. However, in war, battles seldom go according to plan.

At 2:00 A.M., Capt. Doug Gabram, commander of B Company, 1-101st, led elements of his company across the Saudi-Iraqi border. Cody, flying in the front seat of a B Company Apache, recalls that "there was terrible fog, and visibility was bad." While B Company was moving deeper into enemy territory, four OH-58Ds flying in pairs were left behind on the Saudi Arabian side of the border to screen (detect enemy attempts to infiltrate). Being tied by radio to two batteries of nearby 101st artillery, the OH-58D teams had adequate firepower to engage any enemy attempting to infiltrate into the 101st Airborne Division's sector. About the time the B Company Apaches reached fifteen kilometers inside Iraq, an event took place back near the border that forced B Company to alter its mission.

One of the OH-58D teams left near the border had inadvertently entered a fog bank. Both pilots were flying with ANVIS-6 night vision goggles. Captain Tim Gowan managed to recover quickly and commenced flying on his instruments. His wingman, Lt. Gary Stephens, attempted to reestablish ground reference, failed, rolled the aircraft over, and crashed. Stephens and his aerial observer escaped serious injury, but the aircraft caught fire and was destroyed. Gowan contacted Cody by secure radio (voice transmissions are scrambled by the transmitting radio and unscrambled by the receiving set), stating that he had "lost his wingman." Cody instructed Gowan to land and rescue the other OH-58D team, fly south, and attempt to land at TAA Campbell. About that time, Gabram reported that he could maintain only about sixty knots airspeed. Cody recalls:

The Black Hawks and D Models [OH-58Ds] flying with us were flying goggles, we [the Apaches] were flying FLIR and goggles.

The acid test for the weather decision for a Go–No Go for the assault on Cobra was if we could maintain 100 knots [airspeed]. The reason why 100 knots was so critical was because of the distance from PZ [pickup zone] to LZ [landing zone] for the Black Hawks. If they could not hold at 100 knots, they were going to be out of fuel coming back. We were moving all of 1st Brigade in, and then the huge FARRPs would follow. We couldn't afford to suck these FARRPs dry while trying to build up forces in Cobra. So it had to be a round tripper for the Black Hawks. I pulled everyone out of Iraq to regroup and refuel. Knowing that H hour would have to slip, I called the DTOC [division tactical operations center] and let them know that because of weather, aircraft could not exceed 60 knots. I then headed for the crash site.

Following the safe recovery of Stephens and his observer, Cody returned to TAA Campbell, where he contacted General Peay at the division tactical operations center and recommended a one-hour weather delay. Cody promised that he would send out an aircraft every thirty minutes for a weather check. General Peay agreed, and the takeoff time of the first wave was slipped. With this delay went any chance for a night assault.

Just before daybreak on G day, Doug Gabram, flying in the front seat with CWO2 Greg "Turbo" Turberville as pilot, took off for a weather check. The fog bank encountered earlier was still present and still bad enough to prevent the pilots with their night goggles from finding a safe route for the troop-carrying aircraft. Gabram reported his findings to Cody by secure radio and recommended moving H hour back again. Peay did not concur. H hour was set for 7:00 A.M.

Some time before seven, stretching the authorized weather minimums for takeoff, the 1-101st decided to launch its Apache recon mission once more. This time it fell to Capt. Newman Shufflebarger, commander of A Company. It was daylight by the time Shufflebarger led his company north out of Campbell, straight to FOB Cobra. Gabram's B Company was next, and this time B Company's mission was to recon the route to Cobra and insert the pathfinder beacon teams.

Headed north, Gabram flew along one side of the route, closely followed by a pathfinder Black Hawk. Lieutenant Russell Stinger flew the other side of the route. The weather, much improved, allowed for safe flying. Halfway to Cobra, the Black Hawk carrying the pathfinder teams and their navigational beacons landed and dropped off the first pathfinder team. The second team was positioned at the predesignated release point (RP) much closer to Cobra. With the recon mission completed, and no Iraqis found, Gabram led B Company into the future FOB Cobra to search for enemy forces at what would be the touchdown point for the assault wave. B Company was quickly joined by C Company. Before the two companies could begin their recon inside Cobra, they both came under heavy automatic-weapons fire from Iraqi troops in freshly built bunkers. Cody estimates the force to have been "about a battalion, in the northern portion of Cobra across an east-west road, designated by us as Main Supply Route (MSR) Virginia. They were giving us quite a bit of fire, so we started duking it out with them with our Apaches."

It was 8:00 A.M. before the weather would allow the 101st to begin its invasion. Sixty-six Black Hawks made up the first wave of helicopters carrying the assault troops of the 1st Brigade. The enemy force in Cobra forced Cody to move the touchdown point for the first wave several hundred meters to the south of the planned landing spot.

While two companies of the 1-101st were busy trying to pin down the Iraqis firing from their bunkers, the first wave of infantry arrived, disembarked, and immediately began maneuvering north toward the Iraqi bunker complex. As the infantry entered the bunker complex, they assumed responsibility for the ongoing fight. For the Apaches, the main burden of the fighting passed to the men with rifles, and the pilots moved their aircraft to the flanks to provide support for the assaulting infantrymen. One of A Company's Apaches, flown by CWO2 Larry Clark and operating on the right, or eastern, flank of this firefight, began to take heavy ground fire. Clark, realizing that his aircraft had been hit several times, turned around, moved to the rear of the advancing infantry, and landed near a recently arrived battery of field artillery. Clark and his copilot-gunner, CWO2 Lester W. Ramsey, got out to inspect for damage. Four 12.7mm projectiles had left holes in the tail and tail-rotor blades. Several rounds had caused serious damage, severing a hydraulic line and damaging the tail-rotor gearbox. Two days later, after the Apache was repaired where it sat, Clark and Ramsey were back in action.

While the damaged Apache had sought safety behind the infantry, Cody, realizing that the ground fire was intense, ordered his battalion to move all three companies on line, forming an arc from northwest to northeast and pinning down the Iraqis until follow-on air assaults were safely landed in Cobra.

To maintain adequate numbers of Apaches at Cobra, each company commander shuffled assets back and forth between Cobra and Campbell for fuel and ammunition, further complicating the operation.

In the midst of all this, three CH-47 Chinook helicopters flew past Cody and his pilot, CWO2 Greg Gilman, headed north. Before Cody could warn them, the Chinooks crossed MSR Virginia (the northern boundary of Cobra) and into range of an Iraqi S60 antiaircraft gun, which Cody and Gilman were trying to destroy. Contacting the three Chinooks on the air battle net frequency, Cody ordered the Chinooks to turn south immediately before they were shot down. The Chinooks complied. Meanwhile, with their attention diverted by the Chinooks, Cody and Gilman inadvertently flew within range of the S60 gun and began to receive fire. The aircraft flying on Cody's wing and manned by CWO2 Dave Jones and CWO2 Thomas "Tip" O'Neal* destroyed the S60 with one Hellfire.

Historically, during combat operations attack helicopter units have been divided into thirds, usually by company. The battalion commander has one company on station and fighting, one en route, and one at the forward area and rearm refuel point (FARRP) preparing to return to the fight. The location of the FARRP influences the commander's ability to keep combat power in position to fight. In the early hours of the buildup in Cobra, the nearest FARRP was at TAA Campbell.

By 9:30 A.M. things had settled down enough for Cody to hand the battle to Bill Bryan's 2-229th. Also available was Lt. Col. Mark Curran's 3-101st Battalion of Cobras. With this handoff the 3-101st and 2-229th assumed responsibility for support of FOB Cobra. Cody led his battalion to TAA Campbell for fuel.

The Apache's extended station time, once again made possible by the external fuel cells, allowed the 1-101st to provide adequate support for the initial deep air assaults into Iraq and the buildup phase of FOB Cobra. Bryan's similarly equipped 2-229th also added excellent

---

*O'Neal, also known as Gadget, was the battalion's computer hacker. Using his personal computer, Gadget managed to solve confusing map grid line problems plaguing the battalion.

firepower at Cobra. Once again improvisation with Apache paid great dividends. The external fuel tanks, never intended for such use, allowed Apache to accomplish missions it might not otherwise have been able to do. The Cobra, on the other hand, had "short legs," or reduced time on station. The requirement to return to TAA Campbell for fuel reduced AH-1S Cobra's loiter time and hence its overall effectiveness.

With the battle still swirling across FAA Cobra, and the buildup continuing, the 1-101st returned to Cobra and landed after rearming and refueling at TAA Campbell. They had come to Cobra for rest, but it was past 2:00 P.M. before the tired crews could spread out their sleeping bags. Even so, the constant drone of helicopters and firing of artillery and the ongoing battle among the bunkers made sleep difficult. The 1-101st crews, like everyone else for the most part, had been awake for forty-eight hours, fourteen of them spent in the air.

Shortly after the 1st Brigade's arrival in Cobra, its supporting artillery went into action against the dug-in Iraqis. With this considerable increase in destructive firepower, white flags began to appear in bunker doors. A cease-fire was ordered, and the subdued Iraqis began pouring out of their holes. This time it fell to the troopers of the 1st Battalion, 327th Infantry, to round up the 339 prisoners taken inside FAA Cobra. Undetected, this Iraqi force could have caused considerable damage to the U.S. infantry coming out of their airlift aircraft during the opening minutes of the assault on FOB Cobra. However, the fierce attacks by the Apaches followed by the artillery pounding kept the Iraqi force from disrupting the assault of FAA Cobra. Once rounded up, the prisoners were fed and given water, processed, and evacuated to TAA Campbell as aircraft became available.

By 8:00 P.M., as dusk came to the desert just twelve hours after H hour, the 1-101st was back in the air. In preparation for the division's operations the next day (February 25), A Company was dispatched to conduct night reconnaissance in the valley of the Euphrates. Simultaneously, B and C Companies were given the mission of screening the area around the exterior of FOB Cobra to detect any attempt by the Iraqis to attack the now-large firebase.

Inside Cobra, soldiers of the 1st and 2d Brigades were on the ground and dug in. Likewise, much of the 101st's aviation brigade had moved to FAA Cobra. The 3d Brigade, still at TAA Campbell, remained uncommitted but was busy finalizing plans for its assault into area of operations (AO) Eagle near the town of Al Khadir in the Euphrates River valley. For the 101st Division, the major event scheduled for February 25, G day + 1, was to be 3d Brigade's air assault.

As day two (February 25) of the ground war dawned, it found the Allies far ahead of their original schedule. On day one, XVIII Airborne Corps had met light resistance and was in an excellent position to move forward to block the escape of much of the Iraqi Republican Guard south of the Euphrates River. The air assault of 3d Brigade, 101st Airborne, was to be the first step in severing these escape routes.

The 3d Brigade's mission was to conduct a combat assault and establish AO Eagle to cut Iraqi Highway 8, the one remaining avenue of retreat for Republican Guard units fleeing before the U.S. VII Armored Corps farther to the east. Originally 3d Brigade's assault was to have taken place during the early hours of darkness on the night of February 25, but the weather forecast called for a severe desert storm. The need to cut Highway 8 was enough to gamble and move the time of liftoff forward, losing the advantage of darkness.

The assault elements that were headed for AO Eagle were airborne at noon. The second wave departed at 3:00 P.M. By dusk most of the 3d Brigade was on the ground and fighting for portions of AO Eagle. Cody sent 1-101st Apaches forward, deeper into Iraq to support Eagle.

Once in the vicinity of AO Eagle, the Apaches ambushed fleeing Iraqi vehicles or unsuspecting vehicles approaching dug-in 101st troopers. Additionally, Hellfires fired from Apaches dropped bridges in and around AO Eagle to hinder possible Iraqi tank attacks.

The weather forecast proved to be correct. During the night of February 25, American forces experienced their first *shamal,* a fierce desert storm with high winds and blowing sand. Not only were aircraft grounded by the storm, but the force of the storm's high winds came close to damaging the unprotected aircraft. Cody's worries were increased by knowing that he had aircraft stranded for about ten hours at nearby LZ Sand, the FARRP, and elsewhere in AO Eagle. Pilots recall riding out the storm sitting in their aircraft. Those who had erected tents watched as they were snatched up and blown into the dark night. Many feared that the fully loaded Apaches might be blown over.

At first light crews were up and trying to put the aircraft back in order. The first several hours of the day were devoted to removing piles of sand that had collected in the nooks and crannies of their aircraft.

There was enough sand inside the aircraft to add noticeable weight but not enough to affect performance.

While the flight crews were busy with their aircraft, Cody was called to aviation brigade headquarters to plan operations for day four (February 27). Present at the meeting were Cols. Tom Garrett and Ted Purdon, commanders of the aviation and 2d brigades, respectfully; the battalion commanders for the helicopter lift battalions, Black Hawk and Chinook; and the commanders of the 2d Brigade infantry battalions.

The initial plan of day three had called for a brigade-sized task force to air assault into the Iraqi air base at Tallil in the northwestern corner of the division's zone of responsibility. However, the Allied offensive had gone so well that General Peay abandoned his plans for 2d Brigade to seize Tallil. Although Tallil was heavily defended, it was no longer tactically important. Instead, Peay ordered 2d Brigade to the east to assault 160 kilometers in the direction of Basra and the fleeing Iraqi forces. The division's mission was to establish operating base (OB) Viper and to cut escape routes across the Euphrates.

With this change, Peay also ended his policy of day-night Apache battalions. At 6:00 A.M. on February 27, the 2d Brigade was en route to Viper with the 1-101st Apaches leading and providing cover. However, 2d Brigade's assault was not without its complications.

The night before, at what was to become OB Viper, an unfortunate incident had occurred—the type every soldier dreads. Because of a poorly defined boundary between XVIII Airborne Corps and VII Corps, a night fratricide incident involving 3d Squadron, 3d Armored Cavalry Regiment, and a small engineer section from VII Corps had occurred with loss of life. Apparently the engineers had gathered several disabled vehicles on what they believed to be the VII Corps side of the corps boundary. They were to await daylight when they would either fix their vehicles or have them evacuated. Unfortunately, elements from 3d Squadron, screening XVIII Corps' right flank, came upon the unsuspecting engineers. Believing no friendly forces to be in the area, and failing to identify the engineers as friendly, the cavalrymen took the engineers under fire.

The next morning, Cody arrived at Viper early and took the battle handoff from Lt. Col. John Daly, the 3d Squadron commander. The 3d Squadron then moved off to rejoin its regiment. By 10:00 A.M., 2d Brigade touched down in Viper and quickly rounded up forty enemy prisoners.

By 2:00 P.M., 2d Brigade occupied OB Viper. Company A, 1-101st, was tasked to recon west of Viper. Meanwhile, C Company, 1-101st, having spent the night conducting patrols around 3d Brigade's perimeter, was assigned to escort the convoys en route to Viper. The last of the 1-101st companies, B Company, received a mission that was destined to become complex and somewhat historic.

Doug Gabram, the B Company commander, was ordered by the aviation brigade to take his company and move north to attack a causeway that crossed the Euphrates. Gabram recalls that his instructions were neither plentiful nor clear, but they were based on the best information available at OB Viper. About all Gabram received was a general location and a line running east-west, beyond which he was not to fly. There was little intelligence of enemy activity en route or at the causeway. B Company's mission was to block the causeway and deny the Iraqis one of their last routes of retreat across the Euphrates River. They were to engage targets of opportunity.

By February 27, Allied forces were primarily engaged in the destruction of Iraqi army units that continued to resist. Those honoring the Geneva Convention were treated according to the rules prescribed by that convention. However, the Iraqi units trying to flee north of the Euphrates or westward out of the path of the advancing Allied armies were engaged and destroyed wherever found. Those firing on Allied forces were treated harshly.

Not sure exactly where the target lay, Gabram flew north to the Euphrates and turned east. "What they forgot to tell us was that it was like a ghost town up there; there was abandoned Iraqi equipment everywhere," Gabram remembers. Occasionally Iraqi soldiers with white flags were observed wandering about. Fires from burning oil fields and refineries reduced visibility. "We were about twenty kilometers away from the causeway when we started taking fire from Iraqi bunkers. Guys were standing around with white flags on their AKs [Russian-built assault rifles], and when we passed, they'd shoot at you," Gabram said. "We engaged with the 30mm as we went on in."

Finding that visibility at the target extended for only a few yards, Gabram divided the causeway in half, sending Lt. Tom Drew south while he took the north end.

By the time B Company reached the causeway, Gabram recalls that "it was a graveyard. The Air Force had bombed the hell out of them."

There were some Iraqis moving around, but activity was scarce. Gabram recalls flying too close to the causeway. "In fact, we overflew the damn thing." Overflying the enemy at low level invites trouble. This time Gabram was lucky: no one fired.

As B Company engaged targets to block traffic on the causeway, distress calls from an aviator in trouble came over emergency radio frequencies. The distress calls came from an F-16 pilot forced to eject and descend by parachute somewhere nearby. During any wartime or peacetime flight deemed hazardous, pilots carry a small survival radio (AN/PRC 90). As the F-16 pilot slowly descended by parachute toward the hostile desert still under Iraqi control, he tried to describe his location to assist CSAR aircraft in finding him.

At almost the same time as the F-16 pilot's call, Gabram heard one of his chalk 3 aircraft report, "I've lost chalk 4 in the smoke," leaving Gabram wondering if he meant that the reporting pilot had lost sight of chalk 4 or that chalk 4 had been shot down. "That was the worst point for me. The way the radio call sounded, it sounded like he went down," Gabram remembers. Reacting quickly and hoping that he was not faced with two sets of downed airmen, Gabram called for the section of B Company operating on the northern end of the causeway to "stack on me," meaning that all his aircraft were to line up on him so each could be accounted for. The "lost" chalk 3 answered.

In the meantime the F-16 pilot continued to broadcast on guard frequency, describing his location as best he could. Nothing the descending pilot said told Gabram where he might be coming down. Meanwhile, an air force forward air controller (FAC) began talking to the descending pilot. For Doug Gabram, events close at hand were serious. The volume of Iraqi ground fire coming at the Apaches was increasing. Splitting his attention between Iraqi ground forces, controlling his company, and looking skyward trying to locate the endangered air force pilot was too much. Satisfied that the causeway was sufficiently blocked by destroyed vehicles, Gabram ended the causeway mission and ordered both his teams to reassemble. B Company would hunt the parachuting pilot who remained unseen but continued broadcasting. Gabram recalls that the last call from the pilot he was able to understand was that Iraqis on the ground were shooting at him. The 1-101st aviators never heard from him again. "It was damn frustrating. I didn't know where he was and I can remember him saying this:

'I am coming east of the refinery. I see the smoke.' I was really pissed off. The situation was really hectic because of this guy punching out, and we could not seem to find him."

On the return leg to OB Viper, B Company was fired on again by Iraqis waving white flags. "I just put some 30mm on them and they quit." At one location the Apaches discovered several Iraqi armored personnel carriers. Gabram pulled the company up on line, and they destroyed the APCs with their remaining Hellfires.

After landing, Gabram learned that Drew's team had found a much more lucrative target on the southern end of the causeway. He was also informed, incorrectly, that sometime during all this, five Apaches from the 2-229th had moved in close to Drew's team, bringing the total number of Apaches on the southern end to eight. The error lay in the definition of "close." In listening to Gabram describe this action, one can easily detect a sense of frustration. Gabram certainly had adequate cause. First of all, the mission was launched with little intelligence of the enemy situation. Second, smoke from burning oil facilities obscured the area, raising the level of danger to the Apaches. Third, the obvious disregard for the rules of war by Iraqi soldiers, waving white flags one minute and shooting at the Apaches the next, added anger to his level of frustration. Finally, and most importantly, Gabram and his crews were most frustrated by not being able to find and assist the hapless F-16 pilot.

In hindsight, Doug Gabram's experiences during the causeway mission were a classic example of the fog of war. For a long time he wondered if the air force pilot had survived. In June 1992, Cody was able to inform him that he had and that he hopes to find a way to thank the army crews who tried so hard to rescue him.

Not surprisingly, Lt. Col. Bill Bryan saw the causeway fight somewhat differently. In fact, in war it is not unusual for each participant to see things differently. This is a characteristic of the fog of war.

Bill Bryan remembers that soon after his battalion had arrived in AO Viper, three hundred kilometers east of Cobra, he was met by General H. Hugh Shelton, assistant division commander of the 101st, and Colonel Garrett, the 101st aviation brigade commander. It was early afternoon and Viper, although still growing, was austere. The FARRP was busy, and Bryan's battalion was refueling and rearming as he was being briefed. He recalls being told, "Fly due north, hit the Euphrates River, fly east along the river until you hit the causeway." Bryan remembers instructions to stay north of a now-forgotten east-west grid line while he attacked Iraqi troops attempting to flee across the causeway.

Speed was fast becoming a factor. Everyone seemed to be aware that the war was nearing its end, and no one wanted any more of the Iraqi army to survive intact than could be prevented.

Like Gabram, Bryan had little or no intelligence information. Not knowing what lay ahead, he task-organized his battalion to conduct a battalion attack with a phased sequential rotation (one company fighting, one rearming, and one en route). Bryan led with C Company, followed by B and A Companies at thirty-minute intervals. Bryan worried that the small FARRP at Viper, operated by the 2-17th Cavalry, might prove to be a bottleneck. With the external fuel tanks, fuel would not be a problem. Ammunition, on the other hand, might be the limiting factor.

Attaching himself to Capt. Perry Wiggins's C Company and opting to fly in the front seat of an Apache, Bryan and C Company, 2-229th, took off at 3:00 P.M. on February 27.

Arriving at the causeway, C Company came on-line facing east. Bryan recalls:

The visibility was terrible. The smoke from the oil fires sometimes reduced the visibility to less than seven hundred meters. You could not see with the naked eye. The Apache crewmen were forced to use their FLIRs. Although it was 3:30 in the afternoon, it looked like it was dark. We took several missiles, and we shot an SA-6 that was trying to lock on to us. There were abandoned vehicles everywhere. It was like flying into Hell. It was really eerie. There were fires everywhere. I am one of the few Vietnam guys left, and this was one of the most incredible experiences of my life.

Sometimes we could see Gabram's company on our right flank, [the 2-229th was north of Gabram, not south as Gabram was later told] about three kilometers away and sometimes we couldn't. It looked like he had five Apaches on-line near the causeway. As we came on-line, we had a simultaneous engagement, both companies firing for about two or three minutes, and then Gabram was expended and came off-line.

Charlie Company [C Company, 2-229th] stayed on-line for about another thirty minutes until we were expended. We made contact with B Company [2-229th] who came up and relieved us, and we headed back.

About halfway back I know I should be running into A Company, but I never see them. At the same time I am listening to half a conversation from an Air Force AWACS. I could tell that someone had been shot down. Then I heard the AWACS controller say, "Understand the call sign is Bengal 15," a call sign belonging to CWO4 Phil Garvey, one of my Black Hawk pilots.

Bryan had one of his three UH-60s with him and had left the other two at OB Viper low on gas.

As Bryan neared Viper, he began to hear both sides of the AWACS conversation, only to discover that Garvey had, in fact, been shot down. "At this point I don't know how or why or who had given him the mission."

Landing at Viper, Bryan sought out Garrett to learn what had taken place. Garrett explained that the brigade air force liaison officer (ALO) had heard a request (probably from the AWACS) for an urgent CSAR. Bryan realized that "A Company got tied up in the F-16 mission. After I had left [Cobra for the causeway], they decided to do a CSAR to go pick up the downed F-16 pilot. Two of the A Company birds were detached by brigade headquarters to go with the CSAR," Bryan learned.

After the request had come in from the air force, Garrett called the 2-229th to ask if they had an aircraft available to conduct a CSAR for a downed F-16 pilot and was told yes. Garrett asked if they would go, and in Bryan's words, "It was like asking a Beagle if it wants to go chase a rabbit."

Garvey, an old-time aviator with seventy-five hundred hours in the Black Hawk alone, was told to take off, fly north to the causeway, link up with Bryan, and then attempt to recover the downed F-16 pilot.

Garvey departed Viper at the same time A Company lifted off for the causeway. He requested that Capt. Michael Thome, the A Company commander, provide two Apaches for escort of the CSAR. Thome aborted the deep attack mission on the causeway to escort the Black Hawk.

Contacting the AWACS, Garvey was directed straight to the position where the AWACS believed the F-16 pilot had landed and not via the causeway. Garvey was given a heading and distance (eighteen kilometers) to the downed pilot.

Flying at five feet and 145 knots above the desert floor, Garvey's UH-60 led the Apaches toward their objective. Later it was learned that the Apaches had activated their video cameras, recording both the sound and sights of the entire mission.

Nearing the supposed crash site, the Black Hawk called, "Taking fire! nine o'clock! Taking fire!" This was quickly followed by, "Don't put the rotor in the ground, don't put the rotor in the ground, Phil." Then silence.

At the same time the UH-60 was going down, the two escorting Apaches realized that they were receiving heavy ground fire. One was struck by a 23mm round that went through the left engine nacelle, and another round passed through the fuselage. The second Apache escaped without damage.

"They [the Apaches] were both getting the shit shot out of them from about five different directions, so they turned around and came out of there," Bryan stated.

That evening after carefully debriefing the Apache crews, Bryan learned that eight people were aboard the downed bird but no one was sure of the crash location. With the AWACS guiding the aircraft by radar vectors, no one paid much attention to navigating with a map. Bryan realized that perhaps the only means of finding the downed Black Hawk would be the videotape from the two Apaches.

It was the following evening, February 28, before the videocassette recorders (VCRs) could be located to view the film. The battalion's ground vehicle convoy, with its food, water, and other supplies, road-marched twenty-four hours straight through from AO Cobra to catch up. The video equipment was aboard one of the trucks in the convoy.

The videotapes turned out to have been filmed with the FLIR heads locked straight ahead. They weren't useless, but they made Bryan's task harder. Bryan set his two Apache crews and several other officers down with a map and film and was able to recognize some key terrain features and a couple of highways. The data recorded on the film, direction of flight, and airspeed helped. The only information available from the AWACS was the crash site of the F-16, and Bryan estimated that the pilot of the F-16 had landed thirteen to fifteen kilometers away from his F-16's point of impact. Finally Bryan felt sure that he could find the crash site of his lost Black Hawk. Unfortunately, a new set of problems came into play. The cease-fire had been in effect one full day, and his missing aircraft was on the Iraqi side of the cease-fire line in front of the neighboring 24th Infantry Division. After explaining to General Peay, commander of the 101st, where he believed his missing aircraft to be, Bryan and Capt. Joe Mudd flew to the headquarters of the 24th Division to seek General McCaffrey's permission to attempt a recovery. Without hesitation, McCaffrey gave his approval and offered any assistance they might need, including a tank battalion. Bryan accepted the offer for the tanks, and with that the mission was on.

The recovery task force would consist of five Apaches from B Company plus Bryan's two headquarters UH-60s and two medical evacuation Black Hawks. C Company would provide the backup force, landing on the cease-fire line with engines running and remaining on immediate standby.

With Bryan leading, the recovery team crossed the FLOT at 1:00 P.M., taking thirty minutes to find the crash site, which turned out to be five hundred meters from where their film and map analysis had predicted. The tank battalion from the 24th Infantry Division arrived thirty minutes behind Bryan's Apaches and immediately moved to secure the area surrounding the crash site.

The missing Black Hawk had crashed into an earthen berm pushed up by the Iraqis to afford their vehicles some protection. The aircraft's nose had dug into the soft sand on impact, causing it to flip over and come to rest on its back, two feet from an American-built M109 improved tow vehicle (ITV). Bryan credits the soft berm for there being any survivors.

Five bodies were discovered at the crash site. The pilot, Chief Warrant Officer Four Garvey, and copilot, CWO3 Gary Godfrey, had died instantly, as had all the others. Two bodies, those of Sfc. Daniel Butts, the crew chief, and Sgt. Roger Berlinski, a pathfinder, were found inside the wreckage. The fifth body, that of SSgt. Patbouvier Ortiz, was discovered lying just outside the wreckage.

"The Iraqis had scavenged everything of value in the aircraft but had not bothered the bodies or taken any personal effects except for watches. Wedding rings were still on the bodies." Looking about the deserted site, Bryan believed that "the Iraqis had literally walked off the day before we arrived, leaving all their equipment, including the M109 improved tow vehicle (ITV), stolen from Kuwait."

With the discovery of but five of the bodies known to have been aboard the aircraft, Bryan knew that he had three missing and still unaccounted for. A search of nearby abandoned Iraqi bunkers revealed no more bodies. But Bill Bryan did discover a clue that perhaps the three missing were prisoners. In one of the bunkers, several yards from the crash site, he found a blood chit (see the glossary) belonging to one of the missing crew members. These serially numbered chits were issued to each flight crewman, and with it the owner could be identified. This one belonged to one of the missing crewmen, and Bryan was now reasonably sure that the three missing crewmen were prisoners of the Iraqis.

After spending four hours at the site searching for any clue to the fate of the missing personnel, and after removing sensitive equipment overlooked by the Iraqi scavengers from the UH-60, Bryan ordered his team to load up for the flight back to Viper.

Five days after the search party returned from the crash site, the 2-229th learned that their three missing comrades were POWs and would soon be released. The captured crew chief, SSgt. Daniel Stamaris, suffered a severe break in one leg and came close to losing it. The second pathfinder on board was Sgt. Troy Dunlap. He had been thrown clear of the aircraft on impact and was uninjured, not even qualified for the Purple Heart. The senior member of the crew, Maj. Rhonda Cornum, the battalion flight surgeon, had a shoulder wound, knee injuries, and two broken arms.

With their return behind friendly lines, the 2-229th's war had ended. Later they were to learn that they had suffered more casualties than any other unit in the 101st. Although not proud of the losses, the 2-229th believes that it more than carried its weight and earned the Valorous Unit Award, which was presented on May 29, 1992. For "School Troops" they had done one hell of a job.

Chapter Twelve

THE VICTORY DIVISION WINS ANOTHER

During the 24th Division's lightninglike 150-kilometer slash across southern Iraq to the banks of the Euphrates River, the Vipers' Apaches operated around the clock in support of the division's ground maneuver forces. Like the infantrymen, tank crewmen, and artillerymen, Apache pilots and crews put aside personal comfort and hygiene and drove themselves and their equipment toward the division's objectives.

One of those Apache crewmen was CWO2 Adam Heinicke. He had enlisted in the army from San Diego, California, in 1987, coming in under a program entitled High School to Flight School, which was popular with youngsters wanting to learn to fly. Heinicke's interest in flying had begun years earlier, and he had earned his private pilot's license by age seventeen. Fascinated with helicopters and hearing of the army's helicopter flight program, Heinicke enlisted in the army and graduated from Fort Rucker in September 1988. He remained at Rucker to attend "graduate school" and became an Apache pilot, one of the first warrant officer ones to do so.

Reporting to 1-24th Aviation in February 1989, Heinicke was disappointed to discover that the unit was still Cobra equipped, but he knew that it would convert to Apaches within six months. In July 1989, the 1-24th deployed to the Apache training brigade at Fort Hood. For a charged-up young aviator, the six-month wait for Apaches was a long

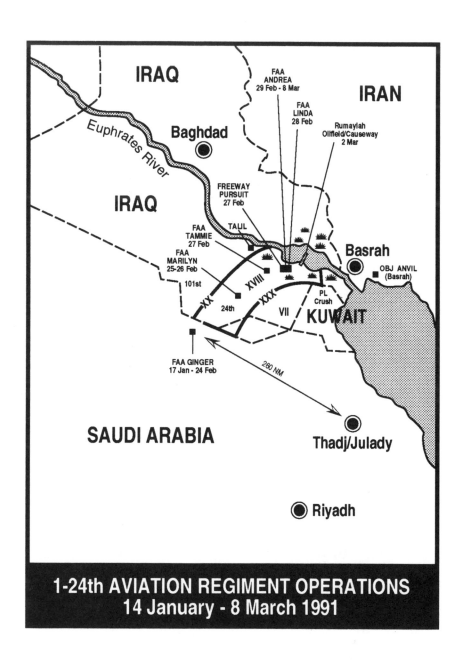

**1-24th AVIATION REGIMENT OPERATIONS
14 January - 8 March 1991**

time. In fact, it was almost a year after graduating from Rucker before Heinicke would again fly an Apache. "A long, almost unbearable wait," he recalls.

Sometime during their stay at Fort Hood, Heinicke's unit, C Company, 1-24th, nicknamed itself the Outcasts. Heinicke reasons, "We're a tight company. We work hard, party hard. We have fun." Heinicke knew he had joined a group of special soldiers. As all soldiers feel about their units, Heinicke feels his assignment to C Company was a stroke of luck. In fact, luck played a large role in Heinicke's life in the 1-24th.

While at Fort Hood, Heinicke was paired with CWO3 John Sullivan, a highly qualified aviator. Sullivan, an Apache instructor pilot and instrument examiner, started Heinicke flying in the backseat, an almost unheard-of break for a Wobbly One. "In a unit with a lot of WO1s, he did me a great service. I became a PIC [pilot in command] before anyone else," Heinicke remarked. By the time the 24th Division moved to Operation Desert Shield, Heinicke felt good about his ability to handle the Apache.

The long wait in Saudi Arabia for their aircraft to arrive was disheartening for the 1-24th. All around, others were training and preparing while Heinicke and his company mates made the best of their accommodations in the abandoned cement factory. Heinicke remembers the excitement that swept the company when the aircraft finally arrived. "Now we had something to do besides laying [sic] around in Cement City."

The move to Thadj saw no improvement in living conditions. In fact, they got worse. "Since OR [operational rate] is the body count of the '80s, operating in the desert made life tougher," Heinicke commented.

Two days after the air war began, January 18, C Company found itself moving to the far west of Saudi Arabia, to forward assembly area (FAA) Cheese. They were to use their mobility and firepower to provide security for the growing logistical base and the division's forward tactical operations center (DTOC). "Being at Cheese was entertaining. We were twelve miles from the border," Heinicke recalls. Being in close proximity to the enemy adds melodrama to life.

The aviation brigade of the 24th Infantry Division completed its move west on January 21 and established TAA Ginger. C Company, 1-24th, would remain at Cheese until January 29. In the meantime, on January 23, C Company flew the 1-24th's first combat mission, a recon of an Iraqi border outpost at Nisab. Until the ground war began on

February 24, Heinicke recalls spending most of his time participating in training and preparation for war. The cross-border recon missions at first added new meaning to their being in Saudi, but they too soon became routine.

For the 24th Division, the invasion of Iraq began at 11:00 A.M. on February 24, 1990. Taking a famous saying from World War II, "The shortest way home is through Berlin," the men of 1-24th greeted each other with, "The shortest way home is through Iraq."

One mission historically given to cavalry in a movement to contact is to get well ahead of the main force to locate the enemy before he locates the friendly force. On February 24, 2d Squadron, 4th Cavalry Regiment of the 24th Division, was out front. The mission given to the 1-24th was to find Iraqi forces while keeping itself in position to react quickly to the division's needs and to assist the 2-4th Cavalry to develop any situation that might arise. Much to the disappointment of the Apache crewmen, no calls came that first day.

By dark the battalion was tucked into FAA Marilyn, about midway between the Saudi-Iraqi border and the Euphrates River. That night they experienced the same storm that battered the 1-101st. It was a storm so intense that it came close to seriously damaging the unprotected Apaches. Before the storm had roared down on them, some crews had attempted to put up tents and lean-tos, which were quickly carried away with the arrival of the high winds.

Bob Glover recalls that he spent the night of February 23 (the night before G day) sleeping in his cockpit because of the weather. The night of February 25 was again spent in the front seat, again because of weather. For most of the Americans participating in Desert Storm, this was their first *shamal*.

Memories of the night of the twenty-fifth remain fresh in Bob Glover's mind.

We caught up to the company about halfway to the Euphrates Valley at FAA Marilyn. Right about dark, the wind picked up and the clouds rolled in. We had forty to fifty knots' sustained winds all night. By 9:00 or 10:00 P.M. it was blowing so hard you could hardly walk in it. I am thoroughly convinced that if we hadn't had those aircraft loaded down with eight hundred pounds of missiles, another thousand pounds of rockets, about twelve hundred pounds of 30mm, plus full bags of gas, if we'd had empty airplanes, they would have probably rolled over. The helicopters rocked and rolled all night long. We also had two boxes of MREs, a five-gallon can of water, each crewman's personal kit bag with extra clothing, two folding cots, one general-purpose small tent [pup tent or GP tiny], and all the aircraft's extra gear on board.

Glover remembers the night of the twenty-fifth for other reasons. Unaware of the storm about to strike, Glover decided that rather than sleeping two nights in an Apache cockpit, he would sleep outside on his cot. Tying his poncho and pup tent together, he draped them over the stabilator of his Apache. He then placed his cot under this Apache-supported tent. Finally Glover tied the poncho-tent rig to the cot. Pleased with this temporary home-away-from-home, Glover lay down just as the wind began to blow. All too soon, he realized that there was no way this rig was going to last in a storm this strong. Loose canvas began to beat him on the head, to the point of pain. The comforts of the cockpit became more appealing. Disassembling his "house," Glover rolled the canvas into a ball and set it on the ground. It was immediately blown away, coming to rest under the front wheel of his aircraft. As he stood to fold his cot, the force of the wind caused it to press firmly against his body and rise with him. Afraid that if the cot got away it might seriously damage a nearby aircraft, Glover sat back down, disassembled the cot while still sitting on it, and stuffed it in his aircraft. Looking back, Glover still does not understand how a wind of such force did not flip the exposed Apaches. The desert winds had no respect for rank. Colonel Burt Tackaberry, commander of the 1-24th Aviation Regiment, watched as his tent collapsed, forcing him to seek shelter in a HMMWV.

The total weight of all the extras aboard the Apaches remains unknown and probably should stay that way. True weight figures might not be well received at the Department of the Army. But during the *shamal,* this weight—the fuel, ammo, and personal gear—may have kept the aircraft upright. Even so, it causes old-time army aviators to wonder whatever happened to weight and balance forms.

February 26 dawned with the weather still bad, but it improved during the early afternoon. Once again the ground forces charged ahead while the Apaches of 1-24th stayed close by on strip alert (aircraft ready to crank with crews nearby). Midafternoon saw the battalion displace to FAA Tammie, arriving at 5:30 P.M. While this move was in progress, 1st Brigade reached the southern edge of the Euphrates River valley and, after a quick pause, continued their attack. The speed of this daring attack confounded the experts.

Arriving in Tammie at about the time 1st Brigade launched its attack (5:30 P.M.), A Company, 1-24th, was ordered to move with the brigade and support it as needed. The tanks and mechanized infantry were moving so fast that when they encountered the enemy, they became entangled in a vehicle-to-vehicle slug match. The 1st Brigade directed A Company's Apaches to support one of its fast-moving battalion task forces. With each unit attempting to contact the task force commander, the volume of radio traffic on the task force's command-and-control frequency made coordination almost impossible. The pace of battle was so fast moving that the task force commander had his hands full keeping track of the location of his ground maneuver units and supporting artillery. Unable to keep an accurate FLOT in the 1st Brigade area, Tom Stewart, commander of the 1-24th, became concerned about a possible fratricide, recalled A Company, and placed it on strip alert at Tammie, where they spent the night.

The third night of the war was much better for the tired flight crews. For most of the aviators it was their first good night's sleep since February 23. But for Glover and Douglas, the night was short.

At 4:00 A.M. they were awakened for guard duty. The division and the 1-24th had moved so far and fast that their convoys with their support personnel and equipment were having a tough time catching up. This lack of support forced the pilots to perform such duties as aircraft maintenance, refueling, and guard duty, which were normally accomplished by the ground crews. With only two Apache crew chiefs at FAA Tammie, the pilots were needed to guard the perimeter.

Glover and Douglas were assigned to a guard post located on the north side of the perimeter. Sitting on the edge of their two-man foxhole wearing night vision goggles, they watched the magnificence of volley after volley of telephone pole–sized rockets from the division's multiple-launched rocket systems (MLRS) climbing into the dark night skies toward the Iraqi air base at Tallil. Glover remembers thinking about the beating the Iraqi aviators were taking that night.

To keep close to divisional operations and to be in position to respond to the division's requirements, Col. Burt Tackaberry joined 1-24th at Tammie. Using the 1-24th command post's communications equipment, Tackaberry directed his brigade's operations through the night.

At 4:00 A.M. on February 27, Tackaberry passed the order that the 1-24th had been waiting for. The division had moved as far north as it would go. Like General Patton during the Battle of the Bulge, General McCaffrey wheeled his division ninety degrees to the right and ordered an attack to the east, toward Basra. The mission was to attack and destroy the fleeing Iraqi Republican Guard. McCaffrey ordered his Apaches to get out front and destroy everything in their path.

An elated Tom Stewart passed the attack mission to his companies with the additional order for them to be prepared to rotate on station, enabling the division's attack to maintain its momentum.

Beginning at 7:00 A.M., the first Apaches, the helicopters of A Company, were airborne. Using Iraqi Highway 8, which ran east-west parallel to the southern bank of the Euphrates, as their axis of advance, the marauding Apaches of the 1-24th sped eastward, destroying everything of military value. By radio, McCaffrey informed Stewart that recent intelligence indicated two Iraqi battalions moving west on the six-lane Highway 8. McCaffrey, whose radio call sign was Victory 6, commented to Stewart, "You are in the right place at the right time." Stewart understood what was to be done.

To the aviators of the 1-24th, February 27 is known as Highway Day, the day they acquired the name Iraqi Highway Patrol. Their mission was to "ticket" everything moving.

B Company relieved A Company around 8:00 A.M. and was task-organized into two teams of three Apaches and one Scout each. One team moved along the north side of the highway and one on the south.

Glover recalls hearing his team being instructed to "get on down the road and destroy anything that looks military." Captain Woods led one team and sent his OH-58C Scout, piloted by CWO2 Patrick "Pat" Donnelly, forward. On board the OH-58 with Donnelly was Sp4 Robert Mullenix, a trained scout observer. Woods positioned two of the Apaches immediately behind the unarmed Scout. Woods rode in the front seat of one of the forward Apaches with CWO2 Samuel "Sammy" Harris in back. The second Apache was piloted by tall and lanky CWO2 Larry

Lundberg. With Lundberg was CWO2 Sean Gilpin. Douglas and Glover were in the third Apache and flew in the trail slot to prevent attack from the rear.

"We went about twenty miles, blowing up anything that got in the way," Glover recalls. At one point three vehicles were found hiding under a highway overpass. Two of the vehicles were large fuel tankers and the third appeared to be a command vehicle. One Hellfire streaked into one of the tankers. "That was the wildest explosion I have ever seen," Glover remembers. "It was great." The three vehicles were totally destroyed as the bridge collapsed on them. Moving on, Glover destroyed an armored personnel carrier with a Hellfire and several trucks with 30mm cannon. Then, about the time to turn for home, the Scout got into trouble.

Suddenly Donnelly reported that the Scout was taking heavy fire from a large number of Iraqi soldiers. Glover and Douglas instantly moved to provide supporting fire with Hellfire and rockets. Seconds after opening fire, their 30mm, which had not failed them all day, jammed. Captain Woods moved to support the vulnerable Scout. While Woods fired his 30mm, Glover fired several multipurpose submunitions (MPSM) rockets. In the confusion, the Scout was able to withdraw. He had experienced several near misses. Now safely out of range, Woods gave a battle handoff to the C Company team arriving to replace them.

Several hours after landing at AA Arlene, Glover's crew chief discovered that his Apache had taken a 12.7mm round in the "turtle back" (service doors behind the rotor mast). The damage was light and was not repaired until after the end of the war. But Glover remembers the queasy feeling he had when the maintenance officer presented him with the spent round. He carries it in his pocket to this day.

Adam Heinicke was with the C Company team when it replaced B Company. Heinicke recalls, "We knew where we were going. We task-organized into two teams of two Apaches and one Scout, with a team on each side of the highway." As Heinicke and Sullivan, his pilot, worked their way east, they heard B Company on the radio talking about being in contact with the enemy.

Tension was increasing the closer we got to B Company. It was almost chaos, not quite, but it was a mess. Seeing so many Iraqis trying to walk home was hard to handle. Our guidance was to leave them alone if they were unarmed and walking north. Carrying a weapon was another case. Armed enemy could be taken under fire. What was really scary was flying past all the fixed antiaircraft gun emplacements, some still manned.

After relieving B Company, Heinicke recalls that keeping their over-eager Scout under control became a chore. "He kept wanting to get a thousand meters out in front, and I'd have to hammer him by radio and order him back."

Moving along the flanks of Highway 8, the C Company Apaches found themselves in the midst of a smorgasbord of Iraqi targets. "As we ran into moving vehicles, we took them out," Heinicke recalls. "There were tanks and tank carriers, and trucks full of equipment everywhere." At about the same place the B Company Scout had gotten into trouble, Heinicke and his team came upon an area full of troops, vehicles, and antiaircraft guns. They approached cautiously. It had begun to rain, reducing visibility. Not wanting to take undue risk, Heinicke moved his wingman up into firing position, and together the two Apaches opened fire with Hellfire missiles and MPSM rockets.

"It was my first exposure to MPSM. They are impressive. There were guys running around until the MPSM landed; then there was no one else running around."

Reacting to an Iraqi mortar round that landed between the two Apaches, they moved to a new position. Almost as soon as they arrived in their new location, they were engaged by an Iraqi surface-to-air missile. Heinicke saw the missile's smoke trail right above his cockpit. "That caused me to have a lot more faith in the 144 [ALQ-144 infrared jammer]," he stated.

While Heinicke's team was busy on the north side of the highway, their companion team on the south side was also busy. One of the Apaches, piloted by CWO2 John Lenander, took hits in the tail rotor and one engine. Indications from the aircraft's instruments revealed that the damage required immediate precautions. Lenander pointed his damaged aircraft westward, and after reaching the safety of the lead elements of the division's advancing troops, he landed to check the aircraft.

A Company relieved C Company on station, and Heinicke recalls that during the return to FAA Ginger,

> We were kind of high on the tempo of events. Once again we were flying over all those guys walking home. Some would wave at you and some were too dejected. I didn't have a good feeling flying over them. I was flying trail [last in formation]. We flew over a couple of guys, and as we flew over them, I was thinking there is something wrong with this picture. A couple had guns.

The Apache to Heinicke's front warned of the armed Iraqis and turned hard left. Heinicke saw one Iraqi drop to his knees and raise his weapon to fire. Heinicke turned his aircraft to avoid overflying the Iraqis. He recalls, "We took those guys out with the 30mm. It's a hard thing to handle when you see it that close. Nobody is made for that. I had trouble handling that for a couple days. That was too up close and personal." This was not an unexpected reaction for a young soldier in his first close-in combat.

A word about logistics. Just as combat elements are placed in formations for attacking the enemy, the logistic elements of each unit are placed into "trains," formations for supporting the combat elements.

Prudent commanders attempt to keep their trains as close to the combat elements as safety permits. By doctrine trains follow along two terrain features behind the combat elements, ready to move forward to resupply or repair whenever the battle tempo allows. The two-terrain-feature concept is used to allow the trains to remain out of sight of the enemy.

The deserts of Saudi Arabia and Iraq raised new problems for unit trains. First, the terrain failed to offer much in the way of recognizable terrain features suitable for concealing vehicles. Therefore trains were positioned to remain out of range of enemy weapons. Second, desert warfare often is conducted at speeds not seen in other regions of the world. Desert Storm saw combat units moving distances not seen since the closing days of World War II. The heavily ladened logistics vehicles found themselves constantly trying to catch up to the fighting elements of their units.

To facilitate the 1-24th's move westward to its forward assembly area prior to G day, Tom Stewart created Task Force (TF) John, which consisted of seventy-two personnel and twenty-six vehicles. Task Force John was tailored to move fast and provide essential resupply—fuel, ammunition, food, water, mechanics, and parts—to the battalion's forward elements. The remainder of the trains would travel in their normal places with brigade trains.

On February 24, G day, TF John moved ahead of the battalion's combat elements but behind the division's ground combat forces, to establish FAA Marilyn inside Iraq. Marilyn was occupied by 3:00 A.M. on February 25. However, the battalion's aircraft remained at FAA Ginger most of G day, moving to Marilyn at 10:30 A.M. on the twenty-fifth. That evening, winds in excess of fifty knots forced cancellation of aircraft missions until after 3:00 A.M. on February 26.

At 11:45 A.M. TF John was again sent well forward, this time to establish FAA Tammie. In the meantime the remainder of the battalion's logistic vehicles, the battalion trains, remained miles to the rear but moving as fast as they could to catch up. The aircraft and TF John arrived at Tammie together and spent the night preparing for operations the following day.

While the battalion aircraft fought their way along Highway 8, on February 27, the battalion trains moved overland toward FAA Tammie, arriving at noon, just in time to stretch their legs, refuel their vehicles, and move out to FAA Arlene in the Euphrates River valley.

The site selected for FAA Arlene proved to be a former stronghold of an Iraqi airborne division. It was best described as a mess. Abandoned and wrecked equipment was strewn everywhere. Tired, hungry, and dejected Iraqi soldiers sat idly watching the aircraft conduct their recon. None showed any inclination to resist.

The battalion trains began arriving at FAA Arlene around midnight, followed by TF John at 1:40 A.M. on February 28. For the soldiers riding in the trains' vehicles, it had been an emotional journey. They had spent much of their time driving past disarmed and dejected Iraqi soldiers with neither food nor water. Sympathetic to the plight of fellow soldiers, the men of the 1-24th gave food and water to their vanquished opponents.

Shortly after its arrival at FAA Arlene, TF John was dispatched farther east to establish FAA Linda and did so by 7:00 A.M. The battalion had been alerted to be prepared to support the division's eastward push toward the city of Basra, pleasing the soldiers of the battalion who were anxious to carry the war into Iraq's second largest city. It was not to be.

At 8:00 A.M. on February 28, 1991, Stewart was handed a message declaring an immediate cease-fire, and the fighting ended. It was a bittersweet message. For some, it came too soon. The devastation brought about by Saddam Hussein's barbarous invasion of Kuwait caused some to wish for a chance to repay Iraq with interest. To those of calmer spirit, it came as a blessing. The war was over and Allied losses had been light. Now, all that the men of the 1-24th wanted was to go home and get clean, fast.

Later that afternoon, at 3:00 P.M., the 1-24th moved again and established AA Viper, close to the 24th Aviation Brigade's headquarters. For the first time since February 24, the entire battalion was together.

At 7:30 A.M. on March 2, almost three days after the cease-fire became effective, reports began coming in announcing that an Iraqi armored column was moving west toward FAA Linda. Stewart ordered C Company to get airborne and verify or discount the report. About the time that C Company lifted off, Iraqi artillery began shelling the 1st Brigade. C Company found nothing moving toward FAA Linda and was ordered to return. Counterbattery fire from 24th Division Artillery soon stopped the Iraqi shelling. Quiet returned.

The Vipers were glad to be together again. For the last day and a half, the convoys had been slowed by the carnage left by the Apaches and the division's armored forces. Day and night, the convoys were forced to slowly pick their way east through the destruction littering Highway 8. By the time they arrived in Viper, these young soldiers understood the destructive power of their modern weaponry.

What Glover remembers most about the early hours of the cease-fire was having the opportunity to tend to three long days of neglected personal hygiene. A bath and shave made him feel better, almost young again. Being deep in enemy territory, no one was allowed to relax completely, but with guards posted, much-needed sleep was actively pursued. Even in this damnable desert, soldiers worked to bring life back to pre–G day conditions. Unfortunately, the serenity brought by the cease-fire was not to last. The next day, March 2, with little warning, danger rumbled down the road from the east. The order to saddle up rang across FOB Viper.

The second day of the so-far-unilateral cease-fire started with the promise of good things. Rumors, the constant companion of soldiers, spoke of starting for the ports in Saudi Arabia. These rumors allowed soldiers to make the next leap in logic: ports equal ships, and ships mean travel, and travel means—home?

For most of the still-fleeing Iraqi army, Basra offered their best chance of escape. However, the air force had earlier destroyed the bridges across the Euphrates in Basra, forcing the Iraqi troops to turn west and up Highway 8.

A few miles west of Basra the Euphrates River appears to be marshy; in places the river widens, forming lakelike areas. Located in the vicinity of the village of Shaibah are the Rumayalah oil field facilities, built into the marsh on a man-made causeway. A road leading north from Highway 8 traverses the causeway and crosses the Euphrates by bridge. From there the road leads north to Baghdad, making it an ideal escape route for the Iraqi soldiers deflected by broken bridges in Basra.

For the 24th Infantry Division, March 2 began early and with great excitement. By 7:30 A.M. divisional radio traffic spoke of enemy forces moving toward the 1st Brigade, in apparently deliberate violation of the cease-fire. Acting on orders from Brig. Gen. James T. Scott, Tackaberry ordered the air cavalry troops of the 2-4th Cavalry to the north end of the causeway. Hearing Tackaberry's order to the cavalry, Stewart alerted his companies for action.

The 1-24th flight crews, assisted by their long-missed crew chiefs, began readying aircraft. The news that 1st Brigade had been taken under fire caused Tom Stewart to take off immediately in his Black Hawk command-and-control helicopter. Stewart flew to the 1st Brigade's area to offer the assistance of his AH-64 Apaches if they were needed. Anticipating acceptance of his offer, Stewart ordered his A Company into the air and to a holding area convenient to 1st Brigade. Company A arrived in their assigned holding area by 8:15 A.M.

Bob Glover was eating breakfast when he heard the A Company aircraft beginning to crank. The speed of A Company's departure told Glover and the rest of the battalion that something serious was in the offing. With A Company still in sight, news reached the other companies that they were now on alert.

Everyone laid aside their unfinished breakfasts and started for their aircraft. Glover recalls a moment of humor during this unexpected emergency. Chief Warrant Officer Two Steve Morris, normally an easygoing, pleasant man, always felt a great need for breakfast. However, if circumstances prevented Morris from having his morning meal, his mood was less than pleasant the rest of the day. With the announcement to man their aircraft, Morris let go a stream of profanity about people who denied others breakfast. Cursing and grumbling, he picked up his flight equipment and stalked toward his Apache, strapping on equipment as he went.

Pilots were briefed alongside their planes. Crews rushed to get protective covers off the aircraft and complete preflight inspections. Bob Glover's crew chief, Sgt. Eric Peterson, had arrived first and began helping the crew with their preflight inspection and engine start-up.

Reports said that an Iraqi convoy of tanks and other vehicles was headed west on Highway 8 and was turning north to cross the Euphrates via the causeway. With that news, B Company took off. Once in the air, 1-24th aircraft switched to the 1st Brigade radio frequency (also called freq, push, or net). "We heard that what was left of an Iraqi division coming out of Kuwait was trying to escape via the causeway," Glover recalls.

Air force fighter-bombers had earlier destroyed the bridge across the river at the causeway. With the air force observing the cease-fire, Iraqi engineers had constructed a crude bypass, and some vehicles were already across. Scouts and AH-1S Cobras from 2-4th Cavalry occupied blocking positions north of the causeway and killed the lead vehicles with well-placed TOW missiles. The cav's first TOW hit was a lucky shot: The lead vehicle turned out to be an ammunition truck, which continued to explode for several minutes, effectively blocking the route to the rest of the one-hundred-plus-vehicle Iraqi convoy.

After making a personal reconnaissance, Stewart ordered A Company to a holding position to the northwest of the causeway out over the Euphrates marsh. The 1st Brigade was using artillery against the Iraqis until the Apaches arrived. Once the Apaches appeared overhead, 1st Brigade lifted the artillery. Stewart then ordered A Company to attack targets north of the QU 90 grid line while ground elements of the 1st Brigade attacked targets south of the QU 90 grid line.

A Company's first strike hit a large fuel tanker fleeing north. With one thirty-five-hundred-foot Hellfire shot, the tanker stopped fleeing, and the subsequent fire made it difficult for the Iraqis to pass the flaming truck. With the northern end of the causeway effectively blocked, A Company systematically worked its way along the stalled column of enemy vehicles. At first, the desperate Iraqis returned fire, but they quickly recognized the futility of confronting the lethal Apaches. Most abandoned their vehicles and weapons and fled north on foot.

At 10:15 A.M. A Company was relieved by B Company, and by 10:40 all the enemy vehicles in the 1-24th's share of the target area had been destroyed. Glover remembers:

> We had no opposition. None. We sat out at four to five kilometers and just lobbed missile after missile, and nobody even thought about firing back. It was unreal. We were far enough away that they probably never saw us or where the missiles were coming from. All their tanks were lined up pointed north toward Baghdad. They never tried to get off the road, to take defensive positions. They were just trying to get out and made the unfortunate mistake of firing up the lead elements of the division [the U.S. 24th], and the division commander got ticked off, and it was wild.

Early in the battle Tom Stewart remembers overflying a large formation of Iraqi soldiers standing in ranks, at attention, with white flags in front of each platoon. Stewart flew over the same group near the end of the battle and it appeared that not an Iraqi had moved. At 11:00 A.M., C Company arrived on station to relieve B Company, but they were too late; the fight for the causeway was over. Tanks and infantry from 1st Brigade swept the smoking battlefield, destroying what was left untouched and rounding up prisoners.

But even this late, C Company would get lucky. At first they were ordered to land and remain on standby. Shortly after noon, reports filtered in of additional Iraqi forces moving toward the division. At 1:00 P.M., C Company launched a team of three Apaches and one Scout to move to the south side of Rumayalah and recon to the east. Arriving in the designated area, the C Company team located several T72 tanks with crews aboard. Clearance to engage was slow in coming, but finally the T72s were destroyed by Hellfires. A second C Company team replaced the first team. The new team continued discovering and engaging deployed tanks, Roland antiaircraft vehicles, and tanks either neatly hidden or in the process of being hidden. By this time no sign of an organized reinforcement of the causeway could be identified. For the Iraqi soldiers it had become a war of "each man for himself."

By 3:00 P.M. the Battle of the Causeway was over. For the 1-24th, so was the war. The battle damage assessment shows the total vehicles destroyed by the 1-24th and the 1st Brigade to be 32 T72 tanks, 49

BMPs, 37 trucks, 1 jeep, 6 FROG missile launchers, and 9 other types of enemy vehicles. The Apaches of 1-24th were credited with 69 of this 134 total. This number, of course, fails to reflect all kills. A Hellfire impacting on a vehicle fully loaded with fuel and ammunition explodes with such force that it leaves a shallow crater and no sign the vehicle ever existed. These graphic examples of the level of Apache lethality caught the attention of military leaders everywhere, and for some, they raise the question of whether or not Apache can dominate future battlefields. The Apache's success reinforces the position of those who no longer believe in the need for armored vehicles. However, these people fail to remember that in many other types of terrain, attack helicopters have limitations. The power and violence that armor brings to the battlefield are still required to seize and hold ground. In truth, modern warfare demands both.

As quiet returned to the battlefield, the Hammurabi Division of the Iraqi Republican Guard and remnants of several other Iraqi divisions had been, for all intents and purposes, deactivated on the Hammar Causeway effective at 3 P.M. on March 2, 1991.

March 3 was a day of recovery. The 24th Infantry Division had covered in excess of three hundred miles in thirty-six hours. According to Lt. Gen. Gary Luck, commanding general of XVIII Corps, the 24th Division's slashing drive across southern Iraq to the Euphrates and then east to Rumayalah had blocked the Iraqis' chance of escape from Kuwait. Later, General Schwarzkopf used the threat of further drives by the 24th and others in his formal cease-fire negotiations with the Iraqis. Iraqi negotiators caught the point of Schwarzkopf's threats and accepted the terms offered by the United Nations. The world breathed a sigh of thanksgiving. Within days of the formal cease-fire, advanced parties from U.S. and other UN forces began moving to Saudi airfields for their trip home. Not far behind the advanced parties, the remainder of the largest armored armada since 1943, perhaps ever, and certainly the largest ever to fight under the UN flag, reversed course and began withdrawing. Within weeks the ports and airfields of Saudi Arabia were again teeming with soldiers, this time with men and equipment who were homeward bound. And the soldiers' thoughts turned to home and loved ones and gave them energy to get everything in order and ready to move when their turn came. No one wanted to be the last to leave.

So it ended, this war in the desert. Over the years historians will pore over the reams of documents seeking to explain why Desert Storm occurred, what worked, and what didn't. Each military service will study and record lessons learned. In all the postwar analyses, factions will try to ensure that their piece of turf is portrayed in a favorable light. Prewar skeptics of this or that system will strive to prove that they had been correct all along, some with justification and others without. But one thing is certain: In Desert Storm, Apache exceeded everyone's expectations. Under the worst of conditions, America's high-tech equipment worked. And more importantly, the sense of duty, the loyalty, and the dedication of the American soldier also exceeded everyone's expectations. From the inception of the all-volunteer force, naysayers have insisted that it would not work and that it surely would not fight. Desert Storm proved them wrong. The soldiers of Desert Storm won the right for Americans to be proud . . . again.

Epilogue

Older men declare war.
But it is youth that must fight and die.

Herbert Hoover

For the soldiers of the Allied forces, the victory celebrations following the cease-fire were reserved. Deep in Iraq there was little with which
to toast the uneasy peace. In fact, snoring may have been the most
conspicuous sound to greet the news that the war had ended. In forward bases deep in the Euphrates River valley, the shortage of alco-
holic beverages limited those who might have been moved to celebrate
in the usual American style. No longer taken up exclusively by war,
soldiers' thoughts, regardless of nationality, automatically flashed home.
For young Americans, their duty done, it was time to "sky up," and
strap on a freedom bird headed for the good ole U S of A. Unfortunately, it would not be that simple. It took months to recover Allied
forces from Operation Desert Storm. In fact, this great event has taught
us the need to keep some troops permanently in Kuwait and Saudi Arabia.

For others, the end meant disappointment. Soldiers from North
Carolina's Apache-equipped Army National Guard 1st Battalion, 130th
Aviation Regiment, were mobilized and sent to Fort Hood for refresher
training and deployment to Saudi Arabia. Within days of their arrival
in central Texas, the Tar Heels of the 1-130th were designated combat ready and deployable. If needed, other National Guard Apache
battalions, one each from South Carolina and Florida, were slated to
follow the 1-130th. The abrupt cessation of hostilities ended deploy-

ment preparations for the guardsmen. However, other reserve component personnel did deploy and serve. Many were still at work long after their active-duty brothers and sisters had returned home. Some died. To help in the back-hauling of millions of tons of supplies and equipment from Saudi Arabia, troops other than those who fought were rotated in and out of Saudi Arabia at set intervals.

Units that had engaged in the fighting were shipped home as fast as possible. Even so, for those waiting to leave, the process seemed slow and painstaking.

First, the units had to retrace their tracks, making long, dusty road marches across the deserts of Iraq to Saudi Arabia. Once in Saudi Arabia, American soldiers spent seemingly endless days cleansing each piece of equipment to the satisfaction of members of the United States Department of Agriculture, known to the troops as "pencil-necked geeks." They had been flown in to inspect every item being returned to the United States. It took the 1-24th eight days before the "gentlemen" from the Department of Agriculture approved their equipment for shipment. The 1-24th's after-action report states:

> We braved the heat, the cold, the enemy and the desert storms with little to no problem; yet, the Department of Agriculture Inspectors . . . brought us to our knees.

In any case, the time spent cleaning really did not matter to these combat veterans. There was a huge, slow-moving queue in the ports. Mercifully, those in charge recognized the waste in time, manpower, and money, and arranged transportation so that once a unit's equipment passed inspection, passenger aircraft were waiting to take the soldiers home. If the wait for ships was to be long, it was better for the morale of both the soldiers and their families for them to wait at home.

These returning soldiers, unlike those who had come home from Vietnam to be greeted by catcalls and spit, were welcomed by a grateful nation, which was prepared to express its heartfelt thanks. With the activation of members of the National Guard and reserves, most regions of the nation found that they had a personal stake in this endeavor. The use of the reserves had forced most of the country to buy in to Desert Storm.

Romans reminded their returning heroes that glory was fleeting. In time, the men and women of Desert Storm also discovered this to be true and found themselves once again preparing for possible crises. With the arrival of its equipment, the army returned to preparation for war. Normal training resumed. Maintenance of equipment and all the other mundane requirements of stateside life moved to the forefront once again.

By late May 1992, large training exercises were back in full swing. Elements of the XVIII Airborne Corps, including Apaches from the 1-24th, were again loaded aboard ships in Savannah harbor, but this time they were sent to the beaches of North Carolina. This was an exercise involving army, navy, Marine Corps, and air force players. The training scenario called for a joint force to invade a theoretical country overrun by a ruthless neighbor. The scenario had a familiar ring to it.

During the night of July 22, 1992, a reinforced brigade of the 101st Airborne Division (Air Assault), six thousand men and women strong, arrived at the Marine Corps Air Station (MCAS) in Beaufort, South Carolina. Around the clock for two days and nights, C-5s and C-141s landed, disgorged their cargos of soldiers and equipment, and took off again to gather the next load.

Among the first to arrive at MCAS Beaufort were the veteran crews and tank-killing Apaches of the 1-101st, veterans of the Iraqi deserts. Exercise Sand Eagle was another joint exercise requiring the expulsion of an invading aggressor from an overrun, but this time fictitious, friendly nation. It, too, evoked memories of Desert Storm. Nearby Fort Stewart, Georgia, was the site for this exercise. In the sprawling tent city erected to temporarily house the troopers of the 101st, Lt. Tom Drew, the competent and adventurous young lieutenant selected to lead White Team during the raid into Iraq by TF Normandy, was busy in the battalion operations center. Drew's soldierly appearance would have made him an ideal candidate for a recruiting poster. But his experience made him too important for just posing. After returning from Desert Storm, he became the battalion's intelligence officer (S-2).

Exercise plans called for paratroopers from the 82d Airborne Division to jump in and be quickly reinforced by troopers from the 101st. When the troopers of the 82d and 101st arrived in the operations area, they would discover soldiers from the 10th Infantry Division, some of whom would later serve in Somalia, already on the ground there, playing the role of occupying aggressor forces.

A few tents away from Drew's operations center, Tim Vincent, another TF Normandy veteran, newly promoted to chief warrant officer two, tried to rest for the long night ahead. Row upon row of general-purpose (medium) tents, erected on the grassy areas adjacent to the runways, were filled with cots and soldiers trying to rest. The intense heat precluded sleep. Noise from departing marine jets interrupted conversation as well as rest. Again, shades of Desert Storm.

MCAS Beaufort's spacious aircraft parking ramps were crowded with CH-47D Chinooks, UH-60 Black Hawks, and Apaches, all in various stages of reassembly or being towed from the congestion of the ramps for test flights.

On the ramp, SSgt. Bobby Gunter was busy. A large man, Gunter was not reluctant to add his strength to the tasks at hand. His brawn and experience made the reassembly process go quickly. Like Drew, Gunter would make a fine recruiting poster. His stern gaze spoke of competence, strength, and professionalism, and like all good NCOs, Gunter turned everything into a learning experience for younger soldiers in his care.

The Apaches, both at Hunter with the 1-24th and at Fort Campbell with the 1-101st, veterans of the war against Iraq, are little changed since their return. Those that were battle damaged have been repaired and are operational. Crew members point out how and where their Apaches took punishment and how they brought them safely home. Listening carefully, one can sense that the men feel real affection for the machines. Unfortunately, all too soon the army's ever-fluid personnel system will cause that to end. After all, in the army, the most consistent thing is change. Some of the old hands are already gone.

Dick Cody relinquished command of the 1-101st soon after returning to Fort Campbell. He has been selected for promotion to colonel and is finishing studies at the Army War College. For their daring raid on the Iraqi radar sites, members of the 1-101st received individual awards.

On June 4, 1992, in one of the large, hot hangars at Hunter Army Airfield, Tom Stewart passed the colors of his much-loved 1-24th to his successor. Having completed the Naval War College at Newport, Rhode Island, Stewart is responsible for assigning all the army's aviators.

He departed the 24th Division pleased to know that the 1-24th received the Valorous Unit Award for its operations in Iraq. Likewise, at Fort Rucker, Bill Bryan reluctantly passed the colors of the 2-229th to his replacement. He was proud that the 2-229th received the Valorous Unit Award for its service during Desert Storm. Bryan remained at Fort Rucker to become the director of Training and Doctrine for the Aviation Center.

Historically combat has been the best means to test men and material. Desert Storm was no exception. As the result of Apache's experiences in the desert, certain shortcomings were discovered.

Critical for future employment is the need for an on-board, satellite driven, global positioning system (GPS), a fix already underway. Of equal importance is Apache's need to be able to communicate over long distances while flying nap of the earth.

Rotor blades will be enhanced to further reduce noise and lessen sand erosion along their leading edges. The already improved 30mm feed chute system, a fix coming from experience gained in Panama, will continue to replace faulty feed chutes in early Apaches.

As new technologies become available, they must be considered and, if found useful, be incorporated into Apache. Several programs in progress will greatly enhance the Apache. If Congress approves, 227 AH-64As will be rebuilt and equipped with the Longbow radar system. Once completed, these Apaches will be redesignated as AH-64Ds. The first Longbow prototype flew on April 15, 1992.

The Longbow-equipped AH-1D consists of a fire control radar (FCR) targeting system most noticeable by a dome positioned above the main rotor. This system, scanning 360 degrees around the aircraft, will increase the range at which Apache can detect, classify, prioritize, engage, and destroy multiple enemy targets, ground and air. Information gathered by the FCR is automatically and instantaneously sent to the Longbow-compatible Hellfire. It will fire the new fire-and-forget Hellfire equipped with a radio-frequency seeker or the air-to-air Stinger. All of this allows AH-1D to reduce its exposure time to enemy fire. It improves the Apache's day-night, all-weather capability. Imagine the effect of one AH-1D being able to engage an enemy armored formation by ripple-firing sixteen fire-and-forget Hellfire missiles without ever being seen by the enemy. By using data burst transmissions, Longbow can transmit all the information it has gathered to army, air force, and navy command centers. If asked, the Longbow FCR is capable of designating specific areas as no-fire zones, reducing the chance of fratricide. The FCR's air-to-air system contains an air targeting mode (ATM). The ATM provides 360-degree coverage against possible air threats and allows the AH-64D to engage enemy aircraft with the air-to-air Stinger missile.

Enhanced AH-1D Longbow-equipped Apache survivability is made possible by the improved onboard computer. Crews are able to load battlefield overlays, safe routes, radio frequencies of other units, and much more information into the aircraft computer by means of a data transfer cartridge. This information allows for increased battlefield awareness by the crew. It allows the pilot to fly a route displayed on the screen using the FCR in the terrain profile mode to avoid dangerous terrain. AH-1D survivability is further improved by the incorporation of radio frequency warning and radio direction-finding equipment, allowing the crew to pinpoint and engage enemy radio transmitters.

Needless to say, all this increase in capability does not come without a price. The additional weight of Longbow and other improvements requires the power output of the engine to be upgraded.

Other Apaches, to be designated the AH-64C, will receive less expensive improvements. This version will not have Longbow but will be able to receive input from Longbow-equipped AH-64Ds, display the information, and engage targets with the same fire-and-forget lethality as the D model.

Nevertheless, Apache is but a metal object. It takes the likes of Tom Drew, Tim Vincent, Bob Glover, and the thousands of soldiers who service and maintain Apache to bring it to life. Even with Apache's planned improvements, the United States must find, train, and support the magnificent young soldiers who are so willing to "strap on Apache" and ride it into battle.

One reason for the United States' unquestioned success during Desert Storm was its willingness to pay the price of conducting research and development to keep the soldiers equipped with the best weapons available. The performance of U.S. equipment against forces manning the latest Soviet weaponry was beyond everyone's expectations. As the events of Desert Storm unfolded, the world stood in awe of American technology. Many countries have subsequently placed orders for the technological stars of Desert Storm. But maintaining such a lead requires a continued search for improvement.

Congress seems willing to pay the price to ensure fortunately, that our soldiers will continue to have superior equipment. Currently Apache's replacement is beginning to take shape. The RAH-66 Comanche will enter service several years from now with state-of-the-art technology. It will be a significant improvement over Apache. In fact, Comanche will have the necessary systems to be both a scout and an attack helicopter, and it will have considerably enhanced survivability. Other new systems, both ground and air, are currently on the drawing board or in mock-up stage. It seems we have finally begun to understand that the world is indeed a dangerous place and likely to remain so for the foreseeable future. In the words of Flavius Renatus Vegetius, "Let him who desires peace prepare for war." As a nation we owe that to our sons and daughters who will have to fight our future wars.

NOTES

Chapter Three. In the Beginning

1. Jonathan M. House, *Towards Combined Arms Warfare: A Survey of 20th Century Tactics, Doctrine, and Organization* (Fort Leavenworth, Kans.: Combat Studies Institute, U.S. Army Command and General Staff College, 1984), 77.

2. William E. Butterworth, *Flying Army: The Modern Air Arm of the U.S. Army* (Garden City, N.Y.: Doubleday and Company, Inc., 1971), 78.

Chapter Four. Damned If You Do and Damned If You Don't

1. House, *Towards Combined Arms Warfare*, 47.

2. Ibid., 131.

3. Ibid.

4. Butterworth, *Flying Army*, 35.

5. Richard P. Weinert, Jr., *A History of Army Aviation—1950–1962* (Fort Monroe, Va.: Office of the Command Historian, Headquarters, U.S. Army Training and Doctrine Command, 1991), 4.

6. "Forty Years of Army Aviation: Part 2, Building a Training Program," *U.S. Army Aviation Digest*, July 1982.

7. Edward M. Flanagan, Jr., *The Angels: A History of the 11th Airborne Division* (Novato, Calif.: Presidio Press, 1989), 120–24, 126, 130–31.

8. James M. Gavin, *War and Peace in the Space Age* (New York: Harper and Brothers, Publishers, 1958), 121.

9. Key West Agreement, April 21, 1948.

10. Weinert, *History of Army Aviation*, 10.

11. Ibid., 39.

12. Gavin, *War and Peace in the Space Age*, 110.

Chapter Five. Growing Up . . . Again

1. William D. Ellis, *Clarke of St. Vith* (Cleveland: Dillon-Liederbach, 1974), 195.

2. Richard S. Tipton, *They Filled the Skies* (Fort Worth, Tex.: Bell Helicopter Company, 1983), 1.

3. Ellis, *Clarke of St. Vith*, 195–96.

4. "Forty Years of Army Aviation."

5. Ibid., 32.

6. Weinert, *History of Army Aviation,* 19.

7. Ibid., 159.

Chapter Six. Clear and Untied . . . Blades Are Comin' Through
Information contained in chapter six was derived from personal experiences of the author, colleagues, interviews with participants, private and government documents, and from Kenneth Peoples, *Bell AH-1 Cobra Variants.* Aerofax Datagraph 4. Arlington, Texas: Aerofax, 1988.

1. Weinert, *History of Army Aviation,* 118.

2. Ibid., 119.

3. Charles E. Canedy, interview with the author, April 1992.

4. "Armed Helicopters Around the World," *U.S. Army Aviation Digest,* September 1971.

5. Ibid.

6. John R. Burden, Sr., Cheyenne test pilot, interviews with the author, 1991–92.

7. Report, Air Cavalry Troop Evaluation, Headquarters, U.S. Army, Europe, and Seventh Army, September 15, 1970; and Preliminary USAREUR Report, Joint Attack Helicopter Instrumented Evaluation, July 3, 1972.

8. Ibid.

9. Engineering Evaluation, AH-56A Compound Helicopter with Advanced Mechanical Control System, Final Report, U.S. Army Aviation Systems Test Activity, Edwards Air Force Base, Calif., March 1973, 17.

10. Report, Air Cavalry Troop Evaluation, and Preliminary USAREUR Report.

11. Nick J. Primis, International Division, Bell Helicopter, interviews with the author, 1991–93.

Chapter Seven. Birth of a Brave
Information contained in chapter seven was derived from personal experiences of the author, colleagues, interviews with participants, private and government documents, and from the ARCO Military Book *AH-64,* Modern Fighting Aircraft (series) vol. 12. New York: Prentice Hall, 1987.

1. James R. Hill, former division chief, Armor Agency, Fort Knox, Ky., interviews with the author, hereafter referred to as Hill interviews.

2. Ibid.

3. John R. Burden, Sr., deputy test director, Operational Test II, TOW Cobra, interviews with the author, 1991–93.

4. Nick J. Primis, interviews with the author, 1991–93.

5. Samuel G. Cockerham, After-action Report by the Advanced Attack Helicopter Program Manager, April 15, 1973–May 31, 1976.

6. Hill interviews.

7. Cockerham, After-action Report.

8. Ibid.

9. Edward M. Browne, Advanced Attack Helicopter Program Manager, April 1976–December 1982, interviews with the author, 1991–92.

10. Cockerham, After-action Report.

11. Browne, interview.

Chapter Ten. The Eagle's Talons

1. William H. Bryan, written comments to the author, June 1992.

2. Ibid.

Glossary

AAH   Advanced attack helicopter.

ADEN/DEFA   Type of round developed by British and French and adapted to Apache's 30mm cannon.

Aerodynamic doghouse   Streamlined cowling enclosing most of the main rotor mast and push-pull tubes. Designed to reduce drag, thereby increasing speed and fuel efficiency.

All-American   Moniker for the 82d Airborne Division. Their red, white, and blue shoulder patch carries *AA* in its center.

ANVIS-6   Night vision goggles that depend on ambient light.

ARTEP   Army training and evaluation program. Sets unit training standards and how to evaluate.

ATM   The army aircrew training manual; also, air targeting mode.

AWACS   Air force airborne warning and control system.

Blood chit   An 8½- by 11-inch paper printed in several languages, promising a reward if the bearer is returned to American control.

BMP   Soviet-built armored personnel carrier.

CAIG   Team of cost analysts working for the secretary of defense who validate projected program costs.

C&C   Command and control.

CENTCOM   Central Command, General Schwarzkopf's headquarters.

Chalk   Number used to identify individual aircraft.

CMS   Combat mission simulator. Aircraft simulator programmed to place aircrews into situations found in war.

COMSOCCENT   Commander, Special Operations Command, Central Command.

CSAR   Combat search and rescue.

Drop zone   Area designated for dropping an airborne unit.

DTOC   Division tactical operations center.

E date   Start date for training for Apache units undergoing Apache transition.

EDRE   Emergency deployment readiness exercise.

EPW   Enemy prisoner of war.

EW   Electronic warfare. Includes the jamming of communications, radar, and guidance systems, and measures to defend against such jamming.

FAA Forward assembly area.

FAC Air force forward air controller. Responsible for directing air strikes.

FARP Forward area refuel point.

FARRP Forward area rearm and refuel point.

FFAR Folding fin free flight aerial rocket, either 2.75 inch or 72mm.

FLIR Forward looking infrared night and bad weather viewing device.

FLOT Front line of own troops.

FOB Forward operating base.

FROG Type of Soviet missile and launcher similar to American Honest John.

Front line trace Line denoting the forward edge of friendly units.

G day February 24, 1991, the day the Allied ground offensive began.

GTV Ground test vehicle. Fully configured attack helicopter prototype used exclusively for testing that does not involve flying.

Guard frequency Designated frequency reserved for emergency use only. All aircraft are expected to monitor "guard."

Gun cover Slang term meaning to have armed aircraft overhead.

HMMWV "Humvee" or "Hummer." High mobility, multipurpose, wheeled vehicle.

IAT Image auto tracking.

ICAP Program to improve AH-1G Cobras by adding TOW missiles and sighting devices.

IHADSS Integrated helmet and display sight system.

JAAT Joint air attack team, composed of Apaches and A-10s.

Landing zone Area selected for helicopter-borne troops to be landed.

LOA Limit of advance.

LRSD Long-range surveillance detachment.

MiG Designation given to Soviet-built fighter aircraft, usually accompanied by a number.

MPSM Muitipurpose submunitions.

Murphy's Law If something can go wrong, it will.

NETT New-equipment training team.

NOE Nap of the earth. Flying in such a way as to make use of terrain masking.

OR Operational rate. The percentage of a type of equipment in operational condition.

ORT   Optical relay tube.

Overwatch   Locating one combat unit so as to provide support by firepower if the maneuvering unit needs assistance.

PASS in Review   Department of the Army committee formed to evaluate usefulness of AH-1 aircraft during 1975–85.

Pathfinder   Airborne soldiers specially trained to be inserted ahead of airborne or airmobile assaults to guide air force transports or army helicopters to the drop or landing zone.

PIP   Product improvement program.

Pitch-change links   Rods connecting rotor blades to the swash plate, the movement of which induces pitch change to the rotor blades.

PNVS   Pilot's night vision sensor.

Push-pull tubes   Hollow tubelike linkages between the pilot's cyclic and collective controls leading to the swash plate.

RFP   Request for proposal. Document used to invite industry to enter bids on proposed equipment program.

RP   Release point.

SA-6   Soviet-built tracked vehicle with three surface-to-air missiles.

SA-7   Soviet shoulder-fired, heat-seeking, antiaircraft missile.

Stabilator   Horizontal control located near the end of the tail boom designed to automatically or manually level the helicopter aerodynamically in flight.

Standard European day   Used to measure a helicopter's ability to hover at two thousand feet on a seventy-five-degree-Fahrenheit day.

Strip alert   Highest readiness condition, requiring crews to sit in their aircraft ready to start engines within seconds of notification.

Swash plate   Two-part device, attached to the helicopter rotor head, which imparts pitch change to the pitch-change links and subsequently to the rotor blades.

TAA   Tactical assembly area.

TADS   Target acquisition and designation system.

Task Force Normandy (TF Normandy)   Code name for 1-101st raiding party.

TOW   Tube-launched, optically sighted, wire-guided antitank missile.

TRADOC   Training and Doctrine Command, headquartered at Fort Monroe, Virginia.

Wobbly One   Nickname for warrant officer one, the lowest warrant rank.

Zone reconnaissance   Zone designated to be reconnoitered with lateral and depth boundaries.

ZPU-4   Russian-built, four-barreled, 23mm, towed antiaircraft gun.

ZSU-23-4   Russian radar-controlled, four-barreled, 23mm antiaircraft gun mounted on a tracked vehicle.

Index